VISUAL QUICKSTART GUIDE

APPLESCRIPT

FOR THE INTERNET

Ethan Wilde

 Peachpit Press

Visual QuickStart Guide
AppleScript for the Internet
Ethan Wilde

Peachpit Press
1249 Eighth Street
Berkeley, CA 94710
(510) 524-2178
(510) 524-2221 (fax)

Find us on the World Wide Web at: http://www.peachpit.com

Peachpit Press is a division of Addison Wesley Longman

Editor: Simon Hayes
Copy Editor: Bill Cassel
Production Coordinator: Amy Changar
Compositor: Owen Wolfson
Indexer: Ann Longknife/Creative Solutions
Cover Design: The Visual Group

ISBN: 0-201-35359-8

0 9 8 7 6 5 4 3 2 1

Printed and bound in the United States of America

Acknowledgments

I'd like to acknowledge the following people without whom this book would never have been possible: My editor Simon Hayes, who found me and helped to make this book happen. Cal Simone, who influenced me with his personal vision of AppleScript. Special thanks go to Chris Espinosa and his AppleScript team at Apple for their advice and time. And finally, a sincere round of applause to the many AppleScript developers who have created a vast universe of free and shareware scripting additions and applications that have raised AppleScript's abilities to new heights.

The book is dedicated to the Schwartzina family, including Simone, Masala and my old friend Scriptosaurus.

Preface

About four years ago, I attended WebEdge 2, a Macintosh Webmasters conference that took place in Austin, Texas. Jon Wiederspan, (then of the University of Washington), who wrote a set of lessons for Webmasters to learn how to write CGIs in AppleScript, gave the first conference session, "AppleScript CGI." The room was filled with over 100 Webmasters, some of whom stood up and said "I'm not a programmer, but I was able to write this cool little CGI in AppleScript that did such-and-such." I was blown away!

The funniest thing about this conference was that, in those days, most people doing AppleScript work were integrating FileMaker with Eudora or QuarkXPress. Those of us who'd been involved with AppleScript since the beginning (1991–1992) had never even heard of CGIs. When I described to some of the folks at this conference what AppleScript was originally designed to do, they asked "Are you talking about the *same* AppleScript?"— they had thought that AppleScript was developed just so that Webmasters could write CGIs!

CGIs written in AppleScript can do anything from keeping simple hit counts to reaching across your LAN to grab data out of a database, throwing it into a graphing program to make a chart, combining it with other data from the database and then either delivering nicely formatted, freshly prepared charts to a user's Web browser or preparing a package of e-mail containing requested information, including enclosures, and sending it off.

AppleScript can also be used for server administration, managing files, updating databases, and formatting data for presentation.

The AppleScript language is a marvel. There are a number of definitions of AppleScript, but mine is this: AppleScript is the system-wide, English-like scripting language for communicating with and controlling off-the-shelf applications.

It's the bane of programmers and the delight of power users (and Webmasters). Programmers find it verbose and inconsistent, while users and Webmasters find it enabling and powerful.

The Internet has produced some interesting changes in certain segments of our society. One aspect of this is that we as humans have a medium in which to explore and express our anarchical nature. Many Internet-meisters tend to view the Internet as the place to do things their own way. And people who wouldn't have otherwise been able to become developers now have access to materials that help them get started.

This book is a testimonial to the power and versatility of AppleScript, and it's continued role in empowering the creative spirit!

Yours in scripting,
Cal Simone

TABLE OF CONTENTS

Chapter 1: Getting to Know AppleScript   1

How does AppleScript work? 3
What can I do with AppleScript? 4
Open Scripting Architecture 5
More on-line! 6

Chapter 2: Learning the Basics   7

The Script Editor 8
Scriptable applications and dictionaries 10
Beware scripting additions 11
Interacting with users 12

Chapter 3: Let's Get Started   13

Making statements 14
Fun with variables 15
Understanding operators 16
A family of values 17
The importance of lists and records 20
Objects and references to them 22
Comparisons and control statements 24
Advanced comparisons for strings, lists,
    and records 26
Combining comparisons 27
Repeat loops 28
Error handling 31
Using with timeout to wait 32
Handlers 33
Using comments to help yourself 35
Simple interaction with the user 36
Asking for a choice 37
Using on run and saving scripts
    as applications 39
Making drag-and-drop applications
    with on open 41
Other ways to save scripts 42

Chapter 4: AppleScript on the Desktop   43

Moving a file or folder 44
Changing creator types 46
Testing for the existence of a file 48

Renaming all the files in a folder 49
Making a folder 52
Creating a file from scratch 53
Customizing the Finder 55
Using folder actions in OS 8.5 57
Customizing the Application Switcher
    in OS 8.5 58
Customizing your Appearance in OS 8.5 60
Customizing File Exchange in OS 8.5 62
Finding files and searching the Web with
    Sherlock in OS 8.5 65
Switching, starting, and stopping Desktop
    printers in OS 8.5 67
Switching Location Manager sets in OS 8.5 69

Chapter 5: Open Transport and Networking   71
Creating a TCP/IP configuration in OS 8.5 72
Enabling multi-homing with TCP/IP 74
Switching TCP/IP configurations 76
Scripting OT/PPP and Remote Access 78
Making a PPP connection 79
Maintaining a PPP connection 80
Making a Remote Access connection 81
Changing your file-sharing status 83
Scripting the Users & Groups control panel 84

Chapter 6: Scripting Your Web Browser   87
Submitting form data from
    Netscape Navigator 88
Submitting form data from
    Internet Explorer 90
Printing local HTML files from
    Netscape Navigator 92
Printing local HTML files from
    Internet Explorer 94
Putting Netscape Navigator into kiosk mode 97
Retrieving HTML source code with
    Internet Explorer 98
Clearing the browser cache 99
Deleting Netscape Navigator's cookies file 100
Running AppleScripts from your browser 102

**Chapter 7: Scripting Emailer and
Outlook Express   107**
Converting mail from Eudora or UNIX 108
Converting mail from QuickMail Pro 116

Filing mail based on keywords 118
Sending replies based on keywords 122
Forwarding mail based on keywords 124
Faxing mail with faxSTF based on
    keywords from Emailer 126
Importing mail into Microsoft Word
    based on keywords 129
Copying mail data to FileMaker Pro 131
Creating a mailing list with FileMaker Pro 134

Chapter 8: Scripting Eudora Pro   **137**
Filing mail based on keywords 138
Sending replies based on keywords 142
Forwarding mail based on keywords 144
Copying mail data to FileMaker Pro 146
Creating a mailing list with FileMaker Pro 148

Chapter 9: Fetch and Anarchie for FTP   **151**
Sending a file via FTP 152
Retrieving a file via FTP 154
Retrieving a directory listing via FTP 155
Updating a remote directory via FTP
    with Fetch 158
Retrieving a file via HTTP with Anarchie 162
Retrieving an entire site's files via HTTP
    with Anarchie 163

Chapter 10: DataComet for telnet   **165**
Reading a UNIX passwd file or restarting a
    UNIX server 166
Adding mail aliases to a UNIX server 171
Retrieving an environment variable from a
    UNIX server 174
Telnet to your Mac with Script Daemon 177

Chapter 11: Building CGIs   **179**
Mac OS 8.5 and CGIs 180
Understanding GET data 181
Parsing form POST data 184
Parsing server variables 189
Returning content via redirection 190
Returning content from other scriptable
    applications 192
Sending partial replies with WebSTAR 194
Creating protected realms and users
    in WebSTAR 196

TABLE OF CONTENTS

Chapter 12: FileMaker Pro for HTML   **199**

Scripting FileMaker Pro 200
Finding records in a content database 201
Sorting the records in a content database 202
Getting data from a record in a
    content database 203
Creating a new record in a content database ... 205
Merging data with templates to create
    HTML files 206

Chapter 13: Microsoft Word for HTML   **209**

Recording a script to modify type styles 210
Modifying a recorded script for
    batch processing 212
Batch exporting Word documents as HTML ... 215

Chapter 14: CyberStudio for HTML   **219**

Modifying, styling, and hyperlinking text 220
Logging errors for a folder of HTML files 222
Importing a tab-delimited file as a table 225
Converting styled text in the clipboard
    to HTML 226

Chapter 15: QuarkXPress for HTML and Images   **229**

Scripting QuarkXPress 230
Importing and formatting HTML
    source code 231
Exporting all pages in a document as
    EPS files 234
Exporting all text from a document 235

Chapter 16: Clip2gif and GifBuilder for Images   **237**

Creating and exporting graphical text
    in clip2gif 238
Creating graphical charts 239
Converting images to GIFs with
    adaptive palettes 240
Converting images to GIFs with the
    Web-safe palette 241
Making interlaced framed GIF images 243
Creating animated GIFs of moving text 246

**Chapter 17: Images with Photoshop
and PhotoScripter**   **249**

Creating and exporting graphical text 250
Exporting each layer of a document

as a separate file 255
Importing a folder full of files into a
    document as layers 257
Adding transparency to grayscale images 260
Creating animations 264
Previewing an animation created as
    separate layers 265
Exporting a layered document as an
    animated GIF with GifBuilder 267

**Chapter 18:   Scripting with
                Apple Data Detectors   269**
Creating Apple Data Detector action scripts . . . 270
Detecting e-mail addresses and adding
    them to an address book 271
Detecting a domain name 273
Detecting a URL and displaying links
    with Alta Vista 274

**Chapter 19:   Using Timbuktu Pro to
                Control Windows   275**
Restarting a Windows NT server 276
Synchronizing a folder on your Mac and PC 278

Chapter 20:   Scripting Mail and List Servers   281
Converting all list subscribers to non-posting . . 282
Subscribing a user to a mailing list 283
Setting a mailing list's subject line prefix 284
Adding a user account to EIMS 2.x 285
Scripting ListSTAR/SMTP 287
Subscribing a user to a mailing list 288
Sending mail to a mailing list's subscribers 289
Enabling and disabling a mailing list 290

Chapter 21:   Marionet for Scripting the Internet   291
Scripting Marionet 292
Resolving a DNS name to an IP address 293
Sending mail directly via an SMTP server 295
Sending a file via FTP 297
Retrieving a newsgroup's article list with NNTP 298
Retrieving files from a Web server with HTTP . . 300

**Chapter 22:   The Big Project:
                A Web Server Monitor   301**
Monitoring a Web server by retrieving a file 302

Chapter 23: Giving Your Scripts a Face   **305**
Creating a window with controls 306
Entering the project script 307
Adding scripts to window controls 312
Saving a project as an application 314

Chapter 24 : Debugging AppleScript   **315**
Debugging with the Script Editor 316
Debugging with Scripter 318
Debugging with Script Debugger 319
Debugging with FaceSpan 320
Proper system software configurations
    for AppleScript 321

Appendix A : AppleScript Reference   **323**
Appendix B : To Learn More About AppleScript   **331**

GETTING TO
KNOW APPLESCRIPT

The concept of the user interface entered popular thinking with the Macintosh. Everything essential to what we think of as the user interface today—including the mouse, the Desktop, icons, and menus—originated for most of us with the Macintosh. All of these innovations made the Mac easier to use, but harder to automate when compared with other operating systems' command-line interfaces.

In wasn't until AppleScript first appeared with the release of System 7 in 1993 that Apple realized a script language that embodied all of the important philosophies of the Mac OS.

Apple's early effort at automating the Mac OS, MacroMaker, let users record their mouse and keyboard actions for later playback. This technology disappeared after the first few versions of the Mac OS as system functions grew more complex.

With AppleScript came a host of unique features that make it the powerful and flexible language we use today:

♦ AppleScript can control many applications over an entire network, not to mention controlling other platforms over the Internet.

♦ In "recordable" applications, AppleScript can automatically create a script based on a recording of your real-time actions. There are a limited number of recordable applications, but those few are great demonstrations of the power of recording. Later on, we'll look at a few recordable applications, including Microsoft's Word 98, to demonstrate the power of this feature.

♦ The AppleScript language is *dynamically extensible*: each scriptable application has its own dictionary of supported commands, classes, and properties. However, you don't always need an entire application to add commands to AppleScript. There is another group of language extensions known as *scripting additions*. Scripting additions are small compiled libraries that also have dictionaries of commands, classes, and properties that extend AppleScript's vocabulary and functionality. In a nutshell, scriptable applications and scripting additions both have dictionaries of additional commands that expand AppleScript.

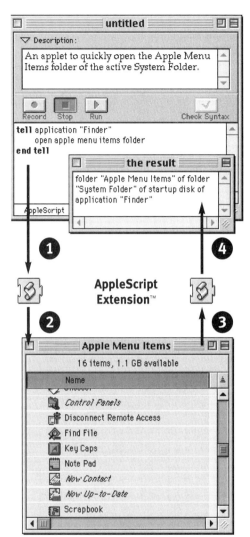

Figure 1.1 The flow of events when an AppleScript is executed. See steps 1 through 4 for a detailed discussion of the process.

How does AppleScript work?

At the heart of AppleScript is the AppleScript system extension. This extension is installed by default—along with the default editing application, the Script Editor—in every Mac OS from System 7 through current versions of System 8. **Figure 1.1** shows the sequence of events that occur when a simple script is run from the Script Editor.

When you write a series of AppleScript statements in an editor and run them, the AppleScript extension translates your script's statements into individual messages for different applications. These messages are called Apple Events. Here's how Apple Events work:

1. AppleScript statements are passed from the running script to the AppleScript extension.

2. The AppleScript extension sends Apple Events corresponding to the script statements to the application. Each of these events requests that the application perform a specific action.

3. The application returns Apple Events that contain results from the actions.

4. The AppleScript extension interprets the Apple Event results and sends them back to the script.

✔ AppleScript is fully PowerPC-native in OS 8.5!

■ As of this writing, AppleScript has just gone through a major revision in the latest System, Mac OS 8.5. It is now finally fully PowerPC-native, which has resulted in a dramatic five-fold increase in script execution speed!

What can I do with AppleScript?

Want to build an e-mail database? Print an entire Web site? Perform complex global search-and-replace routines on text files? Build an entire Web site from a database? Control a UNIX or Windows machine from your Mac? People are using AppleScript to do all of these things right now. The fact that AppleScript is dynamically extensible means that its functions are limited only by the range of scriptable applications that support it.

Historically, AppleScript has been most visible in automated publishing solutions, thanks to the very complete AppleScript dictionary in QuarkXPress. More recently, the Finder and many more System components have become scriptable. The Finder is even recordable in Mac OS 8. Anything you can do with your Desktop and files can easily be automated. Renaming, copying, backing up, and modifying files are easy with AppleScript. And with conditional logic, you can make the Finder do things in a very sophisticated manner.

AppleScript is used extensively on the Internet to create CGIs on Mac-based Web servers. Now, with a super-fast PowerPC-native version of AppleScript available in Mac OS 8.5, AppleScript is an even more powerful CGI programming environment.

Conditional logic: What does it mean?

Conditional logic refers to the concept of testing the state of a variable or property and responding to that state in your script. Examples of conditional logic include the ubiquitous "if...then" statements found in most computer languages:

```
if myvariable > 10 then display
dialog "Big number!"
```

CGI: common gateway interface

"Common gateway interface" is the phrase that was coined to describe the manner in which local scripts on a server receive data from an Internet client and return results at the end of their execution. A group of standards describes the way CGIs communicate on each platform. On UNIX, script and server sometimes share data via environment variables. On the Mac, the natural avenue for CGIs is Apple Events, which makes AppleScript a natural choice for handling the passing of data. We'll cover CGIs in Chapter 11.

Open Scripting Architecture

The system-level framework that underlies AppleScript is called Open Scripting Architecture (OSA). OSA allows the script language used to be translated into the actual Apple Events that are sent to different applications. OSA uses Interapplication Communication (IAC) to send Apple Events to scriptable applications and receive results.

The beauty of OSA is that many different scripting languages and dialects can be implemented on top of it. A number of OSA-compliant script languages are now available for the Macintosh:

- ◆ **Frontier** from UserLand is a complete scripting language that includes some very powerful features not available in AppleScript. Frontier has a built-in database that can be used to store objects and data of all types.

- ◆ **MacPerl** is a port of the very popular text-manipulation scripting language used throughout the Internet.

- ◆ **MacTCL** is a widely used scripting language ported from the UNIX world.

Isn't AppleScript a wonderful idea made real? Now let's get ready to write some elegant AppleScripts using this beautiful and democratic language.

✔ Tip

- ■ The scripts in this book are practical examples of ways that I have actually used AppleScript. As you will see, a little innovative AppleScript can go a long way toward creative solutions to many problems. The sky is the limit.

AppleScript: number two CGI language worldwide

Georgia Tech University's October 1997 survey of Web developers showed AppleScript to be the second most popular CGI scripting language, after Perl. For details, visit GTU's survey online at http://www.gvu.gatech.edu/
→ user_surveys/.

More on-line!

Various factors made it impossible to publish all the material we prepared for this book here in the book. If you have purchased *AppleScript for the Internet*, you can find much more information on AppleScript and applications like BBEdit, RagTime, Macromedia FreeHand, Creator 2, and Web Collage on the support site of the Peachpit Press web site.

Visit this URL for the chapters that didn't make it into the finished book, with complete scripts, detailed explanations and more!

`http://www.peachpit.com/vqs/applescript/`

MORE ON-LINE!

LEARNING
THE BASICS

AppleScript makes it possible for you to control many different applications on your Macintosh. To gain control, you need to write scripts. To write scripts, you need a number of things:

◆ You need to be able to find out what commands each application supports and learn the syntax for those commands.

◆ You need a way to enter scripts and test them.

◆ You also need a way to save your scripts when you're done creating them.

The application we use for these functions throughout this book is Apple's free Script Editor. So to kick things off in this chapter, we'll take a quick look at the Script Editor. In the Script Editor, we'll be able to look at scriptable applications and their dictionaries. We will also check out scripting additions, their dictionaries, and how to properly install scripting additions on your system.

The Script Editor

When you write AppleScripts, you need an application that enables you to edit, compile, and save your scripts. For consistency and accessibility, all of the scripts in this book were written using Apple's free Script Editor. Every version of the Mac OS from 7.1 through 8.5 includes AppleScript and the Script Editor application. **Figure 2.1** shows you what the Script Editor's application icon looks like, while **Figures 2.2–2.5** show the four windows of the Script Editor:

- ◆ **The Script window**: The Script window (**Figure 2.2**) is where you create your script by typing script statements or recording your actions in a recordable application. AppleScript will compile your script and test for syntax errors whenever you click the Check Syntax button in the Script window. Click the Run button to execute your script from the Script Editor. The Script window also has a description field that you can use to describe your script to others. If you roll over your script's icon in the Finder with balloon help on, the script's description will be displayed.

- ◆ **The Event Log window:** The Event Log window (**Figure 2.3**) can be opened from the Controls menu. It displays all events and results generated by a running script, which makes it extremely useful for debugging your scripts.

- ◆ **The Result window**: The Result window (**Figure 2.4**) can also be opened from the Controls menu. It displays the results of the last event.

Figure 2.1 The Script Editor icon

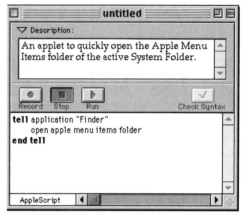

Figure 2.2 The Script Editor's Script window.

Figure 2.3 The Script Editor's Event Log window.

Figure 2.4 The Script Editor's Result window.

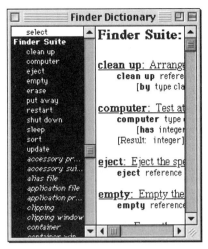

Figure 2.5 The Script Editor's Dictionary window.

◆ **The Dictionary window**: You can open the dictionary of every application or scripting addition in the Script Editor. Dictionaries can provide help with proper syntax and teach you an application's script statements, events, and objects (**Figure 2.5**).

Two other, more complete, commercial editing applications exist: Scripter from Main Event Software and Script Debugger from Late Night Software. You can find out more about these products in Chapter 24. The AppleScript-based application builder FaceSpan also includes a script editing window. We'll cover FaceSpan in Chapter 23.

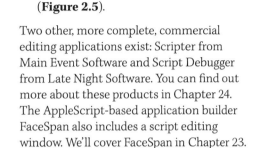

Figure 2.6 Finding the Script Editor in the Finder.

Finding the Script Editor

Use the Finder's built-in Find command (Command-F) to locate the Script Editor on your Mac (see **Figure 2.6**). Most recent Mac OS versions have placed the Script Editor in the AppleScript folder inside Apple Extras. Once you've located the application, make an alias and place it on your Desktop for easy access.

Scriptable applications and dictionaries

Any Macintosh application that supports AppleScript must have a dictionary. The dictionary defines the commands that the application will understand in AppleScript, from the most basic commands like Open to commands unique to that application. Dictionaries also define all objects that you can reference with commands. Objects include things like database records and fields, words and paragraphs in text documents, objects in drawing programs, and URLs in Web browsers. The dictionary also defines what each object's properties are. Properties include things like file names and window positions and sizes.

You can easily learn all of the supported AppleScript commands and objects for an application or scripting addition simply by opening the dictionary from the Script Editor. **Figure 2.7** shows how to open a dictionary from the Script Editor's File menu.

Figure 2.8 shows a sample entry from the Finder's dictionary.

Dictionaries are the only guaranteed way to discover a scriptable application's commands and syntax. With some practice, you will become adept at reading dictionaries in the Script Editor.

✔ Tip

- If you drop a scriptable application or scripting addition icon onto the Script Editor icon in the Finder, Script Editor will open the dictionary for that file.

Figure 2.7 Opening a dictionary from the Script Editor.

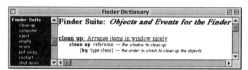

Figure 2.8 A sample entry from the System 8 Finder dictionary.

Figure 2.9 Finding all scriptable applications with File Buddy.

File Buddy

Dictionaries are actually stored inside of the application file (or, rarely, in a related file) as a file resource of the type "aete". The shareware application File Buddy can locate all scriptable applications on your hard drive by searching for all files that contain an "aete" resource. **Figure 2.9** shows how you can do this quickly and easily. File Buddy was written by Laurence Harris and is available at http://www.skytag.com/.

SCRIPTABLE APPLICATIONS AND DICTIONARIES

Figure 2.10 The standard icon for a scripting addition.

Figure 2.11 The Scripting Additions folder.

Beware scripting additions

Many scripts in this book require special files that add commands to AppleScript. These files are known as *scripting additions*, or OSAX by acronym-toting geeks. (OSAX stands for Open Scripting Architecture eXtension, which is the official way of saying that AppleScript lets you add your own command libraries.) Each scripting addition has its own dictionary of commands that are added to AppleScript's set of commands when you put the addition into the Scripting Additions folder in your System folder. **Figure 2.10** shows the standard icon for scripting additions, while **Figure 2.11** shows the Scripting Additions folder icon.

Some scripting additions add very powerful functions to AppleScript's basic command set, including text matching and replacement, control of system components like control panels, and keyboard and mouse control.

Many of the scripts in this book make use of various scripting additions. Wherever a particular scripting addition is required, a note will appear telling you where to get the addition on the Internet. Some scripting additions are available as freeware, but many more are shareware. Be sure to support the Mac development community by purchasing any shareware scripting additions you end up using.

The Scripting Additions folder

The Scripting Additions folder is located directly inside the System folder in all versions of Mac OS 8. Previous versions of the Mac OS placed the Scripting Additions folder inside the Extensions folder. If you are having problems with AppleScript in System 8, make sure there is not a Scripting Additions folder in your Extensions folder. If there is one, copy any additions in it into your real Scripting Additions folder directly inside the System folder, then delete the bogus folder.

Interacting with users

AppleScript is a model of simplicity and elegance in both its underlying structure and its scripting language. In this spirit of simplicity, AppleScript offers only a handful of ways to directly interact with users through the user interface. Using built-in commands, scripts can display dialogs and get user input via buttons and text entry. Most of our scripting examples will make use of these simple ways to query the user and get their input.

However, with FaceSpan, a third-party application from DTI, you get a fully scriptable application builder. FaceSpan is the secret weapon of AppleScripters. Once you've developed a comfortable working relationship with AppleScript, FaceSpan offers a limitless opportunity to create complete stand-alone Mac applications programmed completely in AppleScript.

Every object in FaceSpan is attachable. This means that you can attach an AppleScript to the object that responds to its events. **Figure 2.12** shows the range of objects that can be created and controlled with scripts in FaceSpan.

We'll return to FaceSpan in Chapter 23 after we've mastered the rest of AppleScript.

Figure 2.12 FaceSpan's object creation toolbar.

LET'S GET STARTED

3

Now that we're this far into our tour of AppleScript, you should have a good idea of what it is and how it works. So let's dive into the standard style (or syntax) of AppleScript and really learn how to script on the Mac.

In this chapter, we'll learn about variables and constants, two different kinds of containers that hold values and information. We'll look at handling errors and making handlers. We'll also learn about control statements, or commands that control when and how different parts of scripts are run. The most common control statement, `tell`, is used to indicate which application or other object AppleScript should send commands to.

Other control statements include conditional logic commands like `if...then` and `repeat while`. These commands allow scripts to make intelligent decisions about what to do and how many times to do it.

Now, on to the syntax circus!

Making statements

Every script you write will be made up of a series of statements. A statement is usually just that, a simple English-like sentence with a subject, predicate, and object in the form *noun, verb, noun*. **Figure 3.1** shows what happens after we run the following example from the Script Editor.

```
tell application "Finder" to open
→ disk "Ethan's 1400"
```

Statements are made up of *commands* and *objects*. The target of a statement should be a specific application program, like the Finder in this example.

Commands are like verbs; they're words you use to request an action. The action is usually pointed at an object. Objects are generally nouns; they're things you do stuff to.

In the example statement above, `tell` is directed at the Finder, which is an object. `open` is a command or verb, and `disk` "Ethan's 1400" is its object.

Each object can have parts, or *elements*. This means objects like disks can contain folders and files:

```
tell application "Finder" to open
→   folder "Applications" of disk
→   "Ethan's 1400"
```

In this example statement, the folder `Applications` is an element of the disk object `Ethan's 1400`.

Figure 3.2 shows what happens when we run the above example from the Script Editor.

You may have understood what the example code did intuitively. That's AppleScript syntax at its best.

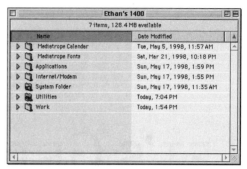

Figure 3.1 At our command, the Finder opens the hard disk's window.

Figure 3.2 Now we've told the Finder to open one of the disk's folders.

More on targets

In AppleScript, you need to specify a target to send a command to. This is done with the `tell` command. The target is the application that you are requesting action from; often the object is a part of that application.

In both examples above, the application `Finder` is the target of the command.

Fun with variables

Variables are where you put values that you are using in your script:

```
set x to "me"
```

Here set, a command, tells AppleScript to set the variable x to the string value "me".

A variable is a kind of object that serves as a placeholder for any information you need to manipulate or share with other applications. There are a few short rules for variables in AppleScript:

◆ The names of variables must start with a letter.

◆ Variable names can only contain letters, numbers, and underscores (_).

◆ Variable names cannot be words that are reserved for commands or objects.

Different people have different attitudes about naming variables. Some people type in short, cryptic variable names in the interest of expedience. I suggest using descriptive variable names, even if it means a little extra typing.

✔ Tip

■ Variables come in many different flavors, including strings, numbers, and Booleans. When you assign a value to a variable, you can tell AppleScript what kind of value it is. This is important because commands often expect to receive values of particular types. We'll look at types in the spread *A family of values* on page 17.

Properties are variables with persistent values

Your script can define its own properties. Properties are variables that keep their values across executions of its handler. This means the value in a property when it stops running will be the same the next time it starts running. You define properties, usually at the beginning of your script, like this:

```
property myUser: "Jay"
property myDelay: 15
```

Understanding operators

AppleScript lets you perform a number of different operations on values and variables. The type of operator you choose depends on what you are trying to accomplish and the kind of value that your variable holds.

You can combine strings together using the concatenation operator, &, like this:

```
Set x to "Hello"&"World"
```

Figure 3.3 shows the result of the above code.

You can also add items to a list using &:

```
Set z to {"apple","pear"}&"banana"
```

Figure 3.4 shows the result of adding an item to a list.

There are many operators that you can use on variables in AppleScript. **Table 3.1** lists numerical operators.

The spread *Combining comparisons* on page 27 discusses logical or Boolean operators.

Figure 3.3 Two strings concatenated together.

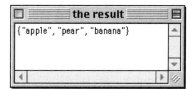

Figure 3.4 Adding an item to a list.

Table 3.1

Numerical Operators		
OPERATOR	MEANING	EXAMPLE
^	Raise to the power of	2^4=16
*	Multiply	1*3=3
+	Add	2+7=9
-	Subtract	5-2=3
/	Divide	8/2=4
div	Divide without remainder	11 div 2=5
mod	Divide, returning remainder	11 mod 2=1

A family of values

A *value* in AppleScript is typically a number, a string, a date, a list, or a record which you store inside a variable. Values in variables serve all kinds of purposes in your scripts. Values are manipulated by scripts and returned by applications as results of commands. You exchange information—either between applications and AppleScript, or between lines of code within your script—with values. When you send commands to applications, you usually accompany them with values.

In most languages, values have *types,* or classes,—such as integer, string, or array—associated with them. AppleScript tries to set a value's type automatically unless it's explicitly defined. This automatic typing of values is almost always OK. Sometimes, however, you will concatenate strings or lists together and need to explicitly tell AppleScript what type of value you want as a result. Or you may need to coerce a string value to be a reference to a file. In those cases it's safest to explicitly set the types of your variables. Let's look at some of the different value types and how you would set them in the Script Editor.

To set a string value

◆ `set x to 1 as string`

Strings are the most ubiquitous value types you'll see in this book, since we're dealing with the Internet and the text file is its standard fare. In this case, we specify that the value x will contain a 1, and we force, or coerce, the value to be a text string by specifying `as string`, even though 1 is a numerical digit. x will have the value 1 in it after this line of code. This coercion of a numerical value to a string is different than our other examples, since they only specify the value type that

Unit types in OS 8.5

AppleScript 1.3.2 adds new value types for units of length, area, volume (liquid and solid), and temperature. To use these types, you'll need to coerce the value using *as*. OS 8.5's Help Center has a complete list of these new types. These new types let you convert values between measurement systems, for example:

```
set myEnglishLength to 10 as inches
set myMetricLength to
→ myEnglishLength as centimeters
```

AppleScript would have automatically chosen anyway. **Figure 3.5** shows how this looks in the Script Editor.

◆ `set x to "me and you"`
  `get the first word of x`

  A string can be referenced by its elements: paragraphs, words, and characters. In this case, after we set x to a string, we ask AppleScript for the first word of that string with the command get. **Figure 3.6** shows the result of this code in the Script Editor.

◆ `set x to "you and I" as text`

  Setting a value's type to text is the same as setting it to string.

To set a number value:

◆ `set k to 1+3.5 as number`

  A number is either an integer or a real number. AppleScript tries to be as casual and carefree about value types as possible. Unless you insist on a type, AppleScript will try an pick one for you, based on the data stored in your variable.

◆ `set j to -2 as integer`

  An integer is a positive or negative number without decimals. By forcing this value type, you can have AppleScript eliminate any decimal values from a calculation.

◆ `set q to 1.222 as real`

  A real value is a positive or negative number including decimals.

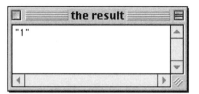

Figure 3.5 Coercing a number into a string.

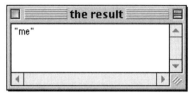

Figure 3.6 Getting the first word of a string.

Incorrect Values

`set x to "you" as real`

Setting the type for your value explicitly is sometimes necessary. But trying to coerce some values to certain types just doesn't make sense to AppleScript. This line of code will generate an error in AppleScript, because a real value must be numerical.

A FAMILY OF VALUES

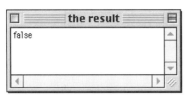

Figure 3.7 Setting a variable to a Boolean value.

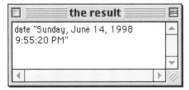

Figure 3.8 Setting a variable to the current date.

Setting other values:

◆ `set x to false as boolean`

A Boolean value can only be true or false. `if...then` statements always test a Boolean value and Boolean variables are useful for storing the state of such tests. Think of them as on/off or yes/no flags. **Figure 3.7** shows the result of this code in the Script Editor.

◆ `set i to the current date`

Dates are their own value type that specify a day of the week, month, year, and time. You can coerce a date into a string by using `as string`. **Figure 3.8** shows the result of this code in the Script Editor.

◆ `set c to the class of {1,2,3}`

Classes are special value types that describe the value type of other values. If you get the class of a variable or literal value, AppleScript will return the value type. This command will generate the result of `list`.

◆ `tell application "Finder"`
   `→ to set d to the startup disk`

A reference value holds a pointer to an object. In this case, an alias reference will be stored in our variable d that points to our startup drive.

✔ Constant values

■ *Constants* are values that are predefined by AppleScript. These terms cannot be changed, but are available to use in your code. Using them makes scripting easier. After all, `tab` is simpler than `ascii character 9`.

More value types

In OS 8.5, the `unicode text` value type has been added to implement support for multi-lingual Unicode text in AppleScript. Along with this new addition, AppleScript also supports the types `international text`, `styled text`, `class` and `script`.

The importance of lists and records

Once you have defined variables for a script, you can then manipulate those variables, store information in them, and reference them later. Variables typically hold a single value, or complex values like lists and records that hold a bunch of values together at one time (each of which can be of a different type like numbers, string, even other lists).

The advantage of storing your values in lists and records is that it makes it much easier to establish relationships between values and to find values quickly and easily. It also saves you a lot of typing time!

To define a list:

1. ```
set k to {"apple","orange",1,2,3}
get item 3 of k
```

   A *list* is an ordered (or linear) collection of values separated by commas. You can create your own lists by specifying each element of the list when you define the list value.

   Lists can be addressed as a whole or by each individual comma-delimited value, also known as a list's *items*. **Figure 3.9** shows the result of this code in the Script Editor.

2. ```
get items 2 thru 3 of k
```

   This line of code will yield the resulting list: {"orange",1}.

3. ```
set k to k & "hey"
```

   You can add a new value to the end of a list using the concatenation operator: &.

4. ```
set item 4 to "me"
get k
```

   You can also modify individual items within a list. If you want to change the value if a single item, just reference it by number. You can have numbers and

Figure 3.9 Requesting the third item from a list.

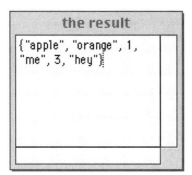

Figure 3.10 Modifying an item and adding a new item.

strings intermixed as items in your lists. **Figure 3.10** shows the result of this code in the Script Editor.

To define a record:

1. `set t to {name: "me",phone:` `→ "111-222-3333"}`

    A *record* is a set of properties. More simply, records are lists where each item is made up of a name-value pair. As you can see in this example, you define a record in the same way that you define a list, each item separated by commas, but in the case of a record each item has two parts, an item name and a value for that name.

2. `set q to name of t`

    In a record you must address an item by name, instead of by position as you do in a list.

3. `set myProperties to length of t`

    The length property will tell you how many properties a record has. But you need to know the specific property names to access the values in records, unless you coerce them into being lists. This line of code will return the result 2.

4. `set myList to (t as list)`

    This line of code will generate the list `{"me","111-222-333"}`.

✔ Types of lists and records

- Just as you sometimes force AppleScript to recognize a variable as holding a particular kind of value—a string, or a real number, or an integer—no matter what is stored in it, you can specify a type for individual items in lists and records. For instance, a record property or list item can hold a string value right next to an item that is a numeric value.

Objects and references to them

Objects are the things in applications, AppleScript, and the Mac OS that respond to script commands. Application objects are objects stored in applications and their documents, like text objects, database objects, and graphic objects. Objects can contain data, in the form of values, properties, and elements, that you can access or change from your scripts.

Each object belongs to an object class. Each object class is a category for objects that defines their properties and elements that we can access from AppleScript. Object classes include applications, documents, windows, databases, fields, graphic elements, and characters. Dictionaries define object classes and indicate the object's properties and elements that can be set. Properties contain values, while elements are themselves objects that can be referenced separately from your script. **Figure 3.11** shows a dictionary entry for the character object class in QuarkXPress.

You can store references to objects, like character 2 of document 1, in variables, just like other value. This way you can simplify your code when you need to refer to an object many times in a script.

Object examples

1. ```
tell application "QuarkXPress"
    get character 2 of word 3 of text
    → box 1 of document 1
end tell
```
   This code will return a single character as the result from QuarkXPress.
2. ```
tell application "Finder"
    set myFile to alias "HD:Test File"
end tell
```

Figure 3.11 A dictionary entry for the character object class in QuarkXPress.

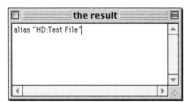

Figure 3.12 The reference stored in myFile as displayed in the Script Editor's Result window.

This code will return a reference to the file Test File stored on the volume named HD. The reference will look like this: alias "HD:Test File".

3. tell application "Finder"
    open myFile
    end tell

This code will make the Finder open the file Test File on the volume HD, since we stored this file reference in the variable myFile above. **Figure 3.12** shows the reference stored in myFile as displayed in the Script Editor's Result window.

✔ The object model

■ The best AppleScript dictionaries follow a coherent structure that includes commands (verbs) and objects (nouns) that scripters know from other programs or that make intuitive sense. Such an approach is called following the object model.

OBJECTS AND REFERENCES TO THEM

23

Comparisons and control statements

One of the most powerful features that AppleScript offers you is the ability to introduce logic along with automation. At its most basic, logic means making decisions based on comparisons between values. These values can be stored in variables or used literally.

To put these comparisons to good use you need a command to use with them. The hands-down conditional command favorite is

if...then...else...

The examples below show some comparisons using the if command. We can use basic comparisons with numbers, strings, and Booleans to good purpose.

To compare values:

1. `if 4 > 2 then beep`
   `if 4 is greater than 2 then beep`
   In these two examples we are asking AppleScript to evaluate whether one value is greater than another. In the first example we have AppleScript beep if 4 is greater than 2, which of course it is. The second example is the same, only we have written the command in words, rather than symbols. AppleScript lets us do this for added clarity.

2. `if 1 < 8 then beep`
   `if 1 is less than 8 then beep`
   In this example we are making the same kind of comparison as in step 1, but in this case we are asking AppleScript to tell us which of the values is less than the other.

3. `if 3 ≥ 1 then beep`
   `if 3 is greater than or equal to 1`
   `→ then beep`

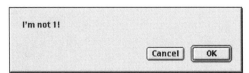

Figure 3.13 A dialog generated by our conditional test.

In this comparison we make AppleScript evaluate two values and tell us if the first is either greater than or equal to the second. The statement evaluates to `true` if that is indeed the case, as it is here. The ≥ character is generated by typing Option-. (period).

4. `if 1 ≤ 3 then beep`
`if 1 is less than or equal to 3`
`→ then beep`

This time, we'll have AppleScript see if 1 is less than or equal to 3. Since it is, we'll get a beep. The ≤ is generated by typing Option-, (comma).

5. `if 3 = 3 then beep`
`if 3 is equal to 3 then beep`

Equality is the most typical comparison, and it works just the way it looks. Since 3 does still equal 3 our Mac will beep to this.

6. `if 1 ≠ 2 then beep`
`if 1 is not equal to 2 then beep`

For every force there must be an opposing force. Not equals is the dark side of equals. And since we do enjoy beeping so, our example will generate another beep. This character is generated by typing Option-= (equals sign).

Using else with if

Comparisons using `if` can also respond to failures by including an `else` clause. **Figure 3.13** shows what happens when we run the script below.

```
set x to 10
if x = 1 then
    beep
else
    display dialog "I'm not 1! "
end if
```

In this example, since we explicitly set `x` to equal 10 on our first line, our initial `if` test will fail, triggering our `else` statement. Thus, we will see the dialog displayed.

Advanced comparisons for strings, lists, and records

You can also use powerful character-matching comparisons like `starts with`, `ends with`, and `contains` with strings, lists, and records. Using these commands, you can make tests that tell you useful information about the values you use in your programs.

Using starts with, ends with, and contains

1. `if "Help me" starts with "Help"`
`→ then beep`

In this example we ask AppleScript to test where the string `Help` appears in the string `Help me`. If it appears at the start of the string, then the expression is true and AppleScript will beep.

2. `considering case`
`    if "Help me" starts with "help"`
`    → then beep`
`end considering`

Usually, comparisons aren't case sensitive. But when we invoke the `considering case` statement, AppleScript will consider case. This code will not generate a beep.

3. `if "Take off" ends with "off"`
`→ then beep`

This time we test whether the string `off` appears at the end of the first string. If `off` appears at the end of the string, then the expression is true and we will hear a beep.

Testing Lists

◆ `if "Red apple tree" contains`
`→ "apple" then beep`
The least restrictive of these three comparisons is `contains`. In this example, if `apple` appears anywhere within the first string, our test will be true. And don't forget the beep.

◆ `if {1,4,5} starts with 1 then beep`
This test on a list will generate a beep since the list does start with a 1.

◆ `if {"me","you","them"} contains`
`→ "you" then beep`
This `contains` test on a list will get us another beep since the list does contain an item with the value you.

Table 3.2

Logical/Boolean Operators		
OPERATOR	MEANING	EXAMPLE
and	Returns true if both tests are true.	x and y returns true only if x is true and y is true.
or	Returns true if either test is true.	x or y returns true as long as either x or y is true.
not	Returns true if test is false; returns false if test is true.	not x returns false is x is true.

Combining comparisons

To add to the usefulness of comparisons, there are three logical operators, and, or, and not, that you can use to create compound if...then statements. Using these command words you can create much more elaborate comparisons that test many values at once. **Table 3.2** lists the logical operators and shows how they work.

Using logical operators

1. `if i contains "yes"`
`→ and j>5 then beep`

Using the logical operator and here lets us combine two if... then tests into one. Both conditions must be true for the overall test to return true and then beep. Here, the string i would have to contain "yes" and the number inside the variable j would have to be greater than 5 to return true. As in all comparisons, AppleScript will only go on to the rest of the statement (and in this case beep) if the comparisons return true.

2. `if i contains "no" or j=1 then beep`

With or we can combine multiple if...then tests and return true for the overall test if one or more of the constituent tests is true. In this case, if either the string i contains "no" or if the number inside the variable j equals 1 then we'll hear a beep.

3. `if not (q contains "maybe")`
`→ then beep`

In this example we tell AppleScript to check the value of q and see if it contains the letters "maybe". If this test is true the not reverses the result, generating a failure and bypassing the beep. We enclose our comparison in parentheses to ensure that AppleScript sees it as a whole phrase to evaluate. We don't want it to think we want to do something with the value not q.

✔ Strings use quotes

- The quoted text in the above examples is a string value. String values are enclosed in quotes in AppleScript.

Repeat loops

Now that we know AppleScript has the smarts provided by comparisons, let's look at the brute force added to AppleScript by repeat loops. A repeat loop makes a comparison continuously over a range of values until it gets a true result.

The repeat loop is one of AppleScript's most essential features, since it lets you do many things over and over again in your scripts, saving a great deal of work that would otherwise be done by your own poor fingers. Repeat loops in their simplest form are infinite. The following script creates such a loop. It is displayed in its entirety in **Code 3.1**.

Running an infinite loop

1. `set myList to {}`

   With this first line, we tell AppleScript to create an empty list variable `myList`.

2. `repeat`

   Now we start a repeat loop without any modifiers. This type of simple repeat will loop until an `exit repeat` command is encountered.

3. `   set myList to (myList & "me")`
   `→ as list`

   Now we append the string `me` as a new item to our list `myList`. We tell AppleScript to set this variable as a list for clarity and just to make sure, but in this case it would do so anyway.

4. `end repeat`

   Finally, we conclude our repeat, sending our script execution back to the line immediately after `repeat` and starting the cycle all over again. If you run this script, the result will be that the variable `myList` will fill up with an infinite number of me's.

Code 3.1 An infinite repeat loop.

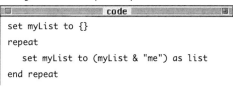

```
set myList to {}
repeat
    set myList to (myList & "me") as list
end repeat
```

Code 3.2 An infinite repeat loop with an exit.

```
code
set myList to {}
repeat
    set myList to (myList & "me") as list
    if the number of items in myList > 10 then
    → exit repeat
end repeat
```

Figure 3.14 Adding items to a list in a repeat loop.

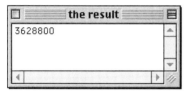

Figure 3.15 Looping from 1 through 10 and multiplying each successive number to get the factorial of 10.

Code 3.3. A counting repeat loop

```
code
set x to 1
repeat with i from 1 to 10
    set x to x * i
end repeat.
```

Exiting from an infinite loop

AppleScript gives us a way out of the infinite loop, however, as demonstrated in the following script, which is also shown in **Code 3.2. Figure 3.14** shows the result of this script.

1. `set myList to {}`

We begin this script just like as the last, by defining an empty list variable.

2. `repeat`

Again, we start an infinite repeat loop.

3. `set myList to (myList & "me")`
`→ as list`

Now we append the string me as a new item to the list myList.

4. `if the number of items in myList`
`→ > 10 then exit repeat`
`end repeat`

Here's the trick! This time we test the number of items in our list. Once it exceeds 10, we exit the loop.

Using a counting repeat loop

Repeat loops can also count using a variable. The next example (**Code 3.3**) will calculate the factorial 10 using the variable i by looping through the numbers 1 through 10 and multiplying the previous result by the next number, i.e., 1*2*3*4*5*6*7*8*9*10. **Figure 3.15** shows the result of this calculation.

1. `set x to 1`

We start by setting a variable outside of the repeat loop to hold our factorial result.

2. `repeat with i from 1 to 10`

By defining a variable and a counting range with this repeat, we tell AppleScript to execute the loop as many times as it takes to get from the starting value to the ending value (from 1 to 10 in this case).

This technique allows us to limit the number of loops through the repeat when we start it, rather than inside the loop itself.

3. `set x to x * i`

Here we set the value of x to equal its current value multiplied by the current counter value in the variable i.

4. `end repeat`

Finally, we end the loop.

Notice that we didn't need the conditional test we used in the previous example to exit this repeat loop, as we took care of that in step 2.

Using a conditional repeat loop

In their most exotic form, repeat loops are conditional, much like if commands. After each loop, the following script (**Code 3.4**) will check to see if x is greater than 100.

1. `set x to 1`

First we initialize a variable to hold an increasing value.

2. `repeat until x>100`

By defining a conditional test after the word until, we have told AppleScript that this loop should repeat until the condition returns a value of true. In this case, our loop will repeat until the variable x holds a value larger than 100.

3. `set x to x+x`

Inside the repeat loop we'll change the value of x by adding it to itself. Our script will keep doubling x from 1 to 2 to 4 and so on until it hits 128, causing the loop to end. Each time it adds x to itself, the first line of the repeat loop is checked by AppleScript again to see if x is greater than 100.

4. `end repeat`

Now we end the loop.

Code 3.4. A conditional repeat loop.

```
set x to 1
repeat until x>100
    set x to x+x
end repeat
```

✔ Skipping and going in reverse

■ You can also skip numbers using the by modifier. Here we'll count from 2 to 50 by 2s, skipping all odd numbers:

```
repeat with j from 2 to 50 by 2
```

■ You can use negative numbers in a by modifier to count down. Here we'll go from 100 to 1 backwards:

```
repeat with j from 100 to 1 by -1
```

✔ Moving through a list with repeat

■ AppleScript has another special repeat loop construction that automates the process of moving through each item in a list. In this code, the values of the three items in myList will each individually be put into the variable myItem, one item for each cycle in the loop. We display the item's value in a dialog:

```
set myList to {1,2,3}
repeat with myItem in myList
    display dialog myItem
end repeat
```

Code 3.5 Handling an error with try.

```
try
    tell application "Finder" to open disk
    → "Blank"
on error myErr
    display dialog myErr
end try
```

Figure 3.16 Our script displays this dialog thanks to the try...on error statement in Code 3.5.

Code 3.6 Ignoring errors with an empty on error handler.

```
try
    tell application "Finder" to open disk
    → "Blank"
on error
end try
```

To ignore errors altogether

You can also use the try statement to keep your script from failing by having it ignore errors completely. You do this by leaving the on error block empty:

```
on error
end try
```

If anything goes wrong, our script silently fails and just continues along its way.

Error handling

As our scripts in this book get more robust and user-friendly, they will need to deal intelligently with errors. Errors happen. AppleScript gives us a way to intercept execution errors in our scripts with the try statement, as **Code 3.5** demonstrates. If we didn't use the try statement in this script, AppleScript would halt execution and display an error message.

To intercept errors with try:

1. try

   We begin by invoking error handling with the try statement.

2. tell application "Finder" to open
   → disk "Blank"

   Next, we ask the Finder to open a disk named Blank. We're using this example because we know Blank doesn't exist, so an error will be created.

3. on error myErr
       display dialog myErr
   end try

   Finally, we create a handler to let AppleScript know what to do if the actions in our script fail. A *handler* is a small piece of code that only runs if something asks it to. In this case, if our tell command fails, the try statement generates an error, which makes this handler run. The handler then displays a dialog with the error's name. To learn more about handlers, see *Handlers* later in this chapter.

Figure 3.16 shows what happens when the disk can't be opened. If everything goes OK, execution of the script will simply continue past the end try statement.

ERROR HANDLING

Using with timeout to wait

Another failure-proofing command you'll want to know is with timeout, which is demonstrated in **Code 3.7**. Commands inside of a with timeout statement will only execute for a specified duration of time, then the script will generate a timeout error.

To control how long your script will wait for results:

1. try

   with timeout of 50 seconds

   We start with a try statement to prevent any timeout errors from stopping the execution of our code. Then we let AppleScript know that we want to restrict the amount of time allowed for our code to run to 50 seconds.

2. tell application "Netscape
   → Navigator™ 4.04" OpenURL
   → "http://applescript.
      → apple.com/"
   end tell

   Now we ask Netscape to open a window with the AppleScript Web site in it. Normally, our script would wait quite a while for Netscape to finish. Inside of the with timeout, however, our script will continue executing after waiting 50 seconds. The same is true for all AppleScript statements we include inside the with timeout statement.

3. end timeout
   on error
   end try

   Finally, we let AppleScript know that we're done with the code for which we're defining the with timeout. We close our try statement with an empty on error handler so that errors are ignored.

Code 3.7 Using with timeout to set an allowable duration for a script's execution.

```
try
    with timeout of  50 seconds
        tell application "Netscape Navigator™
        → 4.04" OpenURL
        → "http://applescript.apple.com/"
        end tell
    end timeout
on error
end try
```

✔ Tip

■ Place your with timeout statement within a try... on error statement to prevent your script from stopping when a timeout occurs. Sometimes you don't want your script to wait forever for something to happen.

Code 3.8 A simple handler with a main line to call it.

```
on testValue (x)
    if x>100 then set x to 100
    if x<1 then set x to 1
    return x
end
set z to testValue(200)
```

Handlers

Handlers are very important. A handler is simply a short modular script that performs one specialized task. If you have heard of a function or subroutine before, then you will understand what a handler is. AppleScript lets you create handlers with input values and output values. Some of the scripts we'll create early in this book can be used in conjunction with each other as independent handlers, or functions, that can be combined to make more complex scripts.

Writing simple code based on handlers makes that code especially easy to reuse. As you become a regular AppleScripter, you'll find that many handlers you create for one purpose are in fact useful over and over again.

AppleScript makes it easy to define a snippet of code as a handler. You simply have to use the on statement and give your handler a name. **Code 3.8** shows a simple handler.

To define some AppleScript as a handler:

1. `on testValue (x)`

By placing thse comparisons within a handler we create a snippet of code we can use whenever we want this comparison made, instead of having to type it out every time. We define the handler by typing on, followed by the handler name. If we want to be able to pass data to our handler, we also need to define a variable in the first line of our handler in order to hold that data. Here we use x. Variables are always placed within parentheses in an on statement.

2. `if x>100 then set x to 100`
`if x<1 then set x to 1`

These two lines are the comparison which works inside our handler, setting

Saving script libraries

◆ You can save a separate compiled script with many handlers to disk as a library. Any script can then easily access the subroutines you've defined in the library. Once you save your handler as a compiled script named "mylib", this code will get the same result that step 1 below yields:

```
set myLibrary to load script
 → "HD:mylib"
tell myLibrary to set z to
 → testValue(200)
```

◆ Your saved script library can have many handlers defined within it. Just reference the appropriate handler name in the tell statement you send to your script library, for example:

```
tell myLibrary to doHandler1()
tell myLibrary to
 → doHandler2("hi","hey")
```

the value of x, which is the data we passed to the handler when we called it.

3. `return x`

This important line tells AppleScript to "return" the value in x to the rest of our script.

4. `end`

The end line stops the handler.

This handler, named `testValue`, will test a value passed to it, ensuring that the value is within the range of 1 to 100, and then return the adjusted value.

Each handler can be placed anywhere in your script outside other handlers.

Calling handlers is just as easy as defining them. You can pass a handler many values of any type, including strings, numbers, and lists. Separate multiple values with commas.

✔ Multiple variables

■ If we want to define a handler which has multiple variables passed to it we would create an on statement like this:

```
on testMax(x,y)
    if x>y then
        return x
    else
        return y
    end if
end textMax
```

✔ Handlers are functions too!

■ Handlers in AppleScript are based on the same programming concept as functions. AppleScript calls them "handlers" because they are routines called to handle something. Simple enough.

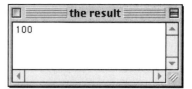

Figure 3.17 The result of our sample handler.

Calling handlers

◆ `set z to testValue(200)`

Here in our one line of main code, we call our handler `testValue`, passing it the value 100. Our handler will return its results into the variable z.

Figure 3.17 shows the result of this example script.

After scripting for some time, you will find yourself with a folder full of handler scripts that you reuse. Efficient use of handlers, like clear variable names, is an important part of good scripting technique.

Figure 3.18 The two types of comments as displayed by the Script Editor.

Using comments to help yourself

Good scripting techniques always seem to take longer at first, but save time later on. You've probably heard this before. In fact, I find that good scripting techniques help not only when you come back to your script later, but also as you're in the process of creating it. Using clear variable names and handler-based scripts helps to keep your thinking clear and uncluttered.

Even more important than both of these techniques is the use of comments to annotate your scripts with additional information. **Figure 3.18** shows what comments look like in the Script Editor. Comments are where you leave important notes for later visits to a script, but they also help you clarify your thinking process while you're engaged in your scripting effort. How? By letting you have some free space in which to outline your scripting approach.

AppleScript gives you two ways to enter comments in a script. The first syntax is for one-liners. You simply type two dashes to start a one-line comment:

```
--this is a quick one-line comment
```

AppleScript, always trying to be flexible, also gives the long-winded a chance to write many lines of comments quickly and easily. For a long comment, you start with an opening parenthesis and asterisk and close with another asterisk and a closing parenthesis.

```
(* this is a long rambling tale of my
greatest hopes for this feeble script
that it may one day be great *)
```

✔ Tip

- Be generous with yourself as you go through the thinking process while scripting. Take the time to write out what you're doing while you're doing it. You will not regret this effort later, and it's a good way to keep yourself organized.

Simple interaction with the user

AppleScript gives you a few simple and elegant commands for getting input from the user while your script is running. You can get textual data and button choices by using the display dialog command. The following script (**Code 3.9**) uses most of the interactive commands of AppleScript. **Figure 3.19** shows the result.

To ask the user for information:

1. display dialog "Please enter your
   → name" default answer "" buttons
   → {"First","Last","Cancel"}
   → default button "Cancel"

   This code has AppleScript stop executing and display a dialog box asking the user to supply a name. **Figure 3.20** shows what happens if we enter "Steven" and push the button labeled "First." In this example we also define a default answer, which sets the initial string that appears in the dialog's editable text field. In this case we set it to an empty string. If we didn't include the default answer then AppleScript would not show a text field in the dialog.

2. set x to the button returned of
   → the result

   Here we access the results of display dialog. Once this line is executed, the variable x will equal the string value First.

✔ Tips

■ You can define up to three buttons in a display dialog.

■ We tell AppleScript to make the Cancel button the default button, which makes that button show up with a thick border and causes it to be triggered when the user presses the Return or Enter keys.

Code 3.9 Asking the user for input. Nothing happens until the user clicks one of the three buttons here labeled "First," "Last," and "Cancel."

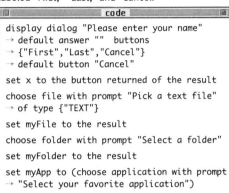

```
display dialog "Please enter your name"
→ default answer ""  buttons
→ {"First","Last","Cancel"}
→ default button "Cancel"

set x to the button returned of the result

choose file with prompt "Pick a text file"
→ of type {"TEXT"}

set myFile to the result

choose folder with prompt "Select a folder"

set myFolder to the result

set myApp to (choose application with prompt
→ "Select your favorite application")
```

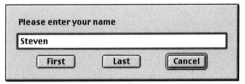

Please enter your name

Steven

[First]   [Last]   [Cancel]

Figure 3.19 A dialog generated by our display dialog command.

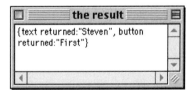

the result

{text returned:"Steven", button returned:"First"}

Figure 3.20 The result of user input to our display dialog command.

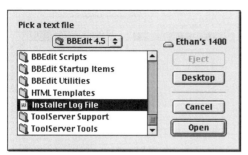

Figure 3.21 A file-selection dialog generated by a choose file command, limited to text files only.

Figure 3.22 The result of a user selection from the Choose File dialog.

Table 3.3

Some File Types to Use with choose file	
FILE TYPE	DESCRIPTION
EPSF	An EPS (encapsulated PostScript) image file
JPEG	A JPEG image file
PICT	A PICT image file
GIFf	A GIF image file
PDF	An Adobe Acrobat™ file
FMP3	A FileMaker Pro 3.0 database file
APPL	An application file
osas	A compiled AppleScript file

Asking for a choice

You can also interact with the user by asking them to pick and choose. AppleScript contains commands that you can use to display standard Macintosh dialogs that let users find files, folders, and applications from their hard drive.

To ask users to pick a file:

1. `choose file with prompt "Pick a`
   `→ text file" of type {"TEXT"}`

   Here we ask the user to select a file via the standard file-selection dialog box with the choose file command. **Figure 3.21** shows this dialog box; note that only text files appear in it. If you want the user to be able to pick other kinds of files, substitute one of the values from Table 3.3 for TEXT in the line above.

2. `set myFile to the result`

   This stores the reference to a file returned by choose file in the variable myFile.

   Figure 3.22 displays the result of the user's selection , which is an alias pointing to the selected file.

To ask users to pick a folder:

1. `choose folder with prompt`
   `→ "Select a folder"`

   choose folder works in a similar way to choose file, except the dialog box only displays folders.

2. `set myFolder to the result`

   Here we store the reference to the folder chosen with choose folder in the variable myFolder.

ASKING FOR A CHOICE

37

To ask users to choose an application

1. `set myApp to (choose application`
   → `with prompt "Select your favorite`
   → `application")`

   We can use `choose application` to have AppleScript ask the user to select a scriptable application from any running application on the local machine or other machines on the network. With this feature we can allow the user to select the target for portions of a script. This time we store the reference returned by `choose application` directly into the variable `myApp`. **Figure 3.23** shows the dialog generated by this command.

Figure 3.23 The application-selection dialog generated by a `choose application` command.

✔ Mac OS 8.5 tips

■ In OS 8.5 `display dialog` has a new optional parameter, `giving up after`, that allows you to specify how long (in seconds) a dialog should appear before the script automatically continues; for example, `display dialog "Hello" giving up after 5`.

■ OS 8.5 also introduces a new interaction command, `choose from list` that allows you to show the user a list of choices that they can choose from, for example, `choose from list {"a","b", "c"} with prompt "Make a choice"`. **Code 4.18** and **4.19** in Chapter 4 show how to use this new command.

Code 3.10 A simple on run handler with one line of main code.

```
on run
    display dialog "hey! "
end run
```

Using on run and saving scripts as applications

We've already seen how you tell AppleScript that you want to define a handler in a script by using the on...end statement in conjunction with a handler name.

We've also seen the special try...on error...end try handler that AppleScript uses to deal with error handling during execution of a script. Well, AppleScript has set aside two other on...end handlers for special purposes. We'll cover one here and the other in the next section.

The most fundamental on...end handler is the on run...end run handler. This handler defines the main chunk of code that is executed when the script is run. **Code 3.10** shows a simple on run handler.

Every script you write starts with an implied on run and ends with an implied end run command whether you type them in or not. In scripts where numerous handlers are defined, it is usually good practice to use the on run and end run commands to make it clear where the main code exists in the script.

If no on run handler is explicitly defined, AppleScript will run the first line of code it finds. However, you can't have both loose code and define an on run handler in one script.

Defining a run handler

1. on run

We begin our script's main portion of code with on run to let AppleScript know that we want it to execute this code first whenever the script is run.

2. display dialog "hey! "

In this example, our main code is simply this one line that shows the user a dialog box.

3. end run

> To let AppleScript know that our main code is over, we close our handler with an end run statement.

Saving your script as an application

When you save a script with an on run handler as an application, the main code within the handler will execute when a user double-clicks your script's icon. **Figure 3.24** shows the Save dialog that appears when you choose to save your script as a stand-alone application. This will be the way we save most of the scripts throughout this book.

Making your script into an application makes it very easy for a user to run the script. Double-click it and it is running.

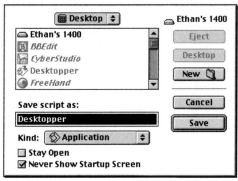

Figure 3.24 The Script Editor's Save dialog, ready to save a script as a stand-alone application.

✔ Script application tips

- By selecting the option to never show the startup screen, we avoid AppleScript's default behavior of showing our script's description in a dialog box before every execution.

- Almost every script in this book will work optimally when saved as an application. AppleScript CGI applications should be saved as applications that stay open to eliminate the launching time for the CGI script application.

- Scripts saved as applications are often called "applets."

Code 3.11 A simple on open handler.

```
                   code
on open (somefile)
    tell application "Finder" to move somefile
    → to the desktop
end open
```

Figure 3.25 The standard icon for a drag-and-drop script application.

Making drag-and-drop applications with on open

More interesting than the quite useful on run handler is the on open...end open handler. This is a special handler because when a script with an on open handler is saved as a stand-alone application it becomes a drag-and-drop capable application. **Code 3.11** shows a simple on open handler.

Your script can have both on open and on run handlers defined in it. Each will be executed according to how the script application is being run. If it is double-clicked, the on run code will execute. If items are dropped onto its icon, the on open handler will be run.

Defining an on open handler

1. `on open (somefile)`

A reference to any object that the user drags onto the script's application icon will be passed to the script in the variable somefile used as an argument for on open.

2. `tell application "Finder" to`
`→ move somefile to the desktop`

With a reference to all the objects that we dropped onto our script stored in somefile, we have the Finder move them to the Desktop.

3. `end open`

Finally, we conclude our on open handler with the end open statement.

✔ Tip

■ The use of parenthesis with the on open handler is optional in AppleScript.

Making Droplets

Try entering the sample script above and saving it as an application from the Script Editor, making sure to select the "never show the startup screen" option. **Figure 3.25** shows the standard icon for a drag-and-drop script application.

Now try dragging a file or folder from anywhere other than your Desktop onto the application icon. The icon should become highlighted and when you let go of the button, the script will launch and tell the Finder to move your selection onto the Desktop.

Scripts with on open handlers that are saved as applications are often called "droplets" in AppleScript.

Other ways to save scripts

Scripts saved as applications can only be reopened in the Script Editor by dragging and dropping their icons onto the Script Editor icon or by explicitly choosing the script from the Script Editor's Open dialog. **Figure 3.26** shows the Script Editor's Open dialog with our previous sample script application selected for reopening.

The Script Editor does allow you to save your scripts in other formats, including as compiled scripts. In this format, the script's syntax is checked by AppleScript as it is saved. Once a script is compiled, it can be executed by AppleScript without needing to be recompiled. You can open compiled scripts into the Script Editor simply by double-clicking them in the Finder. This is often a good format for saving handlers that you expect to use as script libraries. **Figure 3.27** shows the standard icon for a compiled script.

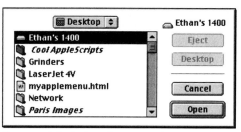

Figure 3.26 The Script Editor's Open dialog.

Figure 3.27 The standard icon for a compiled script.

Figure 3.28 The standard icon for a text-only script.

✔ Saving scripts as text only

■ You can also save your script as text only. If you save your script as text only, you can open it up in any application that can edit text to perform modifications. For example, you might want to reopen your script in a more sophisticated text editor, like BBEdit, to perform cleaning operations such as global search-and-replaces of certain terms. Scripts saved as text do not have their syntax verified, so when they are reopened in the Script Editor, this operation will still need to be performed. **Figure 3.28** shows the standard icon for a text-only script document.

✔ Saving scripts as run-only

■ Finally, scripts can be saved as run-only applications from the Script Editor. Once you've saved your script like this, you will never be able to open it in the Script Editor to change any of its code. This format is available so that you can distribute functional script applications to others without worrying about giving away your AppleScripting secrets!

I avoid saving scripts this way, since most scripts continue to evolve. Always be certain to keep an editable copy of any script you choose to save as run-only or you'll never see your precious code again!

AppleScript on the Desktop

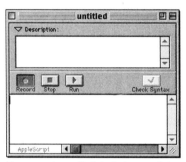

Figure 4.1 A new Script window ready to record your actions.

Figure 4.2 A recorded script from the Finder.

If any one application is more powerful in combination with AppleScript than our 15-year-old friend the Finder, I'm at a loss to name it. We all know the Finder intimately, although we don't usually think of it as an application in the normal sense. However, the Finder is really just another application as far as the Mac OS is concerned. It is, in fact, an extremely scriptable application in its Mac OS 8.x variant. You can even record scripts with the Finder, which provides excellent opportunities for learning its scripting syntax.

Before we dive in, try a quick recording session to get a feel for what the experience can be like. Open a new window in the Script Editor and click the Record button. **Figure 4.1** shows what your window should look like after you do this.

Now select a file in the Finder and drag it into the Trash. Switch back to the Script Editor and click the Stop button. Your recorded script should look similar to **Figure 4.2**. While this amounts to a cheap thrill for now, imagine using this technique when you're desperately trying to figure out some very particular syntax for scripting the Finder (or any other recordable application for that matter).

Moving a file or folder

Have you ever wanted to rearrange a group of files into specific folders based on some attribute of the files? Perhaps you'd like to check the label status of files or folders and move them into different folders based on that status. This would be a quick way to file work you've labeled as finished into an archive folder. **Code 4.1** shows how this can be done with AppleScript.

Before you run this script, prepare by creating two folders on your desktop named No Label and Label.

To move a file or folder based on its label status:

1. `on open (myFileOrFolder)`

   By using the on open handler we create a drag-and-drop script application, as we saw on page 44. Any folder dropped onto this application will be passed to our script in the variable myFolder.

2. `tell application "Finder"`

   Here we inform AppleScript that we want to target all of the following statements to the Finder.

3. `if the label index of`
   `→ (myFileOrFolder as alias) is`
   `→ equal to 0 then`

   Now we test the label index of the object that was dropped onto our script application. If the label index is 0, then it has no label assigned.

4. `move myFileOrFolder to folder`
   `→ "No Label"`

   If our object has no label, we'll have the Finder move it into our folder named No Label.

Code 4.1 It's easy to move objects in the Finder intelligently with AppleScript's conditional logic.

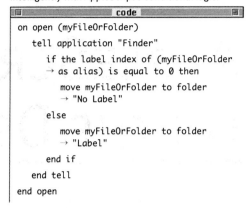

```
on open (myFileOrFolder)
    tell application "Finder"
        if the label index of (myFileOrFolder
        → as alias) is equal to 0 then
            move myFileOrFolder to folder
            → "No Label"
        else
            move myFileOrFolder to folder
            → "Label"
        end if
    end tell
end open
```

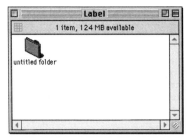

Figure 4.3 A view of the Label folder after a labeled folder is dropped onto the script application.

5. else
```
    move myFileOrFolder to folder
    → "Label"
end if
end tell
end open
```

If our object's label index isn't 0, it must have a label assigned to it, so we'll tell the Finder to move it into our folder named Label.

Be sure to save this script as an application when you've typed it in. Put the application icon on your Desktop. Now drag and drop some labeled and unlabeled objects onto it and see what happens! **Figure 4.3** shows an example of what happens after a labeled folder is dropped onto our script application.

MOVING A FILE OR FOLDER

Changing creator types

Have you ever had a bunch of files that always open in the wrong program when you double-click them? Perhaps they're screenshots, which are automatically tagged as SimpleText files when they're created, but you really want them to open in Photoshop when you double-click them. The Mac uses a file's creator type to decide which application owns the file and should be opened when it is double-clicked. **Code 4.2** makes it quick and easy to change a file's creator type.

To change a file's creator type:

1. `on open (myFileOrFolder)`

   By using the on open handler we create a drag-and-drop script application.

2. `set x to button returned of`
   `→ (display dialog "Change to which`
   `→ application/creator?" buttons`
   `→ {"Photoshop", "CyberStudio",`
   `→ "Cancel"} default button`
   `→ "Cancel")`

   Now we prompt the user to choose one of two applications to be the new creator type for the file and store their selection in the variable x. **Figure 4.4** shows what the dialog looks like. If the user clicks on the Cancel button, AppleScript will exit our script automatically.

3. `if x = "Photoshop" then`
   `    set myCreator to "8BIM"`
   `else`
   `    set myCreator to "GoMk"`
   `end if`

   At this point, we test to see which application the user selected and assign the appropriate creator type to the variable myCreator.

Code 4.2 Changing a file's creator type is painless.

```
on open (myFileOrFolder)
    set x to button returned of
    → (display dialog "Change to which
    → application/creator?" buttons
    → {"Photoshop", "CyberStudio", "Cancel"}
    → default button "Cancel")
    if x = "Photoshop" then
        set myCreator to "8BIM"
    else
        set myCreator to "GoMk"
    end if
    tell application "Finder"
        set myFileOrFolder to myFileOrFolder as
        → alias
        if kind of myFileOrFolder is not
        → "folder" then set the creator type
        → of myFileOrFolder to myCreator
    end tell
end open
```

Figure 4.4 Code 4.2's dialog window with three button choices.

Code 4.3 A script to display creator types.

```
                      code
on open (myFileOrFolder)
   tell application "Finder"
      set myFileOrFolder to myFileOrFolder
      → as alias
      if kind of myFileOrFolder is not
      → "folder" then display dialog
      → (the creator type of myFileOrFolder)
   end tell
end open
```

Discovering creator types

Save **Code 4.3** as an application and drop
any application or file onto it to display
that object's creator type.

4.
```
tell application "Finder"
   set myFileOrFolder to
   → myFileOrFolder as alias
   if kind of myFileOrFolder is not
   → "folder" then set the creator
   → type of myFileOrFolder to
   → myCreator
```

Finally, we instruct the Finder to change
the creator type to our new selection if
the original object dropped onto our
application is not a folder.

Testing for the existence of a file

There are times when all you want to do is make sure something exists on your hard drive. A good example would be when you want to confirm that a particular scripting addition is in the Scripting Additions folder before launching a script that is dependent on commands only available in that addition's dictionary. **Code 4.4** gives us the power to look around our Scripting Additions folder.

To verify the existence of a particular file in the Scripting Additions folder:

1. `tell application "Finder"`

This statement lets AppleScript know that the following commands should be targeted to the Finder.

2. `set x to ((path to scripting` → `additions folder) as text) &` → `"ACME Script Widgets 2.5.1"`

Here we assign a file path to the variable x. This path is made up of the full path to your active Scripting Additions folder followed by the name of a particular scripting addition (ACME Script Widgets, in this case).

3. `if alias x exists then open` → `"Widget User"` `end tell`

If the Finder confirms the existence of our needed addition, we then invite it to open our next script, named Widget User, which resides in the same folder as our first script.

Code 4.4 This short script lets us test for the existence of a particular scripting addition file in the Scripting Additions folder before opening another script dependent on that addition.

```
tell application "Finder"
    set x to ((path to scripting additions
    → folder) as text) & "ACME Script Widgets
    → 2.5.1"
    if alias x exists then open "Widget User"
end tell
```

✔ Other ideas for testing for existence

- If you have a script that moves files around, you might want to test for the existence of a same-named file in the destination folder before moving. Or you might test for the existence of the Scripting Additions folder itself in both the System folder and the Extensions folder to make sure there's only one.

Code 4.5 The Finder is more than happy to do mundane file renaming for you.

```
                    code

on open (myFolder)

    set mySuffix to text returned of
    ⇢ (display dialog "Suffix to add:"
    ⇢ default answer ".jpg")

    AppendSuffix(myFolder as alias, mySuffix)

end open


on AppendSuffix(myFolder, mySuffix)

    tell application "Finder"

        set myFolderContents to every file of
        ⇢ myFolder

        repeat with x in myFolderContents

            if name of x does not end with
            ⇢ mySuffix then

                try

                    set name of x to (name of x &
                    ⇢ mySuffix)

                on error

                end try

            end if

        end repeat

        if number of folders in myFolder > 0
then

            repeat with y in every folder of
            ⇢ myFolder

                AppendSuffix(y, mySuffix) of me

            end repeat

        end if

    end tell

end AppendSuffix
```

Renaming all the files in a folder

Imagine you've just received a Zip disk with 10,000 JPEG images on it. Each of these images has been named with a nice and simple English file name, no file-format suffix like `.jpg` to clutter things up. And now your boss wants you to get each and every one of these files ready for use on a Web site, where file suffixes are a way of life—in fact, an absolute requirement!

Got your Return-key finger ready for 10,000 keystrokes as you furiously type out an endless litany of dot-J-P-Gs? No need—**Code 4.5** will save you the trouble by automatically adding the suffix to every file in a folder.

Be sure to save this script as an application when you've typed it in.

To rename all the files in a folder:

1. `on open (myFolder)`

By using the on open handler we create a drag-and-drop script application, where any folder dropped onto the application will be passed to our script in the variable myFolder.

2. `set mySuffix to text returned of`
`⇢ (display dialog "Suffix to add:"`
`⇢ default answer ".jpg")`

Now we prompt the user to enter a file suffix (or accept the default of `.jpg`) and store that value in the variable mySuffix.

3. `AppendSuffix(myFolder as alias,`
`⇢ mySuffix)`
`end open`

Next we call our function named AppendSuffix, pass it our two variables, coercing myFolder to be a single alias instead of a list with a single item in it, and gracefully end our on open handler.

4. `on AppendSuffix(myFolder,`
`→ mySuffix)`

Here we define our function
`AppendSuffix` and give it two arguments
to receive the main script's variables.

5. `tell application "Finder"`

Now we inform AppleScript that we want
to send subsequent statements to the
Finder.

6. `set myFolderContents to every file`
`→ of myFolder`

We have the Finder return a list of references to every file in our folder and we
store this list in our variable
`myFolderContents`.

7. `repeat with x in myFolderContents`

Here we establish a repeat loop to cycle
through each file in the folder, storing the
current file reference in the variable `x`.

8. `if name of x does not end with`
`→ mySuffix then`

Let's see if the file's name already ends
with the desired suffix.

9. `try`
`set name of x  to (name of x &`
`→ mySuffix)`
`on error`
`end try`
`end if`
`end if`
`end repeat`
`end tell`

We're ready to have the Finder set the
name of the file referred to by `x` by
concatenating `mySuffix` with its current
name. We've placed this command inside
of a `try...on error` handler to keep any
errors that might arise from halting the
script's execution.

10.
```
    if number of folders in
    → myFolder > 0 then
        repeat with y in every
        → folder of myFolder
        AppendSuffix(y, mySuffix)
        → of me
        end repeat
    end if
end tell
```

Now, we check to see if there are any other folders in myFolder. If there are, we loop through each once, sending a reference to the folder to our handler AppendSuffix so nested folders are dealt with.

✔ Learn to batch process

■ Study the structure of this script and you will be able to apply its ability to modify every file in a folder to any script you create. The key command is `repeat with x in every file in folder`. The `every file` reference gets the Finder to return a list of references to each item in the folder specified. By implementing this loop in any of the previous scripts, you could transform them into full-fledged batch processors.

■ The scripting addition command `list folder` can also be used to retrieve a list of the names of all files and folders in a folder. This list differs from the list returned by the Finder for `every file` in that it is a list of file/folder names as strings whereas the list returned by `every file` is a list of references to files. We will use both techniques in this book for batch processing folders of files.

RENAMING ALL THE FILES IN A FOLDER

Making a folder

Sometimes in the course of a script, you'll want to create a folder to hold things. These things might be files and folders your script is moving around or even newly created files spawned by the script itself. **Code 4.6** and **Code 4.7** demonstrate how you can instruct the Finder to make a new folder from scratch.

To create a new folder on the Desktop:

1. `tell application "Finder"`

   This sends all following commands to the Finder.

2. `make new folder at the desktop with`
   `→ properties {name:"holder"}`
   `end tell`

   The make statement tells the Finder to create something, in this case a new folder. The at clause describes the location for the new folder while the properties record defines the folder's name. Additional properties can also be defined at this time.

✔ Mounting network volumes in OS 8.5

- OS 8.5 includes the scripting addition command mount volume to let your script automatically log in as a registered user with a password (or as a guest) to mount a network drive. To mount a drive named "Shared" on a Mac named "My Mac" as user "John" with password "hey" you'd write:

  `mount volume "Shared" on server`
  `→ "My Mac" in AppleTalk zone "*"`
  `→ as user name "john" with password`
  `→ "hey"`

Code 4.6 Creating a new folder on your Desktop is a snap.

```
tell application "Finder"
    make new folder at the desktop with
    → properties {name:"holder"}
end tell
```

Code 4.7 This script create a new folder at a user-selected location on the hard drive.

```
set x to (choose folder with prompt "Choose a
→ destination for new folder:")
tell application "Finder"
    make new folder at x with properties
    → {name:"holder"}
end tell
```

To create a new folder at a location chosen by the user

1. `set x to (choose folder with`
   `→ prompt "Choose a destination`
   `→ for new folder:")`

   Our first order of business is to invite the user to choose where the new folder will be created and then save this reference in the variable x.

2. `tell application "Finder"`

   With this tell command, we instruct AppleScript to send all following commands to the Finder.

3. `make new folder at x with`
   `→ properties {name:"holder"}`
   `end tell`

   In this version of the script our make statement simply has a different location defined, in this case, the reference to the user's selection as defined by x.

MAKING A FOLDER

Code 4.8 Since we've already spent so much time with the Finder, we'll use it to supply some fodder for our script in the form of a list of all the file names in our Apple Menu Items folder.

```
                 code
   set myFolderContents to list folder
    → (path to apple menu items folder)
    → without invisibles

set myFileRef to (open for access file
 → "myapplemenu.html" with write permission)

write "<HTML><HEAD><TITLE>My Apple Menu
 → </TITLE><BODY>" & return to myFileRef

write "<P>An Apple Menu makes or breaks the
 → individual...</P>" & return to myFileRef

write "<P>How do I fare?</P>" & return to
 → myFileRef

write "<UL>" & return to myFileRef

repeat with x in myFolderContents

    write "<LI>" & x & return to myFileRef

end repeat

write "</BODY></HTML>" & return to myFileRef

close access myFileRef
```

Creating a file from scratch

There are many, many reasons why you might want to create a file from within AppleScript. While many scriptable applications support the creation and saving of new documents, AppleScript has its own means of creating text files and writing data to them: the open for access, write and close access commands. For Internet-based purposes, the ability to create text files on the fly is very valuable, since HTML files themselves are simply text files.

Code 4.8 will build a quick HTML page that contains a list of all our Apple menu items to include in our own personal Web site. Because, after all, we certainly know that a person's Apple menu says a lot about who they are.

To create a text file from scratch:

1. set myFolderContents to list
   → folder (path to apple menu items
   → folder) without invisibles

   We'll begin by using the list folder command to gather a list of all the file names (except invisible files) in our Apple Menu Items folder as fodder for our text file.

2. set myFileRef to (open for access
   → file "myapplemenu.html" with
   → write permission)

   Our next step is to open a new text file with write permission. If we didn't specify write permission, AppleScript would open this file as read-only. When AppleScript creates or opens a text file, it returns a reference number that all subsequent commands must use to refer to the now-open file. Since we didn't specify a complete path, this file will be created in the same folder as the current script.

Finding the end of a file (EOF)

AppleScript also lets you determine the length of your currently open file using the get eof command, for example, we can store the length of the file referred to by myFileRef in myFileLength with this line of code: set myFileLength to get → eof myFileRef

---

If we run this script from the Script Editor, the file will be created in the same folder as the Script Editor.

3.
```
write "<HTML><HEAD><TITLE>My Apple
→ Menu</TITLE><BODY>" & return to
→ myFileRef
write "<P>An Apple Menu makes or
→ breaks the individual...</P>" &
→ return to myFileRef
write "<P>How do I fare?</P>" &
→ return to myFileRef
write "<UL>" & return to myFileRef
```

We now have AppleScript write some static text to our new file. This text creates the beginning of a valid HTML page with two paragraphs of text and starts a bulleted list for us.

4.
```
repeat with x in myFolderContents
    write "<LI>" & x & return to
    → myFileRef
end repeat
```

This code puts AppleScript into a loop that repeats once for each item in the list myFolderContents, placing the current item into the variable x. Since myFolderContents is a list of all file names in the Apple Menu Items folder, each instance of x is one of those file names. We then write that file name preceded by the HTML tag to indicate a bulleted list entry and followed by a carriage return to create a clean HTML file.

5.
```
write "</BODY></HTML>" & return to
→ myFileRef
close access myFileRef
```

Finally, we write one more line of static text to complete the proper syntax for an HTML file. Then we close the text file with the close access statement.

For a peek at your handiwork, just drag and drop this new file onto your favorite browser icon to view it. **Figure 4.5** shows a sample HTML file as displayed by Netscape.

Figure 4.5 A sample of this script's output as seen in Netscape Navigator.

Code 4.9 The script sets some of the properties of the Finder's preferences that can be accessed from AppleScript.

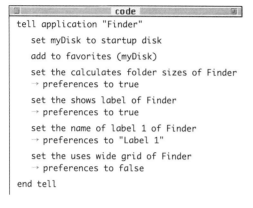

```
                        code
tell application "Finder"

    set myDisk to startup disk

    add to favorites (myDisk)

    set the calculates folder sizes of Finder
    → preferences to true

    set the shows label of Finder
    → preferences to true

    set the name of label 1 of Finder
    → preferences to "Label 1"

    set the uses wide grid of Finder
    → preferences to false

end tell
```

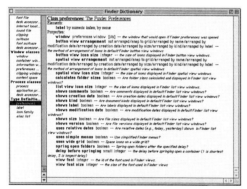

Figure 4.6 The Finder's dictionary entry for Finder preferences.

Customizing the Finder

The Finder has been customizable from AppleScript for some time now, and with OS 8.5, new commands have been added to the dictionary. **Figure 4.6** shows the complete set of properties for Finder preferences that you can set from a script. **Code 4.9** changes some of the settings available from AppleScript. **Code 4.10** shows you how you can also change your Apple Menu Options control panel settings from AppleScript in OS 8.5. All of Code 4.10 and the add to favorites line of Code 4.9 are specific to OS 8.5 and will not work with earlier versions.

To customize some of the Finder's preferences:

1. `tell application "Finder"`

   We begin by letting AppleScript know that we want to talk to the Finder.

2. `set myDisk to startup disk`
   `add to favorites (myDisk)`

   Next, we set our variable myDisk to be a reference to our startup disk. Then we tell the Finder to add our startup disk to the Favorites folder in the System folder.

3. `set the calculates folder sizes`
   `→ of Finder preferences to true`

   Now we tell the Finder to turn on folder size calculations for the standard item view settings.

4. `set the shows label of Finder`
   `→ preferences to true`

   We have the Finder show labels for items in the standard item view settings.

5. `set the name of label 1 of`
   `→ Finder preferences to "Label 1"`

   Then we change the name of the first of the Finder's item labels.

6. `set the uses wide grid of Finder`
`→ preferences to false`
`end tell`

Finally, we have the Finder use tight grid spacing on the Desktop.

To customize the Apple Menu Options control panel

1. `tell application "Apple Menu`
`→ Options"`

We begin by letting AppleScript know that we want to talk to the Apple Menu Options control panel.

2. `set submenus enabled to true`

This line turns on the submenus in the Apple menu.

3. `set recent items enabled to true`

Then we turn on the display of recent items in the Apple menu.

4. `set maximum recent applications`
`→ to 5`

Here we set the number of recent applications to remember to 5.

5. `set maximum recent documents`
`→ to 10`

Now we set the number of recent documents to remember to 10.

6. `set maximum recent servers`
`→ to 3`
`end tell`

Finally, we set the number of recent servers to remember to 3.

Code 4.10 This script sets the properties of the Apple Menu Options control panel that are scriptable in OS 8.5.

```
tell application "Apple Menu Options"
    set submenus enabled to true
    set recent items enabled to true
    set maximum recent applications to 5
    set maximum recent documents to 10
    set maximum recent servers to 3
end tell
```

Code 4.11 A folder action handler that makes a backup copy of every item added to the folder it is attached to.

```
                    code
on adding folder items to myFolder after
receiving myNewFiles

tell application "Finder"

     duplicate myNewFiles to folder "Backup"
     → of myFolder

end tell

end adding folder items to
```

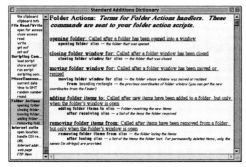

Figure 4.7 Mac OS 8.5's Standard Additions dictionary showing the entries for the new folder action handlers.

✔ Tips

- Folder actions can only be launched when a folder is open. Be aware that the Finder treats all spring-loaded folders as open folders.

- Folder action scripts can be saved on any local drive. There is also a special place you can put them: the folder called Folder Action Scripts in the System Folder's new Scripts folder.

- We could insert any code to manipulate the list of items in myNewFiles within this handler to make a script that automatically processes items added to the folder.

Using folder actions in OS 8.5

Mac OS 8.5 introduces a new set of standard handlers that allow us to attach an AppleScript to a folder in the Finder that responds to changes to that folder! A *folder action script* is attached to a folder by selecting the folder in the Finder and then selecting "Attach Folder Action..." from the contextual menu brought up with a Control-click. There are five action handlers defined in OS 8.5: on opening folder, on closing folder window for, on moving folder window for, on adding folder items to, and on removing folder items from. Each handler statement is defined in **Figure 4.7**, which shows their dictionary entries. **Code 4.11** makes use of the on adding folder items to handler to make a backup copy of every item added a folder.

To duplicate items added to a folder:

1. on adding folder items to myFolder
   → after receiving myNewFiles

   We begin with a on adding folder items to handler, storing a reference to the folder modified in myFolder and a list of items added to the folder in myNewFiles.

2. tell application "Finder"
       duplicate myNewFiles to folder
       → "Backup" of myFolder
   end tell

   Now we have the Finder copy any new files added to a folder named Backup in the same folder that the files were added to. The folder Backup should exist already.

3. end adding folder items to
   We close the handler with an end statement.

Customizing the Application Switcher in OS 8.5

Once you get Mac OS 8.5, you'll notice that the Application menu looks a little different. In fact, the biggest change to the Application menu isn't immediately visible: You can now tear it off! It then becomes a floating palette called the Application Switcher. Even more hidden is the fact that the extension that controls this palette is fully scriptable and highly customizable. **Code 4.12** lets the user customize the Application Switcher by choosing one of three preset styles, including the default settings for the palette. **Figure 4.8** shows the tiles preset style, while **Figure 4.9** shows the task bar preset style.

Figure 4.8
The Application Switcher palette after the tiles preset style has been applied.

Figure 4.9 The Application Switcher palette after the task bar preset style has been applied.

To customize the Application Switcher:

1. ```
   set myAnswer to button returned of
   → (display dialog "Switch the
   → switcher:" buttons
   → {"tiles","task bar","default"})
   ```
   We begin by prompting the user to choose a new style for the Application Switcher. We store their button choice in myAnswer.

2. ```
   tell application "Application
   → Switcher"
   if myAnswer is "tiles" then
      set visible of palette to true
   ```
   Now we check to see if myAnswer shows that the user chose "tiles." If so, we tell the Application Switcher to make the palette window visible. The other choices are responded to by the code that appears after the else statement that follows step 9.

3. ```
      set orientation of palette to
      → vertical
   ```
   ```

Code 4.12 This script lets the user customize the Application Switcher by choosing one of three preset styles, including the default settings for the palette.

```
☐▦▦▦▦▦▦▦▦     code     ▦▦▦ ▣
set myAnswer to button returned of
→ (display dialog "Switch the switcher:"
→ buttons {"tiles","task bar","default"})
tell application "Application Switcher"
if myAnswer is "tiles" then
    set visible of palette to true
    set orientation of palette to vertical
    set button ordering of palette to launch
    → order
    set frame visible of palette to false
    set icon size of palette to small
    set names visible of palette to false
    set position of palette to upper right
    set anchor point of palette to upper left
else
if myAnswer is "task bar" then
    set visible of palette to true
    set orientation of palette to horizontal
    set position of palette to lower right
    set anchor point of palette to lower right
    set button ordering of palette to launch
    → order
    set constraint of palette to one monitor
    set frame visible of palette to false
    set icon size of palette to small
    set names visible of palette to true
    set name width of palette to 140
else
    set visible of palette to true
    set orientation of palette to vertical
    set button ordering of palette to
    → alphabetical
    set frame visible of palette to true
    set icon size of palette to small
    set names visible of palette to true
    set name width of palette to 125
    set position of palette to upper right
    end if
    end if
end tell
```

Then we set the palette to show the application tiles in a vertical column.

4. `set button ordering of palette`
`→ to launch order`

We set the sorting order of the application tiles to display by the order in which they were run.

5. `set frame visible of palette to`
`→ false`

Now we make the palette window's frame invisible to make the palette smaller.

6. `set icon size of palette to`
`→ small`

This sets the size of the application icons in their tiles to the small size.

7. `set names visible of palette to`
`→ false`

Here we make the application names in the tiles invisible.

8. `set position of palette to upper`
`→ right`

We set the palette's position to the upper right of the screen, right under the Application menu icon.

9. `set anchor point of palette to`
`→ upper left`

Finally, we set the anchor point of the palette window to the upper left so that as new applications are launched, the palette gets longer by extending downward.

CUSTOMIZING THE APPLICATION SWITCHER

59

Customizing your Appearance in OS 8.5

The Appearance control panel gains a good number of features in OS 8.5, including the ability to be scripted. And scripted to a great extent! **Code 4.13** demonstrates how you can change many of the standard system settings from AppleScript. This technique would prove highly useful for configuring a large number of machines with identical custom Appearance settings. **Figure 4.10** shows the Appearance control panel with new settings from our script.

To customize your system's Appearance control panel:

1. `tell application "Appearance"`

   We begin by letting AppleScript know that we want to talk to the Appearance control panel.

2. `set highlight color to {255,`
   `→ 255, 0}`

   We set our system's highlight color to maximum red, maximum green, and no blue. Color values range from 0 to 255 in the list with the following order: {red, green, blue}.

3. `set system font to "Charcoal"`

   We set the system font to Charcoal. Any active font name can be used here

4. `set views font to "Helvetica"`

   We set the Finder's window and item font to Helvetica.

5. `set views font size to 10`

   We set the Finder's window and item font size to 10 points.

6. `set font smoothing to true`

   We turn on system-wide antialiasing for TrueType fonts.

Code 4.13 This script demonstrates how you can change many of the standard system settings from AppleScript.

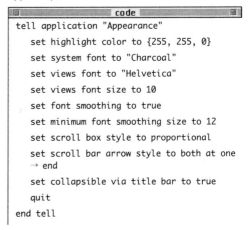

```
tell application "Appearance"
    set highlight color to {255, 255, 0}
    set system font to "Charcoal"
    set views font to "Helvetica"
    set views font size to 10
    set font smoothing to true
    set minimum font smoothing size to 12
    set scroll box style to proportional
    set scroll bar arrow style to both at one
    → end
    set collapsible via title bar to true
    quit
end tell
```

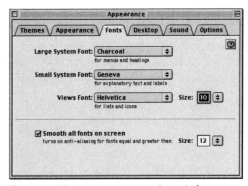

Figure 4.10 The Appearance control panel after our script has set many of the preferences shown here, including turning font smoothing on.

7. `set minimum font smoothing size`
`→ to 12`

We set the minimum point size for antialiasing to 12 points.

8. `set scroll box style to`
`→ proportional`

We set all window scroll boxes system-wide to be proportionally sized.

9. `set scroll bar arrow style to`
`→ both at one end`

We set the scroll bar arrows to both appear at one end of the scroll bar system-wide.

10. `set collapsible via title bar to`
`→ true`

We turn on window collapsing system-wide. This feature is the same as the WindowShade settings from prior versions of the System.

11. `quit`
`end tell`

Finally, we quit the Appearance control panel to make it go away.

✔ Tip

■ You can set both scroll arrows to appear at both ends of your windows' scroll bars by changing step 9 to read (to make the "«" character type option-\, to make the "»" character type shift-option-\):

`set scroll bar arrow style to`
`→ «constant ****dubl»`

Customizing File Exchange in OS 8.5

The functionality of our friendly control panels PC Exchange and Mac OS Easy Open has been integrated into a single control panel, File Exchange, in OS 8.5. File Exchange is nicely designed and very scriptable. **Code 4.14** demonstrates many of the properties that can be scripted in File Exchange as well as how to create a new PC Exchange extension mapping for aif2, associating the suffix with the application Movie Player. I just made up this extension, so you will want to replace the extension string with one useful to you! **Figure 4.11** shows the File Exchange control panel after our script has added the new PC Exchange extension mapping aif2.

To customize File Exchange settings:

1. tell application "File Exchange"

   We start by getting File Exchange's attention.

2. mount now

   Now we have File Exchange mount all PC drives currently available on the SCSI chain.

3. set mapping PC extensions to → true

   We turn on the mapping of PC file name extensions to Macintosh file type and creator codes in the PC Exchange part of File Exchange.

4. set mapping on opening files to → true

   We enable the opening of files without suitable Mac OS types and creators based on any file name extension they might have.

Code 4.14 This script mounts all PC disks available, sets a number of properties, and then adds an extension mapping for the PC file suffix aif2 if one doesn't already exist.

```
tell application "File Exchange"
    mount now
    set mapping PC extensions to true
    set mapping on opening files to true
    set PC disks mount at startup to true
    set automatic translation to true
    set always shows choices to true
    set dialog suppress if only one to true
    set includs servers to false
    set PC file system enabled to true

    try
        get extension mapping "aif2"
    on error
        make new extension mapping with
        → properties {PC extension:"aif2",
        → creator type:"TVOD", file type:
        → "AIFF"}
    end try

    quit
end tell
```

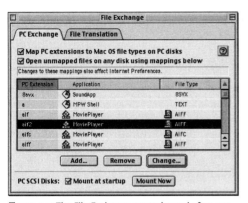

Figure 4.11 The File Exchange control panel after our script has added the new PC Exchange extension mapping for aif2.

5. `set PC disks mount at startup to`
`→ true`

We enable the mounting of all available PC SCSI disks at startup.

6. `set automatic translation to`
`→ true`

We enable the automatic translation of documents when the application program used to create the documents is not available.

7. `set always shows choices to true`

We make sure that the translation choices dialog is always shown even when there is already a translation preference defined for a given file type.

8. `set dialog suppress if only one`
`→ to true`

We enable the suppression of the translation choices dialog when there's only one choice available.

9. `set includs servers to false`

We disable the searching of applications on servers when searching for translation choices. Note the typo in the spelling of includes in this control panel's dictionary. This may be corrected in later versions of the System.

10. `set PC file system enabled to`
`→ true`

We enable the PC file system so that the computer can read and write PC disks.

11. `try`
`    get extension mapping "aif2"`

Next, we try to get an extension mapping from File Exchange for the file extension aif2. If one is returned, we know that a extension mapping already exists for this extension.

CUSTOMIZING FILE EXCHANGE IN OS 8.5

12.
```
    on error
        make new extension mapping
        → with properties
        → {PC extension:"aif2",
        → creator type:"TVOD",
        → file type:"AIFF"}
    end try
    quit
end tell
```

File Exchange generates an error if an extension mapping for the extension aif2 doesn't already exist. If the error occurs, we know that the mapping doesn't exist so we create a new one. The creator type attribute defines the application that File Exchange will launch for aif2 files. TVOD is the creator type for Apple's Movie Player application. The file type attribute is passed to Movie Player when aif2 files are sent to it, so Movie Player knows what kind of file it's opening.

Code 4.15 This script has Sherlock find every file and folder with "buddy" in its name, returning its results in its own window.

```
code
tell application "Sherlock"
    activate
    search for "buddy" with display
end tell
```

Code 4.16 This script uses the Finder to find all files with "buddy" in their names in the System Folder.

```
code
tell application "Finder"
    set myResults to (every item whose name
    → contains "buddy") of entire contents of
    → system folder
end tell
```

Code 4.17 This script has Sherlock search the Web for the term "buddy" using its current search engine settings, returning a list of URLs to our script.

```
code
tell application "Sherlock"
    set myWebResults to (search Internet for
    → "buddy" without display)
    quit
end tell
```

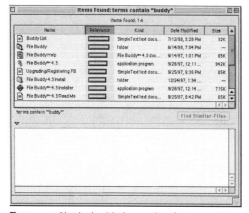

Figure 4.12 Sherlock with the results of our search.

Finding files and searching the Web with Sherlock in OS 8.5

OS 8.5 introduces Apple's long-rumored search technology with Sherlock, a replacement for the Find application in the Apple menu. Sherlock's powers are amazing and a few of them are scriptable! **Code 4.15** shows you how to use Sherlock to search the content of files and folders. **Figure 4.12** shows the results of this script. **Code 4.16** shows how to search just by file name using the Finder. While the Finder is much much slower than Sherlock, with it you can use specific search criteria like file type, size, modification date, etc. **Code 4.17** shows how to search the Web for a term using Sherlock's cool new Internet searching capabilities.

To search for files and folders using Sherlock:

1. `tell application "Sherlock"`
   `activate`
   We begin by bringing Sherlock to the front.

2. `search for "buddy" with display`
   `end tell`
   Next, we have Sherlock search for files and folders with "buddy" in their content. By specifying with display, we have Sherlock return the results in its own window.

To search for files and folders using the Finder:

1. `tell application "Finder"`
   We begin by talking to the Finder.

2. `set myResults to (every item`
   `→ whose name contains "buddy")`
   `→ of entire contents of system`
   `→ folder`
   `end tell`

Next, we have the Finder return a list of every file or folder that has "buddy" in its name in the System Folder of the startup drive. Using the Finder to search through many files is very slow compared to using Sherlock. It's really best to use the Finder to search only a folder or two at most. This script could take very long to run if your startup drive has many files on it. Keep this in mind!

To search the Internet using Sherlock:

1. `tell application "Sherlock"`

   First we let AppleScript know that we want to talk to Sherlock.

2. `set myWebResults to`
   `→ (search Internet for "buddy"`
   `→ without display)`

   Next, we have Sherlock search the Internet for the term "buddy" using its current search engine settings. By specifying `without display`, we have Sherlock return the results only to our script in the variable `myWebResults`, which will contain a list of matching URLs.

3. `quit`
   `end tell`

   Finally, we quit Sherlock.

Using summarize in OS 8.5

The same cool search indexing technology used in Sherlock can be called directly by your AppleScript using the command `summarize` to digest long strings of text into brief summaries. For example, to store a 1 sentence summary of some text in the variable `myBlurb`:

`set myBlurb to summarize "The long`
`→ run-on sentence means nothing to`
`→ me or to you or to anyone. Does`
`→ it? Or does it?" in 1`

Code 4.18 This script lets the user stop the print queues of multiple printers selected from a list of current desktop printers.

```
                    code
tell application "Desktop Printer Manager"
    set myPrinters to the name of every
    → desktop printer
    set myCurrentPrinter to the name of the
    → default printer
end tell
set myNewPrinters to (choose from list
→ myPrinters with prompt "Choose printers
→ to stop:" default items myCurrentPrinter
→ with multiple selections allowed)
if myNewPrinters is not false then
    tell application "Desktop Printer Manager"
        if number of items in myNewPrinters=1
        → then set the default printer to desktop
        → printer (item 1 of myNewPrinters as
        → string)
        repeat with myNewPrinter in
        → myNewPrinters
            set queue stopped of desktop printer
            → (myNewPrinter as string) to true
        end repeat
    end tell
end if
```

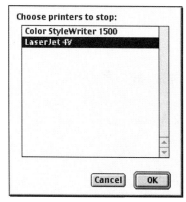

Figure 4.13 The dialog displayed by our script, with all current Desktop printers shown.

Switching, starting, and stopping Desktop printers in OS 8.5

With OS 8.5, we get direct scripting control of any Desktop printer. We can create new printers, change the current default printer, and start and stop an individual printer's print queues, among other things. **Code 4.18** lets the user stop the print queues of multiple printers selected from a list of current Desktop printers. The current default printer is automatically selected. If only one printer is selected by the user, our script makes it the default printer in addition to stopping its queue.

To stop print queues:

1. `tell application "Desktop Printer`
`→ Manager"`

We begin by letting AppleScript know that we want to talk to the Desktop Printer Manager background application.

2. `set myPrinters to the name of`
`→ every desktop printer`

We retrieve a list of the names of all Desktop printers and store it in the variable `myPrinters`.

3. `set myCurrentPrinter to the`
`→ name of the default printer`
`end tell`

Next, we get the name of the current default printer.

4. `set myNewPrinters to`
`→ (choose from list myPrinters with`
`→ prompt "Choose printers to stop:"`
`→ default items myCurrentPrinter`
`→ with multiple selections allowed)`

Now we prompt the user to choose printers from the list of those available. By specifying `with multiple selections allowed`, we let the user choose more than one printer. The list returned is stored in myNewPrinters.

5.
```
if myNewPrinters is not false then
    tell application "Desktop
    → Printer Manager"
```
Now we test our variable myNewPrinters to make sure the user selected at least one printer. If so, we start talking to the Desktop Printer Manager again.

6.
```
    if number of items in
    → myNewPrinters=1 then set the
    → default printer to desktop
    → printer (item 1 of
    → myNewPrinters as string)
```
We check to see if the user selected only one printer. If they did, we make it the default printer.

7.
```
    repeat with myNewPrinter in
    → myNewPrinters
        set queue stopped of
        → desktop printer
        → (myNewPrinter as string)
        → to true
    end repeat
    end tell
end if
```
Finally, we loop through the list of printers the user chose and stop each one's print queue.

Starting print queues

If you change the code in step 7 to:
```
    repeat with myNewPrinter in
    → myNewPrinters
        set queue stopped of
        → desktop printer
        → (myNewPrinter as string)
        → to false
    end repeat
    end tell
end if
```
then your script will start the print queues of the selected printers.

Code 4.19 This script lets the user choose which of the available Location Manager sets to make active.

```
tell application "Location Manager"
    activate
    set myLocationRef to the current location
    set myCurrentLocation to the name of
    → myLocationRef
    set myLocations to {}
    repeat with i from 1 to count of every
    → location
        set myLocations to myLocations & (name
        → of location i) as list
    end repeat
    set myNewLocation to (choose from list
    → myLocations with prompt "Choose
    → location to make active:" default items
    → myCurrentLocation without multiple
    → selections allowed) as string
    set the current location to location
    → myNewLocation
    quit
end tell
```

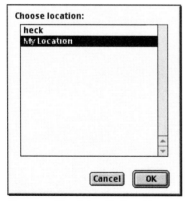

Figure 4.14 The dialog displayed by our script, with all current Location Manager sets shown.

Switching Location Manager sets in OS 8.5

In OS 8.5, the Location Manager becomes scriptable. This means that once you create custom location sets of system settings you can switch the current set from a script. The only drawback of the scripting implementation of the Location Manager is that it always shows a completion dialog that requires user intervention when you have it switch sets. **Figure 4.15** shows the dialog that Location Manager displays. But still, the ability to change most system settings from AppleScript is one of the great improvements of OS 8.5. **Code 4.19** lets the user choose which Location Manager location set to make active from list of available sets.

To change your current location set with the Location Manager:

1. `tell application "Location Manager"`
   `activate`

   We begin by letting AppleScript know that we want to talk to the Location Manager control panel and bring it to the front.

2. `set myLocationRef to the current`
   `→ location`
   `set myCurrentLocation to the`
   `→ name of myLocationRef`

   Next, we retrieve a reference to the current location set and store it in our variable myLocationRef. Using that reference, we get and store the name of the current location set in our variable myCurrentLocation.

3. `set myLocations to {}`

   We initialize a list variable, myLocations, to hold the names of all available location sets.

4.   `repeat with i from 1 to count of`
      `→ every location`
        `set myLocations to`
         `→ myLocations & (name of`
         `→ location i) as list`
      `end repeat`

Now we loop through each location available, appending each location name to the list variable `myLocations`.

5.   `set myNewLocation to (choose`
      `→ from list myLocations with`
      `→ prompt "Choose location to`
      `→ make active:" default items`
      `→ myCurrentLocation without`
      `→ multiple selections allowed)`
      `→ as string`

Now we prompt the user to choose a location set from the list of available sets. By specifying `without multiple selections allowed`, we keep the user from choosing more than one set. The returned value is forced to be a string and is stored in `myNewLocation`.

6.   `set the current location to`
      `→ location myNewLocation`

Now we have Location Manager set the current location to the one chosen by the user. This command will generate a dialog box in the Location Manager.

7.   `quit`
   `end tell`
Finally, we quit the Location Manager.

✔ Using the Location Manager to switch TCP configurations

■ If you want a simple way to change your TCP/IP configuration, use the Location Manager to switch between location sets that you have created. For more control (and more complicated code) see Chapter 5.

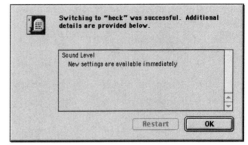

Figure 4.15 The completion dialog displayed by the Location Manager after a set has been activated.

OPEN
TRANSPORT
AND NETWORKING

Now that we've got the basics down, it's time to start using the Internet with AppleScript! The scripts in this part of the book are useful for anyone who works with the Internet, whether they surf the Web, send e-mail, FTP files, or access UNIX systems with telnet.

Before you get onto the Internet, you need to get control of the Mac's networking software, Open Transport, with AppleScript. In this chapter, we'll look at the different capabilities of Mac OS 8 and 8.5 as we script the Open Transport control panels: TCP/IP, OT/PPP, and Remote Access. With these control panels, we'll create new configurations, make remote connections, and make sure we stay connected.

We'll also investigate scripting control of file-sharing states and users and groups, thanks to OS 8's scriptable File Sharing and Users & Groups control panels.

Scripting the
TCP/IP control panel

All the scripts that follow were designed and tested for Mac OS 8 and 8.5.

Any script that relies on features found only in Mac OS 8.5 is specially noted.

Creating a TCP/IP configuration in OS 8.5

The introduction of Mac OS 8.5 has made available a complete set of AppleScript statements to control every aspect of Open Transport, including the creation of new configurations. Here, we'll create a new TCP/IP configuration by calling the application Network Setup Scripting. **Figure 5.1** shows the TCP/IP control panel with the new configuration active. The complete script is shown in **Code 5.1**.

To create a new TCP/IP configuration:

1. `tell application "Network Setup`
   `→ Scripting"`

   We begin by letting AppleScript know that we want to talk to the Network Setup Scripting application.

2. `open database`

   Next, we tell the application to open the Open Transport configurations database.

3. `begin transaction`

   With this line we create an exclusive transaction with the application (in this case the Network Setup Scripting application). This ensures that the database doesn't change while we work with it.

4. `if not (TCPIP v4 configuration`
   `→ "New Config" exists) then`

   Here we make sure that no configuration already exists with the name of our new configuration, "New Config."

5. `make new TCPIP v4 configuration`
   `→ "New Config" with properties`
   `→ {connecting via:"Ethernet",`
   `→ configuration method:"manual",`
   `→ IP address:"206.14.230.16",`
   `→ subnet mask:"255.255.255.0"}`
   `end if`

Code 5.1 Creating a new TCP/IP configuration.

```
tell application "Network Setup Scripting"
    open database
    begin transaction
    if not (TCPIP v4 configuration
    → "New Config" exists) then
        make new TCPIP v4 configuration
        → "New Config" with properties
        → {connecting via:"Ethernet",
        → configuration method:"manual",
        → IP address:"206.14.230.16",
        → subnet mask:"255.255.255.0",
        → implicit search start:"",
        → implicit search end:"",
        → user mode:"basic"}
    end if
    tell TCPIP v4 configuration "New Config"
                make new name server address 1
                → with data "206.14.230.7"
                make new router address 1
                → with data "206.14.230.7"
        end tell
    end transaction
    close database
end tell
```

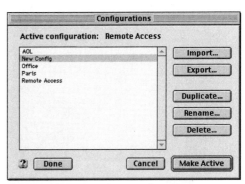

Figure 5.1 The new configuration listed in the Configurations window of the TCP/IP control panel.

Then we create our new configuration, in this case connecting via an Ethernet connection using manual settings for IP address and subnet mask. Be sure to use your own IP address in this line.

6. `tell TCPIP v4 configuration`
   `→ "New Config"`
      `make new name server address 1`
      `→ with data "206.14.230.7"`
      `make new router address 1`
      `→ with data "206.14.230.7"end`

Next, we create a name server address and router address for our new Ethernet TCP/IP configuration. You can get this information from your ISP or system administrator.

7. `end transaction`
   `close database`
   `end tell`

Finally, we can end our exclusive transaction, close the database, and conclude our conversation with the application.

✔ Tips

- If you want to create a new TCP/IP configuration that uses the Point-to-Point Protocol (PPP) instead of Ethernet, simply substitute "PPP" for "Ethernet" in step 5.

- With Mac OS 8.5 you can also create and delete configurations for the AppleTalk, Modem, and Remote Access control panels using the same kind of script we created here.

CREATING A TCP/IP CONFIGURATION IN OS 8.5

Enabling multi-homing with TCP/IP

With multi-homing, your single Mac can respond to multiple IP addresses on a single TCP/IP connection. This configuration enables you to run multiple Web sites or other Internet servers with their own dedicated IP addresses.

Open Transport versions 1.3 and above support multi-homing for manually configured TCP/IP. (Any version of Mac OS 8.1 or above should have at least version 1.3 of Open Transport.) **Figure 5.2** shows the TCP/IP control panel manually configured to allow for multi-homing.

To enable multi-homing in Open Transport, you need to create a specially formatted text file named "IP Secondary Addresses" and save it in the Preferences folder of your System folder. This script, shown in **Code 5.2**, makes it easy. Just set the three list variables at the beginning of the script to include each IP address, its subnet mask, and its router address.

To enable multi-homing with TCP/IP:

1. ```
   set myIPs to {"192.0.0.1",
   → "192.0.0.2", "192.0.0.3"}
   set mySubnets to {"255.255.255.0",
   → "255.255.255.0", "255.255.255.0"}
   set myRouters to {"192.0.0.10",
   → "192.0.0.12", ""}
   ```

   We begin by defining three lists to hold our secondary IP addresses as well as subnet masks and router addresses for each. In this case, we define three additional IP addresses.

2. ```
   set myIPConfig to ""
   ```

   Next, we initialize an empty string variable to hold the constructed text for the special text file we'll create shortly.

Code 5.2 Enabling and configuring multi-homed IP addresses for Open Transport TCP/IP.

```
set myIPs to {"192.0.0.1", "192.0.0.2",
→ "192.0.0.3"}
set mySubnets to {"255.255.255.0",
→ "255.255.255.0", "255.255.255.0"}
set myRouters to {"192.0.0.10",
→ "192.0.0.12", ""}
set myIPConfig to ""
repeat with i from 1 to number of items in
→ myIPs
    set myIPConfig to myIPConfig & "ip=" &
    → (item i of myIPs) & tab
    set myIPConfig to myIPConfig & "sm=" &
    → (item i of mySubnets) & tab
    set myIPConfig to myIPConfig & "rt=" &
    → (item i of myRouters) & return
end repeat
tell application "Finder"
    set myPrefs to the path to preferences
    → folder
    set myIPFile to myPrefs & "IP Secondary
    → Addresses" as text
    if alias myIPFile exists then delete file
    → myIPFile
    set myFileRef to (open for access file
    → myIPFile with write permission)
    write myIPConfig to myFileRef
    close access myFileRef
end tell
```

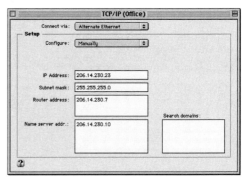

Figure 5.2 For multi-homing to work, your TCP/IP control panel must be set to manual configuration for the primary settings.

3. `repeat with i from 1 to number of`
`→ items in myIPs`

We begin a repeat loop to cycle through each IP address in our list of addresses.

4. `set myIPConfig to myIPConfig &`
`→ "ip=" & (item i of myIPs) & tab`
`set myIPConfig to myIPConfig &`
`→ "sm=" & (item i of mySubnets) &`
`→ tab`
`set myIPConfig to myIPConfig &`
`→ "rt=" & (item i of myRouters) &`
`→ return`
`end repeat`

Now we append properly formatted text to our string to define our new IP and its subnet and router. Here we use AppleScript's built-in string concatenation symbol, the ampersand (&), to join all our strings together and store them in the variable myIPConfig.

5. `tell application "Finder"`
`    set myPrefs to the path to`
`    → preferences folder`
`    set myIPFile to myPrefs & "IP`
`    → Secondary Addresses" as text`

Here we construct a path to the final location of our secondary IP address file starting with the path to our current Preferences folder from the Finder.

6. `if alias myIPFile exists then`
`→ delete file myIPFile`

We check with the Finder to see if the file already exists and delete it if it does exist.

7. `set myFileRef to (open for access`
`→ file myIPFile with write`
`→ permission)`
`    write myIPConfig to myFileRef`
`    close access myFileRef`
`end tell`

Now, we create the text file with write access, write the string defining our new IPs to it, and close up the file.

✔ Tip

- If you omit the values for subnet or router, the primary configuration's settings will apply.

Switching TCP/IP configurations

The ability to easily switch TCP/IP configurations can be very useful if you have different networking environments for your computer. For example, a PowerBook might use a TCP/IP-enabled Ethernet network during the day and a PPP dial-up account at night. Each mode of accessing the Internet requires a different TCP/IP configuration with its own name server, router, and IP information. In this script (**Code 5.3**), we'll use the scripting addition TCP Config to change configurations. **Figure 5.3** shows the Script Editor's Event Log window with the record returned by the statement `TCP config`.

To toggle between two TCP/IP configurations:

1. `set myConfig1 to "Office"`
   `set myConfig2 to "Remote Access"`

   We begin by defining the names of the two TCP/IP configurations we'd like to toggle between.

2. `set myCurrentConfig to current`
   `→ config of (TCP config)`

   Now we store the name of the current TCP/IP configuration in a variable called `myCurrentConfig` (though you can use any name you like).

3. `if myCurrentConfig = myConfig2`
   `→ then`
   `    set TCP config to myConfig1`

   Next, we set up an if/then conditional match check to see if the current configuration matches our second configuration. If it does, we switch the current configuration to our first configuration. (To find out more about if/then matching, see Chapter 3).

Code 5.3 This script toggles between two TCP/IP configurations, switching from one to the other every time it is run.

```
set myConfig1 to "Office"
set myConfig2 to "Remote Access"
set myCurrentConfig to current config
→ of (TCP config)
set myAvailableConfigs to available configs
→ of (TCP config)
if myCurrentConfig = myConfig2 then
    set TCP config to myConfig1
else
    if myCurrentConfig = myConfig1 then
        set TCP config to myConfig2
    end if
end if
```

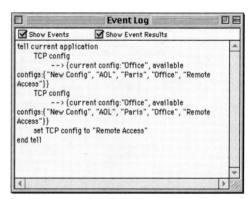

Figure 5.3 The Script Editor's Event Log window displays the record returned by the statement TCP config.

4.
```
else
    if myCurrentConfig = myConfig1
→ then
        set TCP config to myConfig2
    end if
end if
```

Otherwise, we check to see if the current configuration matches our first configuration. If it does, we switch the current configuration to our second configuration. Note that if the current configuration matches neither the first nor the second, nothing gets changed. Keep in mind that the scripting addition TCP Config only lets us switch between existing configurations. See *Creating a TCP/IP configuration in OS 8.5* in this chapter for a script that creates new TCP/IP configurations in Mac OS 8.5.

✔ An easier way to switch configurations in OS 8.5

■ With Mac OS 8.5, the Location Manager control panel is now scriptable! Now the easiest way to change your Mac's TCP/IP settings (among others) is to manually create a number of location sets in Location Manager. Once you do this, use the script in the spread *Switching Location Manager sets in OS 8.5* in Chapter 4.

Scripting with TCP Config

This script requires the scripting addition TCP Config. You must have TCP Config installed in your Scripting Additions folder for this script to work.

TCP Config adds the statements `set tcp config` and `tcp config` to AppleScript, allowing us to set the current configuration by name as well as to get a list of all configuration names along with the current configuration.

The cost of TCP Config is a postcard to the author, who donates them to his son's collection. TCP Config can be found in America Online's software libraries.

TCP Config is published by the generous father and OSAX creator Nigel Perry, who can be reached at `http://smis-asterix.massey.ac.nz/`.

Scripting OT/PPP and Remote Access

Mac OS 8 and 8.5 both offer the same AppleScript statements to control Remote Access and PPP connections via standard scripting additions. This command set doesn't use saved Open Transport configurations for PPP and Remote Access, opting instead to control connections by directly setting the connection's parameters, like the phone number, user name, and password.

In OS 8.5, the two scripting additions Remote Access Commands and PPP Commands have been combined into a single scripting addition called Remote Access Commands. This scripting addition contains the same commands as the two separate additions that came with older versions of the OS. One last system software note is in order here: The functionality of the OT/PPP control panel is completely superseded by the Remote Access control panel of Apple Remote Access 3.1. So don't be alarmed if you don't have an OT/PPP control panel; ARA 3.1's Remote Access control panel will take care of PPP connections for you. **Figure 5.4** shows the Remote Access control panel from ARA 3.1.

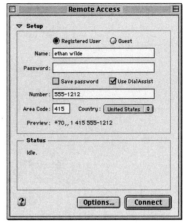

Figure 5.4 The Remote Access control panel of Apple Remote Access 3.1.

Scripting the OT/PPP and Remote Access control panels

All the scripts that follow were designed and tested for Mac OS 8 and 8.5.

None of these scripts relies specifically on OS 8.5.

Code 5.4 This AppleScript initiates a PPP connection.

```
try
    PPP connect address "1-415-555-1212"
    → user name "Fred " password "x2"
    → with quiet mode
on error
    display dialog "PPP Connection Failed"
end try
```

Figure 5.5 The Remote Access control panel with the current PPP connection status displayed.

Making a PPP connection

You're all set to surf the Web, but you still need to connect to your Internet service provider (ISP). Thanks to standard scripting additions provided with Open Transport, making a PPP connection with AppleScript is a snap, as shown in **Code 5.4**. **Figure 5.5** shows the Remote Access control panel with a PPP connection established. If you're using ARA 2.1 or below, the OT/PPP control panel controls your connection and displays your connection status. If you're using ARA 3.1 or above the Remote Access control panel performs these functions.

To make a PPP connection:

1. `try`

   We begin this simple script with `try` to trap any errors that might occur during the connection attempt.

2. `PPP connect address "1-415-555-1212"`
   `→ user name "Fred" password "x2"`
   `→ with quiet mode`

   Now, we attempt to establish a PPP connection to the phone number 415-555-1212 with the user name "Fred" and password "x2". Specifying quiet mode keeps Open Transport's dialogs from appearing during the attempt.

3. `on error`
   `    display dialog "PPP Connection`
   `    → Failed"`
   `end try`

   Finally, we incorporate our error handling routine, displaying a dialog if anything goes amiss.

Maintaining a PPP connection

You're bound to encounter connection interruptions, maybe your ISP restricts the duration of your connection or your phone lines are noisy thanks to a local storm. The quick AppleScript below should be the solution. **Figure 5.6** shows Remote Access renegotiating a PPP connection.

To make and maintain a constant PPP connection:

1. `on idle`

   We begin this script with a very powerful built-in handler: `on idle`. This handler will execute every 30 seconds while your script is running.

2. `set myState to the state of`
   `→ (PPP status)`

   Here we store the current PPP status.

3. `if myState is not "connected" then...`

   Next, we test the variable to see if there is a current PPP connection; if not, we initiate one.

4. `return 30`
   `end idle`

   We return the value 30 to let AppleScript know we want the `idle` handler to run every 30 seconds.

5. `on quit`
   `    continue quit`
   `end quit`

   Finally, we add an `on quit` handler to ensure that our script application will override the `on idle` routine and quit properly when asked. The `continue quit` statement forwards the quit message to AppleScript to make sure everything ends as it should.

Code 5.5 This script constantly tests the PPP connection status and makes a connection whenever one is not active.

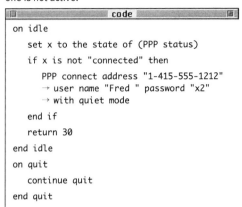

```
on idle
    set x to the state of (PPP status)
    if x is not "connected" then
        PPP connect address "1-415-555-1212"
        → user name "Fred " password "x2"
        → with quiet mode
    end if
    return 30
end idle
on quit
    continue quit
end quit
```

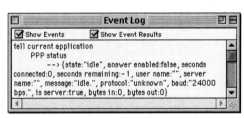

Figure 5.6 The Script Editor's Event Log window showing the record returned by PPP status.

✔ Tips

- Save this script as an application and launch it whenever you want a constant PPP connection.

- If we were to omit the PPP parameters and simply use PPP connect alone, the current control panel settings would be used for phone, user, and password.

Code 5.6 This script initiates a Remote Access connection.

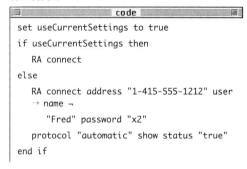

```
set useCurrentSettings to true
if useCurrentSettings then
    RA connect
else
    RA connect address "1-415-555-1212" user
    → name ¬
        "Fred" password "x2"
    protocol "automatic" show status "true"
end if
```

Figure 5.7 The Remote Access control panel displaying the status of our current connection.

Making a Remote Access connection

For some of us, off-site access to the Internet is accomplished through Apple Remote Access 3.1. Thanks to standard scripting additions provided with Open Transport, making a Remote Access connection from AppleScript is just as easy as connecting via PPP, as shown in **Code 5.6. Figure 5.7** shows the Remote Access control panel with an ARA connection established.

To make a Remote Access connection:

1. `set useCurrentSettings to true`

   We begin by setting a variable, `useCurrentSettings`, that we'll later use to decide whether to use the current control panel setting for the connection or use the settings specified in the script below.

2. `if useCurrentSettings then`
   `    RA connect`

   Next, we test that variable and if it returns true, we connect using the current Remote Access control panel settings for phone, user, protocol, and password. You can change the value of `useCurrentSettings` to determine whether to use the current settings or the settings made explicitly in the lines below.

3. `else`
   `    RA connect address`
   `    → "1-415-555-1212" user name`
   `    "Fred" password "x2"`
   `    protocol "automatic" with show`
   `    → status`
   `end if`

   If the test returns false, we make a connection to 415-555-1212 for user "Fred" with password "x2" using whatever

protocol Remote Access can negotiate.
We display a connection status dialog by
including `show status`.

✔ Tips

■ You can add a `display dialog` command
to this script to invite the user to set the
value of `useCurrentSettings` so that they
can decide whether to use the current
settings or the settings stored in the script
when connecting.

■ If we include the parameter `guest`
`access` and omit the `user name` and
`password` strings, Remote Access will
attempt to connect to the server as guest.

■ If we include the parameter `terminal`
`window`, Remote Access will open a
terminal window during the connection.

■ If we include the parameter `quiet mode`,
Remote Access will hide all dialogs while
attempting the connection.

■ The `protocol` parameter can also be set
to "PPP" or "ARAP" to explicitly set the
connection protocol.

Additional parameters

When you use AppleScript to talk to
Remote Access, there are a number of
other parameters you can include in the
script in addition to the ones used in step
3. The complete list of parameters is pre-
sented here:

◆ `address string`
The connection address
(telephone number)

◆ `user name string`
The user name
(cannot use guest access)

◆ `password string`
The user password
(cannot use guest access)

◆ `guest access boolean`
Guest access
(cannot use user name or password)

◆ `protocol PPP/ARAP/automatic`
Protocols attempted for this
connection.

◆ `terminal window boolean`
Open terminal window

◆ `connect script alias`
Use this connect script

◆ `quiet mode boolean`
Don't display dialogs

◆ `show status boolean`
Display status

Code 5.7 This script toggles the state of file sharing and program linking on your Mac.

```
tell application "File Sharing"
    set mySharing to file sharing
    set file sharing to not mySharing
    set myLinking to program linking
    set program linking to not myLinking
    quit
end tell
```

Figure 5.8 The Script Editor's Event Log window displays the file-sharing settings as our script runs.

Changing your file-sharing status

The ability to change your file-sharing status via AppleScript can be very useful. If used as the basis for a CGI, this script (**Code 5.7**) could make it possible for you to remotely toggle the file-sharing and program-linking state of a Web server over the Internet. **Figure 5.8** shows the file-sharing settings in the Script Editor's Event Log window after this script has been run.

To toggle your file-sharing and program-linking status:

1. `tell application "File Sharing"`

   We begin by letting AppleScript know that we want to talk to the File Sharing control panel.

2. `set mySharing to file sharing`
   `set file sharing to not mySharing`

   Next we store the current state of file sharing in a variable we're calling `mySharing,` and set the file-sharing state to the opposite of the variable's Boolean value, toggling it. (A Boolean value can be either true or false, as we saw in Chapter 3.)

3. `set myLinking to program linking`
   `set program linking to not`
   `→ myLinking`

   We do the same thing with program linking, storing the current state of program linking in a variable and then setting the program-linking state to the opposite of the variable's Boolean value, toggling it.

4. `quit`
   `end tell`

   Finally, we tell the File Sharing control panel to quit and end our conversation with it.

Scripting the Users & Groups control panel

With Personal Web Sharing and some other Internet applications like NetPresenz, the Users & Groups control panel takes on the additional function of determining Internet access privileges for users. The AppleScripts discussed in this section show how you can automatically create new users and add users to groups. You could use such scripts to remotely manage access to your Web site and FTP directories. **Figure 5.9** shows a new user window in Users & Groups created by **Code 5.8. Figure 5.10** shows a group containing all defined users created by **Code 5.9**.

To make a new user in the Users & Groups control panel:

1. `tell application "Users & Groups"`

   We begin by letting AppleScript know that we want to talk to the Users & Groups control panel.

2. `set myNewUser to make new user`

   Next we have the control panel create a new user and store a reference to that user in a variable called `myNewUser`.

3. `set the can connect of myNewUser`
   `→ to false`

   We then set the `can connect` property of the new user to `false`.

4. `set the can change password of`
   `→ myNewUser to false`

   We also set the `can change password` property of the new user to `false`.

5. `set the can do program linking of`
   `→ myNewUser to true`

   And we set the `can do program linking` property of the new user to `true`.

Code 5.8 This script creates a new user without a password.

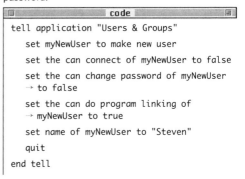

```
tell application "Users & Groups"
    set myNewUser to make new user
    set the can connect of myNewUser to false
    set the can change password of myNewUser
    → to false
    set the can do program linking of
    → myNewUser to true
    set name of myNewUser to "Steven"
    quit
end tell
```

Figure 5.9 Our new user's window in the Users & Groups control panel.

Code 5.9 This script adds all existing users to a group.

```
set myGroupName to "Everybody"
tell application "Users & Groups"
    set myNewGroup to make new group
    try
        set name of myNewGroup to myGroupName
    on error
        delete myNewGroup
    end try
    set myUsers to users
    repeat with myUser in myUsers
        if name of myUser ≠ "Guest" then add
        → myUser to group myGroupName
    end repeat
    quit
end tell
```

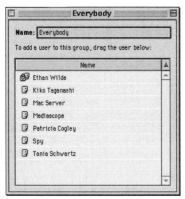

Figure 5.10 The Group window showing all users added to the group.

6. `set name of myNewUser to "Steven"`

Finally, we set the name of the new user to Steven.

7. `quit`
`end tell`

Then we ask the control panel to quit and end our conversation.

✔ Dealing with passwords

■ The Users & Groups control panel will not let a script set a user's password. If you need to script new users complete with passwords, try creating a template user with a password and duplicating that user in your script with the `duplicate` command.

To add all existing users to a group:

1. `set myGroupName to "Everybody"`

We begin by setting the name for our group in a variable called myGroupName.

2. `tell application "Users & Groups"`

Next, we let AppleScript know that we want to talk to the Users & Groups control panel.

3. `set myNewGroup to make new group`

Then we have the control panel create a new group.

4. `try`
`    set name of myNewGroup to`
`    → myGroupName`

Now we try to set the name of the group to our desired name inside of an error handling routine so we won't get an error if the name already exists.

5. `on error`
`        delete myNewGroup`
`    end try`

If we get an error, we delete the new group we just created with the make new `group` command above so we can use the existing group with the proper name.

6. `set myUsers to users`

Now we get a list of all defined users from the control panel and store them in the variable `myUsers`.

7.
```
repeat with myUser in myUsers
    if name of myUser ≠ "Guest" then
    → add myUser to group myGroupName
end repeat
```

We're ready to add each user to the group. "Guest" can't be in any groups, so we add a conditional statement to add users to the group so long as they are not "Guest." Notice the use of the ≠ operator here, which you should read as "does not equal."

8.
```
quit
end tell
```

At the end of our script we quit the control panel and end our conversation with it.

SCRIPTING YOUR WEB BROWSER

Figure 6.1 Navigator's AppleScript dictionary entry for OpenURL as shown in the Script Editor.

Figure 6.2 Explorer's AppleScript dictionary entry for OpenURL as shown in the Script Editor.

Netscape Navigator and Microsoft Internet Explorer are revolutionary software applications that support a number of different Internet protocols, including HTTP and FTP. Our focus on these two popular Web browsers will center on accessing Web pages via HTTP, whether those pages are stored remotely on servers or locally on your own hard drive or local area network.

Each browser has an AppleScript dictionary with some very powerful and rarely used statements—including syntax formed from combinations of nouns and verbs like Open URL. Some of the dictionary statements differ subtly in each browser. **Figures 6.1** and **6.2** show the similar but different dictionary entries in each browser's AppleScript dictionary.

Submitting form data from Netscape Navigator

One of the most powerful scriptable features of Navigator is its ability to simulate user-entered form data for submission to a Web server. Using the post data parameter of OpenURL, we can send form data that a CGI would expect to come from a POST method of submission. In **Code 6.1**, we send POST method data to the www.four11.com personal locator site to search for individuals in their database. The principle illustrated by this script can be applied to any Web site that expects to receive form data via the POST method. **Figure 6.3** shows the dialog prompt for a name generated by our script.

To submit form POST data via AppleScript:

1. set myFirst to text returned of
   → (display dialog "First name:"
   → default answer "John")
   set myLast to text returned of
   → (display dialog "Last name:"
   → default answer "Doe")

   We start this script by prompting the user for a first and last name, which is what we'll search for on Four11. If you're modifying this script to send form data to another site, you'll want to prompt the user for the particular data needed.

2. set my411Defaults to
   → "UseNewLook=yes&Wildcard=
   → yes&Search=Search"

   Next we set some constant form field values for the search that Four11 expects to receive. You can find out the variable names that a particular Web site expects to receive by looking through the HTML source code for the form page that you'll emulate with your script.

Code 6.1 Submitting form POST data to the Four11 Web site, allowing the user to search for people by name from a dialog box.

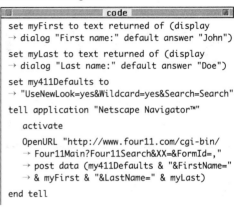

```
set myFirst to text returned of (display
→ dialog "First name:" default answer "John")
set myLast to text returned of (display
→ dialog "Last name:" default answer "Doe")
set my411Defaults to
→ "UseNewLook=yes&Wildcard=yes&Search=Search"
tell application "Netscape Navigator™"
   activate
   OpenURL "http://www.four11.com/cgi-bin/
→ Four11Main?Four11Search&XX=&FormId=,"
→ post data (my411Defaults & "&FirstName="
→ & myFirst & "&LastName=" & myLast)
end tell
```

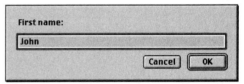

Figure 6.3 The dialog prompt for a name generated by our script.

Quickly opening a URL in OS 8.5

OS 8.5 adds a scripting addition command in its new Internet Suite of commands called open location. This magic command uses your preference settings in the Internet control panel to launch the appropriate application based on the kind of URL you specify. For example, open location "http://www.apple.com" would launch your default browser and send it to Apple's home page. While open location → "mailto:applescript@mediatrope.com" would launch your default email client and create an outgoing message to the address applescript@mediatrope.com.

GET versus POST

The HTTP protocol defines two different ways for Web forms to return form data to the server. The HTML tag <FORM METHOD= "POST" ACTION="script.acgi"> determines the method used for a form.

With METHOD="GET", all field data is appended to the end of the URL that the ACTION tag defines. This field data, also known as the reply string, is appended to the URL with a question mark indicating its start. Each field name and value are paired and separated by an equals sign. Each pair is separated by an ampersand. GET limits the length of form data and lets the user see the form data passed in their browser.

With METHOD="POST", all field data is put into a packet, called the post data, by the user's browser and sent along to the URL that the ACTION tag defines. With POST, form data can be much longer and is hidden from the user when it is submitted.

3. ```
tell application "Netscape
→ Navigator™"
    activate
```
Now we're ready to talk to Netscape and bring it to the front.

4. ```
OpenURL "http://www.four11.com/
→ cgi-bin/Four11Main?
→ Four11Search&XX=&FormId=,"
→ post data (my411Defaults &
→ "&FirstName=" & myFirst &
→ "&LastName=" & myLast)
end tell
```
Finally, we send the OpenURL command with URL and form data. Again, the peculiarities of each Web site will dictate what the URL should look like. You can find out what the correct URL to send to the server is by looking at the ACTION value in the form's HTML source code. We format form POST data *variable1=value1&variable2=value2....*

✔ Tips

- You can easily construct an URL that contains data for a CGI using the GET method of submission, where all data is included in the URL (for example, http://www.yahoo.com/search.cgi?p= → scripting), without using the post data parameter of OpenURL.

- You could use the script above within a repeat loop to conduct a whole series of searches, or you might use a series of OpenURL commands to query a bunch of Web sites with the same search request!

Submitting form data from Internet Explorer

We can use Microsoft Internet Explorer to automatically send form data to a Web server as we did with Netscape Navigator. This time, we'll encode the data we send in the form using the %XX scheme, where XX is a hexadecimal value representing a non-alphanumeric ASCII character. In this way, we'll ensure that special accented characters and symbols like *, ©, and ™ get properly transmitted to the server. Using the FormData parameter of OpenURL, we can send form data that a CGI would expect to come from a POST method of submission. In **Code 6.2**, we send POST method data to Microsoft's corporate search site, search.microsoft.com, to search for key-words in their Web site. **Figure 6.4** shows the dialog prompt for keywords generated by our script.

To submit form post data via AppleScript:

1. `set mySearch to text returned of`
   `→ (display dialog "Search string:"`
   `→ default answer "Internet`
   `→ Explorer Mac")`

   We start this script by prompting the user for terms to search for on the Microsoft Web site. We store the results of the `display dialog` command in the variable mySearch. Again, if you're adapting this script for another purpose, you'll want to prompt for the relevant data.

2. `set myMSDefaults to`
   `→ "MSCOM_SRV=http://www.`
   `→ microsoft.com&SearchCountry=`
   `→ @Locale en-us&Locale=`
   `→ 1033&Boolean=ALL&intCat=10&"`

   Next we set some constant form field values for the search that the Microsoft site expects to find. When customizing

Code 6.2 Submitting form post data to the Microsoft corporate Web site, allowing the user to search the site for keywords.

```
set mySearch to text returned of
→ (display dialog "Search string:"
→ default answer "Internet Explorer Mac")

set myMSDefaults to "MSCOM_SRV=http://
→ www.microsoft.com&SearchCountry=@Locale
→ en-us&Locale=1033&Boolean=ALL&intCat=10&"

set mySearch to Encode URL mySearch

tell application "Internet Explorer 4.0"

    OpenURL "http://search.microsoft.com/
    → results.asp" FormData (myMSDefaults &
    → "SearchString=" & mySearch)

end tell

try

    tell application "Finder"

        set the frontmost of process named
        → "Internet Explorer 4.0" to true

    end tell

on error

end try
```

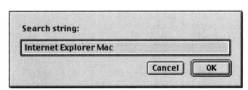

Figure 6.4 The dialog prompt for search terms generated by our script.

Scripting Internet Explorer

All the scripts that follow were designed and tested for Microsoft Internet Explorer 4.0.

Most of these scripts do not work with older versions of Internet Explorer.

Microsoft Internet Explorer is published by the Microsoft Corporation, which can be reached at http://www.microsoft.com/. Screen shots reprinted by permission of Microsoft Corporation. Internet Explorer is a registered trademark of Microsoft Corporation.

this script to call other Web sites, view the form page's HTML source code to determine the form field names used as well as the URL defined by the FORM tag's ACTION parameter.

3. `set mySearch to Encode URL mySearch`

Then we encode special characters in mySearch with the Encode URL statement.

4. `tell application "Internet`
`→ Explorer 4.0"`

Now we're ready to talk to Internet Explorer.

5. `OpenURL`
`→ "http://search.microsoft.com/`
`→ results.asp" FormData`
`→ (myMSDefaults & "SearchString="`
`→ & mySearch)`
`end tell`

Here we send the OpenURL command with URL and form data. We format form data *variable1=value1&variable2=value2*.... The URL string we use as the parameter for OpenURL is found by viewing the HTML source code of the form page we want to emulate and using the ACTION value found there.

6. `try`
`    tell application "Finder"`
`        set the frontmost of process`
`        → named "Internet Explorer`
`        → 4.0" to true`
`    end tell`
`on error`
`end try`

We conclude by telling the Finder to bring Explorer to the front because the activate statement, which we used with Netscape Navigator, is not accepted by Explorer 4.

Scripting with Encode URL

This script requires the scripting addition Encode URL. You must have Encode URL installed in your Scripting Additions folder for this script to work.

Encode URL adds the statement encode URL, which takes a standard string as an argument and returns the string encoded in the URL %XX scheme so that extended ASCII characters are properly transmitted over the Web. You have probably seen strings like %20 in the location field of your browser before. This encoding, %20, stands for a space character, which would otherwise not transmit properly. Other %XX codes exist for all non-alphanumeric ASCII characters.

Encode URL is freeware. It can be found at `http://www2.starnine.com/`
`→ extendingwebstar/osax/`.

Encode URL is written by Chuck Shotton and published by BIAP Systems, Inc., who can be reached at `http://www.biap.com/`.

Printing local HTML files from Netscape Navigator

There are times when you need to print an entire Web site for reference or for ease of reading. This is no easy operation in most cases. Fortunately, AppleScript is here to save your Return-key finger from certain ache. To use the script shown in **Code 6.3**, you need to have all the relevant HTML and supporting graphics files stored locally on your hard drive or network volume. If you're a developer, that's easy for sites of your own creation. For other circumstances, you'll first need to use an application that pulls a Web site's files and saves them locally on your machine.

To print an entire folder of local HTML files:

1.
```
on open (myFolder)
    printHTML(myFolder)
end open
```
We start with an on open handler to pass any drag-and-dropped folder reference in the variable myFolder to our function.

2. on printHTML(myFolder)

Next, we declare our function printHTML.

3.
```
set myFolderContents to list folder
→ myFolder without invisibles
```
We then copy the list of all items contained in the folder myFolder.

4.
```
repeat with myFile in
→ myFolderContents
```
Now, we're ready to loop through each item in myFolderContents.

5.
```
tell application "Finder"
    set myKind to kind of alias
    → ((myFolder as text) & myFile)
    set myName to name of alias
    → ((myFolder as text) & myFile)
end tell
```

Code 6.3 This script prints an entire folder of HTML files, including any in nested folders.

```
on open (myFolder)
    printHTML(myFolder)
end open
on printHTML(myFolder)
    set myFolderContents to list folder
    → myFolder without invisibles
    repeat with myFile in myFolderContents
        tell application "Finder"
            set myKind to kind of alias
            → ((myFolder as text) & myFile)
            set myName to name of alias
            → ((myFolder as text) & myFile)
        end tell
        if myKind is "folder" then
            printHTML(((myFolder as text) &
            → myFile) as alias) of me
        else
            if myName ends with ".html" then
                tell application "Netscape
                → Navigator™"
                    activate
                    ShowFile alias ((myFolder as
                    → text) & myFile)
                    repeat
                        set myPageLoading to the
                        → busy of window 1
                        if myPageLoading is 0 then
                        → exit repeat
                    end repeat
                end tell
                TypeText "p" with Command
                TypeText return
            end if
        end if
    end repeat
end printHTML
```

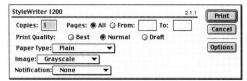

Figure 6.5 The Print dialog moments before our script sends a Return keystroke to continue.

✔ Tips

- See page 41 for more details on using the on open handler to create your own drag-and-drop application. If you're feeling a little fuzzy about creating your own functions, visit page 33 for a review of this concept.

- If your files use a different suffix, like ".htm", change the string in step 7 to match that suffix!

Scripting with Sändi's Additions

This script requires the scripting addition Sändi's Additions. You must have Sändi's Additions installed in your Scripting Additions folder for this script to work.

Sändi's Additions adds the statement TypeText to generate a keystroke as though the user had typed it on the keyboard.

Sändi's Additions is free for noncommercial use.

Sändi's Additions is published by Alessandro Lüthi, who can be reached at sandro@swissonline.ch.

Next, we ask the Finder for the kind and name of the item myFile.

6. `if myKind is "folder" then`
`    printHTML(((myFolder as text) &`
`    → myFile) as alias) of me`

If myFile is a folder, we call the function printHTML again to deal with the nested folder.

7. `else`
`    if myName ends with ".html" then`

Otherwise, we test to see if the file name ends with ".html". If it does, we've found an honest-to-goodness HTML file that we'll want to open in Netscape.

8. `tell application "Netscape`
`→ Navigator™"`
`    activate`

Now we begin talking to Netscape.

9. `ShowFile alias ((myFolder as text)`
`→ & myFile)`

We tell Netscape to open the file myFile.

10. `repeat`
`    set myPageLoading to the busy`
`    → of window 1`
`    if myPageLoading is 0 then exit`
`    → repeat`
`end repeat`
`end tell`

Now we wait for Netscape to finish loading our page by looping and testing the window's busy state.

11. `TypeText "p" with Command`
`TypeText return`
`end if`
`end if`
`end repeat`
`end open`

Finally, we send Command-P and Return keystrokes to Netscape to generate the Print dialog (**Figure 6.5**) and trigger the default Print button.

Printing local HTML files from Internet Explorer

Ever wanted to print out a 100 page Web site for later reference without inducing immediate carpal tunnel syndrome? AppleScript it. You know, I like the way that sounds, don't you?

This script, shown in its entirety in **Code 6.4**, is very similar to the previous one we created for Netscape. This time, however, we'll test for matching file suffixes using a `contains` statement to be sure to catch files ending with `.htm`, `.html`, and `.shtml`. And since Internet Explorer won't recognize the Return key we simulated in our last script, we'll resort to using the very useful control panel known as Okey Dokey Pro to get past the Print dialog, as shown in **Figure 6.6**.

To print an entire folder of local HTML files:

1. `on open (myFolder)`

   We start with an on open handler to pass any drag-and-dropped folder reference in the variable `myFolder` to our function. When we save this script as an application, users will be able to drop a folder full of HTML files on the script's icon in the Finder to execute the script.

2. `try`
   ```
       tell application "Finder"
           set the frontmost of process
           → named "Internet Explorer
           → 4.0" to true
       end tell
   on error
   end try
   ```

   Because Explorer 4 does not accept the `activate` statement, we use the Finder to bring it to the front. The Finder keeps track of all running applications, also known as processes. We can set the

Code 6.4 This script prints an entire folder of HTML files, including any in nested folders.

```
on open (myFolder)
    try
        tell application "Finder"
            set the frontmost of process named
            → "Internet Explorer 4.0" to true
        end tell
    on error
    end try
    printHTML(myFolder)
end open


on printHTML(myFolder)
    set myFolderContents to list folder
    → myFolder without invisibles
    repeat with myFile in myFolderContents
        tell application "Finder"
            set myKind to kind of alias
            → ((myFolder as text) & myFile)
            set myName to name of alias
            → ((myFolder as text) & myFile)
        end tell
        if myKind is "folder" then
            printHTML(((myFolder as text) &
            → myFile) as alias) of me
        else
            if myName contains  ".htm" then
                tell application "Internet
                → Explorer 4.0"
                    print alias ((myFolder as
                    → text) & myFile)
                end tell
            end if
        end if
    end repeat
end printHTML
```

Figure 6.6 Here the Okey Dokey Pro control panel is set to wait five seconds before clicking the default buttons in dialog boxes.

frontmost property of a process to true to force it to the foreground. These lines can be used in place of an activate command in any circumstance.

3. `printHTML(myFolder)`
`end open`

Then we pass the reference to the dropped folder to our function as myFolder.

4. `on printHTML(myFolder)`

Next, we define our function printHTML.

5. `set myFolderContents to list folder`
`→ myFolder without invisibles`

We copy the list of all items contained in the folder myFolder to the variable myFolderContents, ignoring any invisible files like icons or the Desktop database.

6. `repeat with myFile in`
`→ myFolderContents`

Now we're ready to loop through each item myFile in the list myFolderContents.

7. `tell application "Finder"`
`    set myKind to kind of alias`
`    → ((myFolder as text) & myFile)`
`    set myName to name of alias`
`    → ((myFolder as text) & myFile)`
`end tell`

Next, we ask the Finder for the kind and name of the item myFile.

8. `if myKind is "folder" then`
`    printHTML(((myFolder as text) &`
`    → myFile) as alias) of me`

If myFile is a folder, we call the function printHTML again to deal with files in the nested folder.

9. `else`
`    if myName contains ".htm" then`

Otherwise, we test to see if the file name contains ".htm". If it does, we've found an HTML file that we'll want to open in Explorer. By checking for the existence of the string ".htm" in the file name, we catch files that have the suffixes ".htm", ".html", and ".shtml" with one simple test.

10. ```
tell application " Internet
 → Explorer 4.0"
```

Now we begin talking to Internet Explorer.

11. ```
print alias ((myFolder as text) &
 → myFile)
end tell
end if
end if
end repeat
end printHTML
```

Next we tell Explorer to print the file myFile. Okey Dokey Pro will click the OK button in the Print dialog for us (see **Figure 6.6**). We're using Okey Dokey Pro here because Internet Explorer 4 doesn't respond to the simulated keystrokes generated by the scripting addition Sändi's Additions that we used with Netscape Navigator. Without Okey Dokey Pro, this script would get stuck forever waiting at the Print dialog. If we set the delay before the OK button is clicked to enough seconds, Explorer will be able to resolve and draw the entire Web page before printing. Explorer lacks the busy property that we used with Navigator to see if it had finished drawing the page before printing it.

Scripting with Okey Dokey Pro

This script requires the system control panel Okey Dokey Pro. You must have the Okey Dokey Pro extension installed in your Control Panels folder for this script to work.

Okey Dokey Pro automatically clicks the default button in dialog boxes on your Mac. You can set the amount of time it should wait before clicking the default button or restrict its operation to specific applications.

Okey Dokey Pro is free.

Okey Dokey Pro is published by Dan Walkowski, who can be reached at http://www.oneclick.com/click/ okey_dokey_read_me.html.

Code 6.5 This simple script puts Netscape Navigator into kiosk mode.

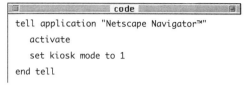

```
tell application "Netscape Navigator™"
    activate
    set kiosk mode to 1
end tell
```

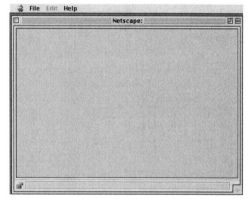

Figure 6.7 This is what Navigator's menu bar and browser window look in kiosk mode.

Putting Netscape Navigator into kiosk mode

One of the most powerful features of Netscape Navigator is one that can only be accessed through AppleScript: kiosk mode. When Navigator is switched to kiosk mode, most of its menu choices and buttons disappear. This state is most useful for presenting Web sites on machines in public settings where you want to restrict the user's options. **Figure 6.7** shows what Navigator's menu and window look like once kiosk mode is invoked. **Code 6.5** is a brief script that switches Navigator into kiosk mode.

To put Netscape Navigator into kiosk mode:

1. `tell application "Netscape` → `Navigator™"`
   `activate`

   We begin by letting AppleScript know that we want to talk to Netscape and bring it to the front.

2. `set kiosk mode to 1`
   `end tell`

   Next, we tell Netscape to begin running in kiosk mode. To switch off kiosk mode, we'd use `set kiosk mode to 0`.

✔ Uses for kiosk mode

■ Have you ever wanted to demo a particular Web site on an unmonitored machine in public? Invariably, people will surf off into the outer limits of the Web, leaving your dedicated Mac and browser displaying unwanted Web pages. Kiosk mode will save you. By eliminating most menus and the location field, kiosk mode makes it much harder for users to take undesirable Web excursions.

■ Kiosk mode is also useful if you want to make a canned presentation to a group from your browser. By invoking kiosk mode, you can guide your audience through a site without any distracting browser controls. Who says a browser-based presentation can't look as slick as something created in a dedicated presentation software package?

Retrieving HTML source code with Internet Explorer

One of the most useful features of Internet Explorer 4.0 is its ability to return the source code for a page directly to a script. This feature can be used to create scripts that intelligently parse HTML source code to traverse sites, mine for data, and perform other functions. The script shown in **Code 6.6** retrieves the current Web page's HTML source code as a string and saves the string to a new text file. Combine this script with an FTP upload routine and you could process and change pages on a Web server and then re-upload them automatically. Hmmm... quite a thought.

To retrieve HTML source code:

1. ```
tell application "Internet
→ Explorer 4.0"
    set currentSource to GetSource
end tell
```
   We begin by asking Internet Explorer to return the HTML source code of its frontmost window to the variable currentSource.

2. `set myFile to new file`
   Next, we have AppleScript display a New File dialog box (**Figure 6.4**) and store a reference to the path of the user's new file name in myFile.

3. ```
set myFileRef to (open for access
→ myFile with write permission)
write currentSource to myFileRef
close access myFileRef
```
   Finally, we write the source code text in currentSource to the file myFile.

Code 6.6. This script retrieves the current Web page's HTML source code as a string and saves the string to a new text file.

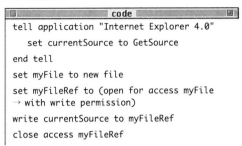

```
tell application "Internet Explorer 4.0"
    set currentSource to GetSource
end tell
set myFile to new file
set myFileRef to (open for access myFile
→ with write permission)
write currentSource to myFileRef
close access myFileRef
```

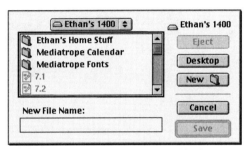

Figure 6.8 The New File dialog displayed by the new file statement.

✔ Parsing search results

- Try using GetSource to retrieve the HTML source code of the frontmost window in Explorer after querying a server using **Code 6.2**. Then parse the code for the search results data!

RETRIEVING HTML SOURCE CODE

Code 6.7 This AppleScript deletes Internet Explorer 4's cache file.

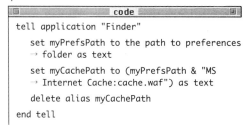

```
tell application "Finder"
    set myPrefsPath to the path to preferences
    → folder as text
    set myCachePath to (myPrefsPath & "MS
    → Internet Cache:cache.waf") as text
    delete alias myCachePath
end tell
```

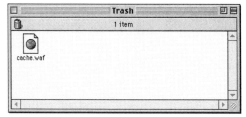

Figure 6.9 Internet Explorer's cache file is in the trash can after the script has been run.

✔ Making this script work with Netscape Navigator

■ See the notes for step 3 to modify this script to work with Netscape Navigator. Instead of deleting Explorer 4's one huge cache file, the modified script deletes the entire cache folder for a specified Netscape user profile. To find out more about user profiles, see *Deleting Netscape Navigator's cookies file*.

Clearing the browser cache

As the browser loads files from remote servers it stores them in a cache to allow quick retrieval for subsequent display. Sometimes, you may need to clear the cache. **Code 6.7** uses the Finder to remove the cache file of Internet Explorer or Netscape Navigator. **Figure 6.9** shows Internet Explorer's cache file in the trash can after the script has been run.

To clear your Internet Explorer cache:

1. `tell application "Finder"`

   We start by letting AppleScript know that we want to speak to the Finder.

2. `set myPrefsPath to the path to`
   `→ preferences folder as text`

   The variable `myPrefsPath` stores the path of our current Preferences folder with AppleScript's built-in `preferences folder` property.

3. `set myCachePath to (myPrefsPath &`
   `→ "MS Internet Cache:cache.waf")`
   `→ as text`

   We construct the full path of our Internet Explorer 4 cache file and store it in the variable `myCachePath`. To change this script to work with Netscape Navigator, replace the string "MS Internet Cache:cache.waf" with "Netscape Users:User Name:Cache *f*". (Change "User Name" to your user profile name. You can look inside the Netscape Users folder to figure out your user profile name, if necessary.)

4. `delete alias myCachePath`
   `end tell`

   Finally, we tell the Finder to delete the cache file pointed to by `myCachePath`.

Deleting Netscape Navigator's cookies file

Browser *cookies* are variables that Web servers store on your hard drive. These variables can be used to track your site preferences, identity, and other attributes. There are times when you want to clear your browser's cookies and start with a clean slate. The simple script in **Code 6.8** uses the Finder to remove Netscape's MagicCookies file. **Figure 6.10** shows this file in the trash can after the script has been run. This scripting concept will not work in the same fashion with Internet Explorer 4.0.

To clear Navigator's cookies file:

1. `set myUserName to "Steven"`

   We begin by defining the user name for our Netscape 4 profile. This user name is defined in a separate application called User Profile Manager that resides in the folder with Navigator. Be sure to change the value of the string "Steven" here to your user profile name. You might also replace the line above with a `display dialog` command to prompt the user for their profile name every time the script is run.

2. `tell application "Finder"`

   Next, we start speaking to the Finder.

3. `set myPrefsPath to the path to` → `preferences folder as text`

   The variable `myPrefsPath` stores the path of our current Preferences folder by using the `preferences folder` reference built into AppleScript.

4. `set myCookiePath to myPrefsPath &` → `"Netscape Users:" & myUserName &` → `":MagicCookie"`

   We construct the full path of our Netscape 4 cookies file in this line and store it in the variable `myCookiePath`.

Code 6.8 This AppleScript deletes Navigator 4.x's cookies file for the defined user.

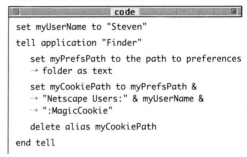

```
set myUserName to "Steven"
tell application "Finder"
    set myPrefsPath to the path to preferences
    → folder as text
    set myCookiePath to myPrefsPath &
    → "Netscape Users:" & myUserName &
    → ":MagicCookie"
    delete alias myCookiePath
end tell
```

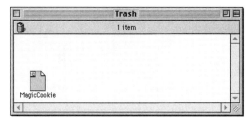

Figure 6.10 Netscape's MagicCookies file in the trash can after the script has been run.

5. `delete alias myCookiePath`
`end tell`

Now we tell the Finder to delete the cookies file pointed to by `myCookiePath`. We use the word `alias` here to tell the Finder that we're actually talking about a reference to an existing file. Within AppleScript, we always let the Finder know that we are referring to an actual file by referencing it as an `alias` object. To make this easier to remember, you might think about the variable `myCookiePath` as though it were itself an alias to the actual file.

Running AppleScripts from your browser

Thanks to Web browsers' ability to receive data files of different types and send these files to other helper applications, we can actually run AppleScripts over the Internet! Practically speaking, however, this technique should only be employed in an intranet situation where you can ensure the security of the scripts and configure users' browsers to receive and run scripts.

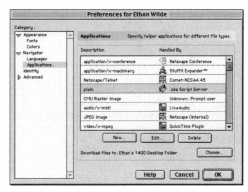

Figure 6.11 Navigator 4's Preferences window with Helper Application selected.

How does it work?

1. First, you need to save a script as a compiled script for use on the Internet.

2. Next, you drop your compiled script icon onto the script application named `.osa Script Converter`. This script, **Code 6.9**, flattens the compiled script into the data fork of the file and resaves the file with the `.osa` suffix.

Code 6.9 Our script to convert compiled AppleScripts.

```
to .osa files: .osa Script Converter
on run
    set myFile to (choose file with prompt "Select script to web-enable:" of type → "osas")
    convertScript(myFile)
end run
on open (myFile)
    set myFile to myFile as text
    tell application "Finder"
        set myType to file type of file myFile
    end tell
    if myType = "osas" then convertScript(myFile)
end open
on convertScript(myFile)
    set myScript to read resource myFile ID 128 type "scpt"
    set myNewFile to (myFile & ".osa") as text
    set myFileRef to (open for access file myNewFile with write permission)
    write myScript to myFileRef
    close access myFileRef
end convertScript
```

Code 6.10 Our script to run .osa files downloaded by our browser:

```
.osa Script Server.
on open myFile
    set myFileRef to (open for access myFile)
    set myScriptText to read myFileRef as script
    close access myFileRef
    try
        tell myScriptText
            activate
            run
        end tell
    on error errmsg number errnum
        display dialog "Error: " & errmsg
        → buttons "OK" default button "OK"
    end try
    tell application "Finder"
        delete myFile
    end tell
    tell application "Netscape Navigator™"
        activate
    end tell
end open
```

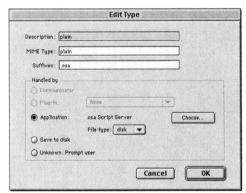

Figure 6.12 Navigator's New Type window with the proper settings to allow .osa Script Server to run any .osa files Navigator downloads.

3. Users must configure their browsers to support the new file suffix, .osa, and launch the second script, **Code 6.10**, as the helper application.

4. **Figures 6.11** and **6.12** show how you should configure Navigator 4 to receive .osa files. **Figures 6.13** and **6.14** show how you should configure Internet Explorer 4 to receive .osa files. Create a new type in the Preferences window, as shown in **Figure 6.11** or **6.13**. Then, enter the values shown in **Figure 6.12** or **6.14** and select your script application as the application to use.

Save **Code 6.9** as an application named .osa Script Converter and save **Code 6.10** as an application named .osa Script Server.

To convert a script for transmission over the Internet:

1. ```
   on run
       set myFile to (choose file with
       → prompt "Select script to
       → web-enable:" of type "osas")
       convertScript(myFile)
   end run
   ```
   We begin with an on run handler to prompt the user to select a compiled script file and pass it to our function below.

2. ```
   on open (myFile)
       set myFile to myFile as text
   ```
   Next, we have an on open handler to store a reference to any file dropped on this script application in the variable myFile.

3. ```
   tell application "Finder"
       set myType to file type of file
       → myFile
   end tell
   ```
   Now we ask the Finder for the file type of myFile.
   ```

4. `if myType = "osas" then`
`→ convertScript(myFile)`
`end open`

If the file is a compiled script we call our function below.

5. `on convertScript(myFile)`

Here we begin the function definition.

6. `set myScript to read resource`
`→ myFile ID 128 type "scpt"`

This line tells AppleScript to retrieve the actual compiled script data that is stored by AppleScript as a resource (always with the ID number of 128) in our script file `myFile`. We store this retrieved data in the variable `myScript`.

7. `set myNewFile to (myFile & ".osa")`
`→ as text`

Now we construct a new file name, the original plus the `.osa` suffix, in `myNewFile`.

8. `set myFileRef to`
`→ (open for access file myNewFile`
`→ with write permission)`
`    write myScript to myFileRef`
`    close access myFileRef`
`end convertScript`

Next, we create a text file named `myNewFile` and store the script resource data in the file's data fork, effectively flattening the file for distribution over the Internet.

To allow your browser to run downloaded AppleScripts:

1. `on open myFile`

We begin with an `on open` handler to receive the `.osa` file `myFile`. When Netscape receives a file it knows should be opened by a helper application, it sends the helper application an Open command with a reference to file.

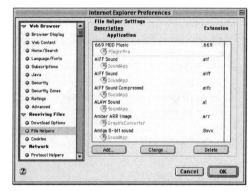

Figure 6.13 Internet Explorer 4's Preferences window with Helper Application selected.

2. `set myFileRef to`
   `→ (open for access myFile)`
      `set myScriptText to read`
      `→ myFileRef as script`
   `close access myFileRef`

We open `myFile` using `open for acess` and `read` the data from it into our variable `myScriptText` as a script. Since we didn't include the phrase `with write permission` in our `open for access` command, the file is opened for read-only access.

3. `try`

Now we begin a `try` error-handling routine.

4. `tell myScriptText`
      `activate`
      `run`
   `end tell`

Now we ask AppleScript to run the script code stored in `myScriptText` as though it were a stand-alone script. This is the magic series of instructions that makes AppleScript execute the `.osa` file downloaded as a script.

5. `on error errmsg number errnum`
      `display dialog "Error: " &`
      `→ errmsg buttons "OK" default`
      `→ button "OK"`
   `end try`

If an error occurs while AppleScript is trying to run our downloaded script, we display a dialog with the error message and number returned by AppleScript.

6. `tell application "Finder"`
      `delete myFile`
   `end tell`

Now that our downloaded script stored in the file `myFile` has run, we can delete the `.osa` file `myFile`.

7. `tell application "Netscape`
   `→ Navigator™"`

Flattening a Mac file's resource fork

By now, you're probably asking yourself: what does "flatten" mean? This term is used to describe the process by which a Macintosh-only file is converted into a simple data-only file. Mac files are normally constructed as two split halves, a resource fork and a data fork. However, when you send a file like this over the Internet, only the data fork gets sent! Well, this won't do at all for transmitting a script, since its code resides exclusively in the resource half of the file. So we flatten it by copying the resource fork to a simple data-only file.

```
    activate
  end tell
end open
```

Finally, now that the show is over, we bring Netscape back to the front with the `activate` command, leaving the user in the same place they were in when they chose to download the `.osa` script file.

✔ Making this script work with Internet Explorer

■ To modify this script to work with Microsoft Internet Explorer, replace the code in step 7 above with these lines:

```
try
    set the frontmost of
    → process named "Internet
    → Explorer 4.0" to true
  on error
  end try
  end tell
end open
```

■ ScriptDemon, from Royal Software, is a Netscape-compatible browser plug-in that offers more features and security for running AppleScripts from Netscape Navigator over the Internet. Royal Software can be contacted at `http://www.royalsoftware.com/`.

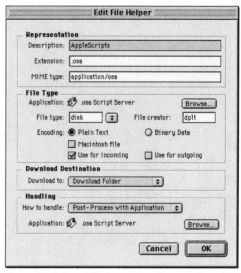

Figure 6.14 Internet Explorer's New Type window with the proper settings to allow `.osa Script Server` to run any `.osa` files Explorer downloads.

Scripting with read/write resource

This script requires the scripting addition read/write resource. You must have read/write resource installed in your Scripting Additions folder for this script to work.

Read/write resource adds the statement `read resource` to allow your script to access resources in standard Mac files.

Read/write resource is shareware and costs 20 French francs.

Read/write resource is published by PAUTEX jf, who can be reached at `http://` → `www.lpmi.u-nancy.fr/FTP.www.html`.

Scripting Emailer and Outlook Express

7

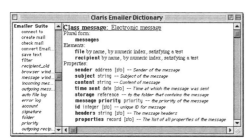

Figure 7.1 Emailer's dictionary entry for its message object.

Figure 7.2 Outlook Express's dictionary entry for its message object.

Emailer's AppleScript dictionary is so exceptionally well-designed that when Microsoft created Outlook Express for the Macintosh, it adopted the vast majority of Emailer's dictionary for Outlook. This brilliant choice to standardize terminology makes our scripting job that much easier, as you'll see in this chapter.

Figures 7.1 and **7.2** show the dictionary entries for the message object in Emailer and Outlook Express. A quick comparison of the two shows the close similarity in terminology.

Either Emailer or Outlook Express makes for a powerful combination with FileMaker Pro to create mailing list databases and mine e-mail for data. Emailer and Outlook's message object is a perfect analog to FileMaker's record object. When you copy properties from an Emailer or Outlook message to cells of a FileMaker record you create a powerful searchable database that can be used to calculate statistics, summarize mail, or send mail back out.

Converting mail from Eudora or UNIX

Code 7.1 will convert a UNIX or Eudora mail file to Emailer or Outlook Express format, extracting each message separately into the In Box. In the UNIX world of `sendmail`, a user's entire mailbox is stored in a single file named after the user. If your file has UNIX line feeds in it, set the variable `myFileIsUNIX` to `true`. The Macintosh version of Eudora stores each mailbox's messages in a single file. If you're using Eudora files, set `myFileIsUNIX` to `false`. **Figure 7.3** shows how Emailer's In Box looks as the script is running.

Figure 7.3 Here we see Emailer's In Box as the script is running. The two messages in the In Box have just been imported into the In Box from a UNIX mail file.

To convert mail from Eudora or UNIX:

1. `on run`
    `set myFileIsUNIX to false`

We begin our `on run` handler defining the variable `myFileIsUNIX` to flag which line feed type to expect in the mail file. You could set this variable to the results of a `display dialog` command to prompt the user for the file type.

2. `if myFileIsUNIX then`
        `set linefeed to ASCII`
    `→ character 10`

Now we test the variable; if it contains the value `true`, then we set the variable `linefeed` to `ASCII character 10`. If you are parsing DOS or PC files, set the variable `linefeed` to both `ASCII character 10` and `ASCII character 13`.

3. `else`
        `set linefeed to return`
    `end if`

If `myFileIsUNIX` contains the value `false`, then we set the variable `linefeed` to `return`, which is a predefined variable set to ASCII character 13.

Scripting Emailer

All the scripts that follow were designed and tested for Emailer 2.0.

Most of these scripts do not work with older versions of Emailer.

Emailer is published by Apple Computer Inc., which can be reached at `http://www.apple.com/`.

Scripting Outlook Express

All the scripts that follow were designed and tested for Outlook Express 4.0.1.

Outlook Express is published by Microsoft Corporation, which can be reached at `http://www.microsoft.com/`. Screen shots reprinted by permission of Microsoft Corporation. Outlook Express is a registered trademark of Microsoft Corporation.

CONVERTING MAIL FROM EUDORA OR UNIX

Code 7.1 A script to import a UNIX or Eudora mail file into Emailer's In Box.

```
                        code
on run
   set myFileIsUNIX to false
   if myFileIsUNIX then
      set linefeed to ASCII character 10
   else
      set linefeed to return
   end if
   set myMailFile to (choose file with prompt
   → "Mail file to import:")
   set myFileRef to (open for access
   → myMailFile)
   set myMailDate to (read myFileRef until
   → linefeed)
   try
      repeat
         set myHeader to ""
         set myMailDateFound to false
         repeat
            set myMail to (read myFileRef
            → until linefeed)
            if myMail = linefeed then exit
            → repeat
            set myMail to (characters 1 thru
            → ((length of myMail) - 1) of
            → myMail as string) & return
            set myHeader to myHeader & myMail
            if myMail starts with "Date: "
            → then
               set myMailDateFound to true
            end if
         end repeat

         if not myMailDateFound then
            try
               set theDayOfWeek to word 3 of
               → myMailDate
               set theMonth to word 4 of
               → myMailDate
               set theDay to word 5 of
               → myMailDate
               set theTime to word 6 of
               → myMailDate
               set theYear to characters 1
               → thru ((length of word 7 of
               → myMailDate) - 1) of (word 7
               → of myMailDate) as string
               set myHeader to myHeader &
               → "Date: "
```

Code continues on next page

4.
```
set myMailFile to (choose file
→ with prompt "Mail file to
→ import:")
```
Next, we prompt the user to select the mail file to import, storing their selection in the variable myMailFile.

5.
```
set myFileRef to (open for
→ access myMailFile)
```
We open the selected file using the open for access command.

6.
```
set myMailDate to (read
→ myFileRef until linefeed)
```
Now we read the first line of the mail file, storing it in a variable named myMailDate. The first line of the mail file often represents a date for the messages contained.

7.
```
try
   repeat
```
Here we start a repeat loop to capture each mail message contained in the mail file.

8.
```
set myHeader to ""
```
We begin the loop by initializing the variable myHeader, which will end up holding the header of the current mail message.

9.
```
set myMailDateFound to
→ false
```
Now we initialize the variable myMailDateFound to false. We'll use this variable to keep track of whether each individual message we find in the file has its own date or not.

10.
```
repeat
```
We begin a nested loop to sequentially read in each line of the mail file that comprises the header of the current message.

CONVERTING MAIL FROM EUDORA OR UNIX

109

11. `set myMail to (read myFileRef`
`→ until linefeed)`

We read characters from the mail file until we encounter the end-of-line character we defined with our variable `linefeed` in step 2 or 3.

12. `if myMail = linefeed`
`→ then exit repeat`

If the variable `myMail` contains nothing but the end-of-line character, it's a blank line. A blank line indicates the end of our header so we exit our loop.

13. `set myMail to`
`→ (characters 1 thru`
`→ ((length of myMail)`
`→ - 1) of myMail as`
`→ string) & return`

We strip the end-of-line character off the variable `myMail`.

14. `set myHeader to`
`→ myHeader & myMail`

Then, we append it to the end of the variable `myHeader`, which we're using to assemble the header of the current message.

15. `if myMail starts with`
`→ "Date: " then`

We test to see if `myMail` starts with the string "Date:".

16. `set myMailDateFound`
`→ to true`
`end if`
`end repeat`

If it does, then the message has its own date, so we set our flag `myMailDateFound` to `true` to indicate that the date exists in the header stored in `myHeader`.

17. `if not myMailDateFound then`

Once we've completed the loop to construct our current message's header, we test our variable `myMailDateFound`

Code 7.1 *continued*

```
                    set myHeader to myHeader &
                    → theDayOfWeek & ", " & theDay
                    → & " " & theMonth & " " &
                    → theYear & " " & theTime
                    set myHeader to myHeader &
                    → return
                on error
                end try
            end if

        set myBody to ""
        repeat
            set myMail to (read myFileRef
            → until linefeed)
            considering case
                if myMail starts with "From "
                → then exit repeat
            end considering
            if length of myMail > 1 then set
            → myMail to (characters 1 thru
            → ((length of myMail) - 1) of
            → myMail as string) & return
            set myBody to myBody & myMail
        end repeat

        set myMailDate to myMail

        makeMessage(myHeader, myBody)

    end repeat
on error
    try
        makeMessage(myHeader, myBody)
    on error
    end try
end try
close access myFileRef
end run

on makeMessage(myHeader, myBody)
    tell application "Claris Emailer"
        make new incoming message with properties
            {long headers:myHeader, content:
            → myBody, read status:read} ¬
                at the in box folder
    end tell
end makeMessage
```

to see if a unique date was found in the header text.

18.
```
try
    set theDayOfWeek to
→ word 3 of myMailDate
```
If the message header doesn't have its own date, we try to reformat the date string we stored in myMailDate earlier. First we capture the day of the week in the variable theDayOfWeek.

19.
```
set theDay to word 5 of
→ myMailDateset theMonth to word 4
→ of myMailDate
set theTime to word 6 of
→ myMailDate
```
Since the date will always be in the same format, we can grab the date, time, and day and store them in our variables.

20.
```
set theYear to characters
→ 1 thru ((length of word
→ 7 of myMailDate) - 1)
→ of (word 7 of myMailDate)
→ as string
```
Finally, we capture the year in the variable theYear, which should reside in the seventh word of our date string. This word also contains the end-of-line character, so we strip off the last character of this word before storing it in our new variable.

21.
```
        set myHeader to myHeader
    → & "Date: "
        set myHeader to myHeader
    → & theDayOfWeek & ", "
    → & theDay & " " & theMonth
    → & " " & theYear & " "
    → & theTime
        set myHeader to myHeader
    → & return
    on error
    end try
end if
```

Now, we're ready to add a properly formatted date entry to our current message's header as stored in myHeader.

22.
```
    set myBody to ""
    repeat
```
Now we initialize the variable myBody to hold the message body and begin a repeat loop to capture the body of the current message.

23.
```
    set myMail to (read
 → myFileRef until linefeed)
```
Within our loop, we read another line of the mail file; its end is indicated by the character stored in our variable linefeed.

24.
```
        considering case
```
We then use the considering case statement to let AppleScript know that the subsequent comparisons need to be case-sensitive.

25.
```
        if myMail starts with
 → "From " then exit repeat
    end considering
```
If the current line of our mail file, as stored in myMail, begins with "From," we know that a new message is starting, so we exit our loop.

26.
```
if length of myMail > 1 then set
 → myMail to (characters 1 thru
 → ((length of myMail) - 1) of
 → myMail as string) & return
set myBody to myBody & myMail
end repeat
```
Otherwise, we strip the last character off the current line and add it to the current message's body that we're storing in the variable myBody.

27.   `set myMailDate to myMail`

When we finish parsing the body and exit the loop, the current line holds the next date, so we save it in the variable that we'll later reformat in steps 18 through 22.

28.   `makeMessage(myHeader, myBody)`
        `end repeat`

Now that we've found the header and body of a message, we call our function `makeMessage` to create a new message in Emailer, passing it the header and body variables.

29.   `on error`
     `try`
        `makeMessage(myHeader,`
          `⇢ myBody)`
     `on error`
     `end try`
   `end try`
   `close access myFileRef`
`end run`

When we finally encounter the end of the mail file, the end-of-file error will trigger this `on error` routine, so we now try to create one final message for Emailer using the current header and body variables. Finally, outside of `on error`, we close the mail file with the `close access` command.

30. `on makeMessage(myHeader, myBody)`

Our `makeMessage` function receives the values for header and body in variables.

31.   `tell application`
      `⇢ "Claris Emailer"`

We begin talking to Claris Emailer now. To make this script work with Outlook Express, replace the string `"Claris Emailer"` with `"Outlook Express"` in this line.

32.
```
make new incoming message
→ with properties ¬
  {long headers:myHeader,
  → content:myBody,
  → read status:read} ¬
    at the in box folder
end tell
end makeMessage
```
Now we tell our mail client application to create a new message in the In Box with a read status indicating that it's already been read. To make this script work with Outlook Express, change the string at the in box folder to at folder "Inbox" and the string long headers to headers.

✔ Making this script work with Outlook Express

- See the notes for steps 31 and 32 to modify this script to work with Microsoft Outlook Express. Outlook's syntax is very similar to Emailer's, except that they refer to the programs' in boxes in a different manner.

Anatomy of a UNIX mail file

Below is a excerpt of a typical UNIX mail file. Line breaks, spaces, and tabs are made visible in this code to help show the file's organization.

```
From◊owner-razanet-l@sfsu.edu◊◊Wed◊Apr◊15◊12:42:26◊1998

Received:◊from◊diana.sfsu.edu◊by◊sgi.mediatrope.com◊via◊ESMTP◊(940816.SGI.8.6
.9/940406.SGI)

X-Sender:◊razanet@apollo.sfsu.edu

Message-Id:◊<v01530504b15aad8537e9@[130.212.1.209]>

Mime-Version:◊1.0

Content-Type:◊text/plain;◊charset="iso-8859-1"

Date:◊Wed,◊15◊Apr◊1998◊12:11:18◊-0700

To:◊razanet-l@sfsu.edu

From:◊razanet@sfsu.edu◊(RazaNet@S.F.◊State◊University◊(CECIPP))

Subject:◊Please◊Forward:◊CineAccion◊Latino◊Film◊Festival◊Director◊announcement

Sender:◊owner-razanet-l@sfsu.edu

Reply-To:◊razanet@sfsu.edu◊(RazaNet@S.F.◊State◊University◊(CECIPP))

Content-Transfer-Encoding:◊quoted-printable

Status:◊0
```

The lines above comprise the message header. Consider modifying your script to parse particular information from the header, like the reply-to address. The header ends with a blank line.

```
CINE◊ACCION'S◊LATINO◊FILM◊FESTIVAL◊SEEKING◊FESTIVAL◊CO-DIRECTOR

◊◊◊◊◊◊◊◊◊◊◊◊◊◊◊◊◊◊◊◊◊◊◊◊◊JOB◊DESCRIPTION

◊◊◊◊◊◊◊◊◊◊◊◊◊◊◊◊◊◊◊◊◊◊◊FESTIVAL◊CO-◊DIRECTOR

>◊◊◊◊◊◊◊◊◊◊◊◊◊◊◊◊◊Cine◊Acci=F3n's◊Sixth◊Annual

>◊◊◊◊◊◊◊◊◊◊◊◊◊◊◊◊◊◊◊Festival◊=A1Cine◊Latino!

>◊◊◊◊◊◊◊(30◊hours/week,◊May◊15,◊1998◊-◊October◊15,◊1998)
```

The end of the body portion of the message is indicated either by the start of the next message or, if it's the last message, by the end of the file. In this case another message starts. Messages always start with at least one blank line followed by a line that starts with the string From.

```
From◊owner-razanet-l@sfsu.edu◊◊Wed◊Apr◊15◊12:43:57◊1998

Received:◊from◊diana.sfsu.edu◊by◊sgi.mediatrope.com◊via◊ESMTP◊(940816.SGI.8.6
.9/940406.SGI)
```

CONVERTING MAIL FROM EUDORA OR UNIX

Converting mail from QuickMail Pro

Code 7.2 will convert a single folder of
messages from QuickMail Pro to Emailer or
Outlook's format, extracting each message
separately into the mail client's In Box. This
script differs from the previous one that
imported UNIX and Eudora mailboxes
because we will actually script QuickMail
as well as Emailer or Outlook, using our
script to create a bridge between the two
applications. Previously, we simply read the
static text files full of messages generated by
Eudora and UNIX. Set the folder name you
want to use in the variable `myFolderName`.
Figure 7.4 shows how Emailer's In Box looks
as the script is running.

To convert mail from QuickMail Pro:

1. `on run`
     `set myFolderName to "Test"`

We begin our `on run` handler by defining
a variable to hold the name of the
QuickMail folder we wish to import into
Emailer. If you would like to prompt the
user for this information, you can use
the `display dialog` command to return
a value.

2. `tell application "QuickMail Pro"`
     `set myMessages to Get Mail List`
     `→ All Folder Name myFolderName`

Next, we begin talking to QuickMail by
retrieving a list of all messages in the
folder `myFolderName`.

3.   `repeat with myMessage in`
     `→ myMessages`

Now we begin looping through each message in `myMessages`.

Code 7.2 This script imports a folder of QuickMail
messages into Emailer's In Box.

```
on run
    set myFolderName to "Test"
    tell application "QuickMail Pro"
        set myMessages to Get Mail List All
        → Folder Name myFolderName
        repeat with myMessage in myMessages
            set mySubject to Subject of
            → myMessage
            set mySender to Who from of
            → myMessage
            open myFolderName Message
            → (Message ID of myMessage)
            set myBody to Body of (Get Message)
            Message Close
            my makeMessage(mySender, mySubject,
            → myBody)
        end repeat
    end tell
end run


on makeMessage(mySender, mySubject, myBody)
    tell application "Claris Emailer"
        make new incoming message with properties
            {sender:mySender, subject:mySubject,
            → content:myBody, read status:read}
            → at folder "In Box"
    end tell
end makeMessage
```

Scripting QuickMail Pro

QuickMail Pro 1.5 is published by CE
Software, who can be reached at
`http://www.cesoft.com/`.

Figure 7.4 Emailer's In Box holds the first message imported from QuickMail Pro as our script is running.

4.
```
set mySubject to Subject
→ of myMessage
set mySender to Who from
→ of myMessage
open myFolderName Message
→ (Message ID of myMessage)
set myBody to Body of
→ (Get Message)
Message Close
```

Here we capture the subject, sender, and body text of the current message and store them in the variables mySubject, mySender, and myBody respectively. To access the body of the message we have QuickMail open the message using the open Message command. Once we've read the body, we close the message using the Message Close command.

5.
```
    my makeMessage(mySender,
    → mySubject, myBody)
  end repeat
 end tell
end run
```

Next, we call our function makeMessage, passing it the sender, subject, and body of the current message, before ending our loop.

6. on makeMessage(mySender, mySubject, myBody)

This function is covered in steps 31 and 32 of the previous spread, which discusses **Code 7.1**.

✔ Making this script work with Outlook Express

■ Since our function makeMessage is the only part of the script that makes reference to the mail client application, follow the tips for **Code 7.1** (steps 31 and 32) to modify this script to function with Outlook Express.

Filing mail based on keywords

Code 7.3 will move messages that contain certain strings in their subjects and/or bodies to a specific message folder, which we'll call the Test folder. **Figure 7.5** shows the appearance of this folder as the script is running.

Figure 7.5 Here we see the folder named Test in Emailer, with two messages that sued to be in the In Box now moved by our script into the folder since they had keyword matches.

In this script, we'll lay the groundwork for most of the subsequent scripts that deal with e-mail. The main portion of the code contained in the on run handler will be reused in all e-mail scripts that deal with keyword matching. It can handle sophisticated searches and/or searching for multiple keywords defined in a list. Both the subject and the body of the e-mail can be searched.

To file mail based on keywords:

1. `global myKeywordMatches`

We begin by defining the variable myKeywordMatches as global so our function and main program can both use it.

2. `on run`

```
    set myKeywords to
→ {"Raza", "Chavez", "Latino"}
    set mySearchType to "or"
    set myIncludeSubject to true
    set myIncludeBody to true
```

Next, we begin our on run handler and define variables to hold our search strings ("Raza", "Chavez", and "Latino"), the type of search to execute ("or"), and Boolean flags indicating whether to search the subject and/or body. These variables are called myKeywords, mySearchType, myIncludeSubject, and myIncludeBody, respectively.

3. `tell application "Claris Emailer"`

Here we begin talking to Emailer. To make this script work with Outlook Express, simply replace the string

Code 7.3 This script moves messages with certain keywords in their bodies and/or subjects to a specific message folder.

```
                    code
global myKeywordMatches

on run

    set myKeywords to {"Raza", "Chavez",
    → "Latino"}

    set mySearchType to "or"

    set myIncludeSubject to true

    set myIncludeBody to true

    tell application "Claris Emailer"

        set myMessages to every message in
        → folder "In Box"

        repeat with myMessage in myMessages

            set myText to ""

            set myKeywordMatches to ""

            if myIncludeBody then set myText to
            → myText & the content of myMessage
            → & return

            if myIncludeSubject then set myText
            → to myText & the subject of
            → myMessage

            set myFound to false

            considering case

                repeat with myKeyword in
                → myKeywords

                    if myText contains myKeyword
                    → then

                        set myFound to true

                        set myKeywordMatches to
                        → myKeywordMatches &
                        → myKeyword & " "

                        if mySearchType = "or" then
                        → exit repeat

                    else

                        if mySearchType = "and" and
                        → myKeyword≠last item of
                        → myKeywords then

                            set myFound to false

                            exit repeat

                        end if

                    end if

                end repeat

            end considering

            if myFound then

                my processMail(myMessage)

            end if
```

Code continues on next page

"Claris Emailer" with "Outlook Express".

4. `set myMessages to every message in` → `folder "In Box"`

Next we retrieve a list of all messages in the In Box. To make this script work with Outlook Express, simply replace the string `"In Box"` with `"Inbox"`.

5. `repeat with myMessage in` → `myMessages`

Next, we start a loop through each message in the list of messages.

6. `set myText to ""`

At the beginning our loop, we initialize the variable `myText` that we'll search for keyword matches.

7. `set myKeywordMatches to ""`

We also initialize the variable `myKeywordMatches` that we'll use to hold all of the matches found in the currently searched message.

8. `if myIncludeBody then set` → `myText to myText & the` → `content of myMessage & return`

If the flag variable `myIncludeBody` is true, we'll add the body of the current message to our variable `myText` so that it is searched for matches below.

9. `if myIncludeSubject then` → `set myText to myText & the` → `subject of myMessage`

If the flag variable `myIncludeSubject` is true, we'll add the subject of the current message to our variable `myText` so that it is searched for matches below.

10. `set myFound to false`

Before we start looping through our keywords to test for matches, we need to initialize a variable, `myFound`, that we'll use to indicate whether any matches are found.

FILING MAIL BASED ON KEYWORDS

11.   `considering case`

Next, we let AppleScript know that we want it to perform all subsequent string comparisons with case sensitivity.

12.   `repeat with myKeyword`
                   `→ in myKeywords`

Now, we start to loop through our list of keywords.

13.   `if myText contains`
                   `→ myKeyword then`

We test to see if our current keyword is found inside of `myText`.

14.   `set myFound to true`

If we find a keyword in `myText`, we first set our flag variable `myFound` to `true`.

15.   `set myKeywordMatches to`
          `→ myKeywordMatches & myKeyword`
          `→ & " "`

We add the found keyword to our variable `myKeywordMatches` to track which matches are found for the current message.

16.   `if mySearchType = "or" then`
              `→ exit repeat`

Next, we check to see if our search is an "or" type search. If it is, we exit our loop.

17.   `else`
                   `if mySearchType = "and"`
`and myKeyword ≠ last item of`
`myKeywords then`
                      `set myFound to false`
                      `exit repeat`
                   `end if`
                `end if`
             `end repeat`
`end considering`

If our search is an "and" search and we haven't tested the last keyword yet, we clear our flag so that the searching continues, ensuring that all keywords are found. In this case, we set our search

Code 7.3 *continued*

```
                           code
        end repeat
     end tell
end run


on processMail(myMessage)
   tell application "Claris Emailer"
      move myMessage to folder "Test"
   end tell
end processMail
```

to be an "or" search in step 2 above. You can change mySearchType to "and" to modify this script.

18.
```
    if myFound then
        my processMail(myMessage)
    end if
  end repeat
end tell
end run
```

If we have a match, we call our function processMail, passing it the current message.

19.
```
on processMail(myMessage)
    tell application "Claris Emailer"
        move myMessage to folder
"Test"
    end tell
end processMail
```

Our function processMail receives a message and tells Emailer to move the message to the message folder named Test. To modify this script to work with Outlook Express, replace the string "Claris Emailer" above with "Outlook Express".

✔ Making this script work with Outlook Express

- See the notes for steps 3, 4, and 19 above to modify this script to work with Microsoft Outlook Express.

Sending replies based on keywords

Code 7.4 will send a reply to the sender of any incoming message that contains certain keywords. This script could be used as a Mailbot to send specific information in response to inquiries that have particular phrases in the body or subject of the incoming message. **Figure 7.6** shows what Emailer's Out Box looks like as the script is running.

To send replies based on keywords:

1. The on run handler of this script is covered in detail in the previous spread, *Filing mail based on keywords* , steps 1 through 18.

2. `on processMail(myMessage)`

   Our processMail function in this script receives a reference to the current message in the variable myMessage.

3. `   tell application "Claris Emailer"`

   We begin by letting AppleScript know that we want to speak to Emailer. To modify this script to work with Outlook Express, replace the string `"Claris Emailer"` above with `"Outlook Express"`.

4. `    set mySubject to "RE: " &`
   `→ (subject of myMessage)`

   Now we define a variable to hold the subject for our new message, basing it on the subject of the message referred to by our variable myMessage.

5. `    set myAddress to sender of`
   `→ myMessage`
   `    set myRecipName to display`
   `→ name of myAddress`
   `    set myRecipAddress to address`
   `→ of myAddress`

Figure 7.6 The outgoing message in Emailer's Out Box was just created by our script as a reply to an incoming message with a matching keyword.

Code 7.4 This script replies to messages that contain the keywords.

```
                    code
global myKeywordMatches
on run
    set myKeywords to {"Raza", "Chavez",
    → "Latino"}
    set mySearchType to "or"
    set myIncludeSubject to true
    set myIncludeBody to true
    tell application "Claris Emailer"
        set myMessages to every message in
        → folder "In Box"
        repeat with myMessage in myMessages
            set myText to ""
            set myKeywordMatches to ""
            if myIncludeBody then set myText
            → to myText & the content of
            → myMessage & return
            if myIncludeSubject then set myText
            → to myText & the subject of
            → myMessage
        set myFound to false
        considering case
            repeat with myKeyword in
            → myKeywords
                if myText contains myKeyword
                → then
                    set myFound to true
                    set myKeywordMatches to
                    → myKeywordMatches &
                    → myKeyword & " "
                    if mySearchType = "or" then
                    → exit repeat
                else
                    if mySearchType = "and" and
                    → myKeyword ≠last item of
                    → myKeywordsthen
                        set myFound to false
```

Code continues on next page

Code 7.4 *continued*

```
                    exit repeat
                end if
            end if
        end repeat
    end considering
    if myFound then
        my processMail(myMessage)
    end if
    end repeat
    end tell
end run


on processMail(myMessage)
    tell application "Claris Emailer"
        set mySubject to "RE: " & (subject of
        → myMessage)
        set myAddress to sender of myMessage
        set myRecipName to display name of
        → myAddress
        set myRecipAddress to address of
        → myAddress
        set myBody to "Thanks for inquiring
        → about " & myKeywordMatches
        make new outgoing message with
        → properties
            {subject:mySubject, content:myBody,
            → recipient:{{address:{display
            → name:myRecipName,
            → address:myRecipAddress},
            → recipient type:to recipient,
            → delivery status:unsent}}}
    end tell
end processMail
```

Next we store the address record of the sender of the current message in a variable, myAddress. From this record, we extract the name and e-mail address of the sender and store them in the variables myRecipName and myRecipAddress.

6.
```
        set myBody to "Thanks for
        → inquiring about " &
        → myKeywordMatches
```
Finally, we set up the body of our new message in a variable, adding a note about which keywords were matched by including the variable myKeywordMatches that our code above constructed for us.

7.
```
        make new outgoing message wit
        → properties {subject:mySubject,
        → content:myBody,
        → recipient:{{address:
        → {display name:myRecipName,
        → address:myRecipAddress},
        → recipient type:to recipient,
        → delivery status:unsent}}}
    end tell
end processMail
```
We then tell Emailer to make a new outgoing message using the variable we just set up. The reply is now ready to be sent.

✔ Making this script work with Outlook Express

■ See the note for step 3 above to modify this script to work with Microsoft Outlook Express. Also, make sure to modify the on run handler as noted in steps 3 and 4 of the previous spread, *Filing mail based on keywords.*

Forwarding mail based on keywords

Code 7.5 will forward any incoming message that contains the keywords. This script could be used as a filter to forward mail to people who would have a particular interest in it. The recipient name and address are defined in variables in our function `processMail`. **Figure 7.7** shows how Emailer's Out Box looks as the script is running.

To forward mail based on keywords:

1. The on run handler of this script is covered in detail in the spread *Filing mail based on keywords*, on page 118, steps 2 through 18.

2. `on processMail(myMessage)`
   `tell application "Claris Emailer"`

   Our `processMail` function in this script begins by letting AppleScript know that we want to talk to Emailer. To modify this script to work with Outlook Express, replace the string `"Claris Emailer"` above with `"Outlook Express"`.

3. `    set mySubject to`
   `    → "Forwarded due to keywords "`
   `    → & myKeywordMatches`

   We define a variable, `mySubject`, to hold the subject for our new message, which is a note about which keywords were matched.

4. `    set myRecipName to "Receiver`
   `    of Forward"`
   `    set myRecipAddress to`
   `    "nobody@nothing.com"`

   We set the name and address of the person to whom we're going to forward the message in the variables `myRecipName` and `myRecipAddress`.

Figure 7.7 These two outgoing messages were created by our script in response to two incoming messages with keyword matches.

Code 7.5 This script forwards messages that contain the keywords.

```
global myKeywordMatches
on run
    set myKeywords to {"Raza", "Chavez",
    → "Latino"}
    set mySearchType to "or"
    set myIncludeSubject to true
    set myIncludeBody to true
    tell application "Claris Emailer"
        set myMessages to every message in
        → folder "In Box"
        repeat with myMessage in myMessages
            set myText to ""
            set myKeywordMatches to ""
            if myIncludeBody then set myText to
            → myText & the content of myMessage
            → & return
            if myIncludeSubject then set myText
            → to myText & the subject of
            → myMessage
            set myFound to false
            considering case
                repeat with myKeyword in
                → myKeywords
                    if myText contains myKeyword
                    → then
                        set myFound to true
                        set myKeywordMatches to
                        → myKeywordMatches &
                        → myKeyword & " "
                        if mySearchType = "or" then
                        → exit repeat
                    else
                        if mySearchType = "and" and
                        → myKeyword ≠last item of
                        → myKeywords  then
```

Code continues on next page

FORWARDING MAIL BASED ON KEYWORDS

Code 7.5 *continued*

```
                    set myFound to false
                    exit repeat
                end if
            end if
        end repeat
    end considering
    if myFound then
        my processMail(myMessage)
    end if
    end repeat
  end tell
end run

on processMail(myMessage)
  tell application "Claris Emailer"
    set mySubject to "Forwarded due to
      → keywords " & myKeywordMatches
    set myRecipName to "Receiver of
      → Forward"
    set myRecipAddress to
      → "nobody@nothing.com"
    set myBody to the content of myMessage
    make new outgoing message with
      → properties
        {subject:mySubject, content:myBody,
          → recipient:{{address:{display
          → name:myRecipName,
          → address:myRecipAddress},
          → recipient type:to recipient,
          → delivery status:unsent}}}
    end tell
end processMail
```

5.
```
        set myBody to the content of
          → myMessage
```
Since we're forwarding the message, we set our variable for the new message's body text, myBody, to hold the body text of the old.

6.
```
        make new outgoing message
          → with properties ¬
            {subject:mySubject,
              → content:myBody,
              → recipient:{{address:
              → {display name:myRecipName,
              → address:myRecipAddress},
              → recipient type:to
              → recipient, delivery
              → status:unsent}}}
    end tell
end processMail
```
We then tell Emailer to make a new outgoing message, ready to be sent.

✔ Making this script work with Outlook Express

■ See the note for step 2 above to modify this script to work with Microsoft Outlook Express. Also, make sure to modify the on run handler as noted in steps 3 and 4 of the spread *Filing mail based on keywords.*

Faxing mail with faxSTF based on keywords from Emailer

Code 7.6 will print any incoming mail that matches the specified keywords to your fax modem using faxSTF. This script could be used as a form-to-e-mail-to-fax gateway for generating faxes from Web forms. The recipient name and address are defined in variables in our function `processMail`.

Figure 7.8 shows faxSTF's FaxStatus control panel as it appears when the script is running.

To fax mail with faxSTF based on keywords:

1. The on `run` handler of this script is covered in detail in the spread *Filing mail based on keywords* in this chapter.

2. `on processMail(myMessage)`
   `    set myRecipOrganization to`
   `    → "Any Company"`
   `    set myRecipFirstName to "John"`
   `    set myRecipLastName to "Doe"`
   `    set myRecipFax to "555-1212"`
   `    set myRecipPhone to "555-1000"`

   We begin our function by storing values for the fax page, including recipient organization, name, and fax and phone numbers, in variables.

3. `    FaxOff`

   Next, we use the scripting addition XCMD OSAX Lite/FAXstf's `FaxOff` command to disable the fax software for other applications.

4. `set oldPrinter to`
   `    → (FaxSwitchPrinter to "FaxPrint")`

   We store the current printer setting in the variable `oldPrinter` while switching to the FaxPrint driver with the `FaxSwitchPrinter` command.

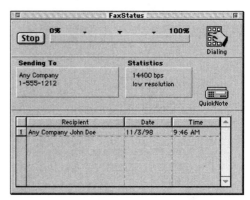

Figure 7.8 Once our script has run, faxSTF will begin sending the fax. Here we see faxSTF's FaxStatus window as our fax is sent.

Code 7.6 This script faxes e-mail messages containing certain keywords using faxSTF and the scripting addition XCMD OSAX Lite/FAXstf.

```
global myKeywordMatches
on run
    set myKeywords to {"Raza", "Chavez",
    → "Latino"}
    set mySearchType to "or"
    set myIncludeSubject to true
    set myIncludeBody to true
    tell application "Claris Emailer"
        set myMessages to every message in
        → folder "In Box"
        repeat with myMessage in myMessages
            set myText to ""
            set myKeywordMatches to ""
            if myIncludeBody then set myText to
            → myText & the content of myMessage
            → & return
            if myIncludeSubject then set myText
            → to myText & the subject of
            → myMessage
            set myFound to false
            considering case
                repeat with myKeyword  in
                → myKeywords
                    if myText contains myKeyword
                    → then
                        set myFound to true
                        set myKeywordMatches to
                        → myKeywordMatches &
                        → myKeyword & " "
```

Code continues on next page

Code 7.6 *continued*

```
                    if mySearchType = "or" then
                    → exit repeat
                else
                    if mySearchType = "and" and
                    → myKeyword ≠ last item of
                    → myKeywords then
                        set myFound to false
                        exit repeat
                    end if
                end if
            end repeat
        end considering
        if myFound then
            my processMail(myMessage)
        end if
    end repeat
    end tell
end run


on processMail(myMessage)
    set myRecipOrganization to "Any Company"
    set myRecipFirstName to "John"
    set myRecipLastName to "Doe"
    set myRecipFax to "555-1212"
    set myRecipPhone to "555-1000"
    FaxOff
    set oldPrinter to (FaxSwitchPrinter to
    → "FaxPrint")
        FaxStartup note "Fax-to-Email Gateway
        → Message" delay 1 coverPage 1
        → archive "" with autoDeletion and
        → callGrouping
        FaxAddADestination organisation
        → (myRecipOrganization) fax
        → (myRecipFax) phone
        → (myRecipPhone) name
        → (myRecipFirstName) surname
        → (myRecipLastName) salutation ("")
    tell application "Claris Emailer"
        open myMessage
        print window 1
        close window 1
        move myMessage to folder "Read Mail"
        FaxShutDown
    end tell
    FaxSwitchPrinter to oldPrinter
    FaxOn
end processMail
```

5. `FaxStartup note "Fax-to-Email`
   `→ Gateway Message" delay 1`
   `→ coverPage 1 archive "" with`
   `→ autoDeletion and callGrouping`

   Then we start an outgoing fax with the **FaxStartup** statement, passing it a note title, a sending delay time, and a cover page to use. Cover pages are referenced by their index, so in this case, the first cover page in faxSTF's settings will be used.

6. `FaxAddADestination`
   `→ organisation (myRecipOrganization)`
   `→ fax (myRecipFax) phone`
   `→ (myRecipPhone) name`
   `→ (myRecipFirstName) surname`
   `→ (myRecipLastName) salutation ("")`

   Finally, we add a destination to the outgoing fax with the **FaxAddADestination** command.

7. `    tell application "Claris Emailer"`
   `        open myMessage`

   Next, we open the message referenced by the variable **myMessage** in Emailer.

8. `        print window 1`
   `        close window 1`

   Since we just opened the message, it will be in the frontmost window, which we can reference by its index: 1. We tell Emailer to print the frontmost window (which it does without a dialog thanks to its well-thought-out AppleScript support) and then close it.

9. `        move myMessage to folder`
   `        → "Read Mail"`

   Then we have Emailer move the message to the Read Mail folder.

10. `        FaxShutDown`
    `    end tell`

    Finally, we send a **FaxShutDown** statement to conclude our printing session the fax driver.

11. `FaxSwitchPrinter to oldPrinter`

Next, we use the `FaxSwitchPrinter` command to change our Chooser settings back to the original printer as stored in the variable `oldPrinter`.

12. `FaxOn`
`end processMail`

We wrap the whole thing up by turning our fax software back on. When we do this, faxSTF sees the new outgoing fax in its queue and starts to process it!

✔ Issues with Outlook Express

■ Outlook Express's dictionary implementation of the Print command does not allow for printing without a dialog box. As a result, the functionality of this script cannot be reproduced in Outlook without using the control panel Okey Dokey Pro, as discussed in the spread *Printing local HTML files from Internet Explorer* in Chapter 6.

Scripting with XCMD OSAX Lite/FAXstf

This script requires the scripting addition XCMD OSAX Lite/FAXstf. You must have XCMD OSAX Lite/FAXstf installed in your Scripting Additions folder for this script to work.

XCMD OSAX Lite/FAXstf adds a series of commands that make faxSTF 3.x scriptable.

XCMD OSAX Lite/FAXstf is free for noncommercial use. It can be found in many AppleScript archives, including `ftp://mirror.apple.com/mirrors/` → `gaea.scriptweb.com/`.

XCMD OSAX Lite/FAXstf is published by Gregory Charles Rivers.

Scripting with faxSTF

faxSTF 3.x is published by STF Technologies, which can be reached at `http://www.faxstf.com/`.

FAXING MAIL WITH FAXSTF

Figure 7.9 Here we see two new Word documents created by script; each document contains the message body of a matching email message.

Importing mail into Microsoft Word based on keywords

Code 7.7 will import into Word the bodies of mail messages that contain keyword matches. Each message will be opened into a new window in Word. **Figure 7.9** shows the new document windows in Word.

To import mail into Microsoft Word based on keywords:

1. The on run handler of this script is covered in detail in the spread *Filing mail based on keywords* in this chapter.

2.
```
on processMail(myMessage)
    tell application "Claris Emailer"
        set myBody to the content of
        → myMessage
    end tell
```
We begin our function by asking Emailer to retrieve the body of the message myMessage passed to the function. We store this string in the variable myBody.

3.
```
    tell application "Microsoft Word"
        activate
```
Next, we tell Word to come to the front with the activate command.

4.
```
        make new document
```
We have Word create a new document.

5.
```
        set contents of selection to
        → myBody
    end tell
end processMail
```
Finally, we set the new document's contents to the text taken from the body of the mail message, as stored in the variable myBody.

✔ Making this script work with Outlook Express

■ See the note for step 2 above to modify this script to work with Microsoft Outlook Express. Also, make sure to modify the on run handler as noted in steps 3 and 4 of the spread *Filing mail based on keywords.*

✔ More on Word 98

■ See Chapter 14 for more on scripting Microsoft Word 98.

Code 7.7 This script imports into Word the bodies of mail messages that contain keyword matches.

```
                                    code
global myKeywordMatches
on run
    set myKeywords to {"subject", "body"}
    set mySearchType to "or"
    set myIncludeSubject to true
    set myIncludeBody to true
    tell application "Claris Emailer"
        set myMessages to every message in folder "In Box"
        repeat with myMessage in myMessages
            set myText to ""
            set myKeywordMatches to ""
            if myIncludeBody then set myText to myText & the content of myMessage & return
            if myIncludeSubject then set myText to myText & the subject of myMessage
            set myFound to false
            considering case
                repeat with myKeyword in myKeywords
                    if myText contains myKeyword then
                        set myFound to true
                        set myKeywordMatches to myKeywordMatches & myKeyword & " "
                        if mySearchType = "or" then exit repeat
                    else
                        if mySearchType = "and" and myKeyword ≠ last item of myKeywords then
                            set myFound to false
                            exit repeat
                        end if
                    end if
                end repeat
            end considering
            if myFound then
                my processMail(myMessage)
            end if
            —end if
        end repeat
        —end if
    end tell
end run

on processMail(myMessage)
    tell application "Claris Emailer"
        set myBody to the content of myMessage
    end tell
    tell application "Microsoft Word"
        activate
        make new document
        set contents of selection to myBody
    end tell
end processMail
```

Figure 7.10 Our FileMaker Pro database displays a new record created by our script from an incoming email message.

Creating the sample database

Before using this script, create a new database in FileMaker Pro. Define the following fields, using the "text" type for each:

◆ sender name

◆ sender address

◆ subject

◆ content

◆ time sent

Copying mail data to FileMaker Pro

Code 7.8 will copy data from any messages in the In Box that contain the keywords to a new record in a sample FileMaker database. This script can be used to transfer e-mail information to a database using sophisticated keyword searching of many mail messages. **Figure 7.10** shows what the FileMaker Pro database looks like as the script is running. Refer to Chapter 12 for more information on scripting FileMaker Pro.

To copy mail data to FileMaker Pro:

1. We start this script, like the others in this chapter, with the on run handler described in *Filing mail based on keywords*.

2. on processMail(myMessage)
    tell application "Claris Emailer"
      move myMessage to folder
      → "Read Mail"

We begin our function by telling Emailer to move the message to the Read Mail folder so that we don't repeatedly process it. To modify this script to work with Outlook Express, replace the string "Claris Emailer" above with "Outlook Express".

3.   set mySender to sender of
    → myMessage
    set mySenderName to display
    → name of mySender
    set mySenderAddress to
    → address of mySender
    set mySubject to subject of
    → myMessage
    set myContent to content of
    → myMessage
    set myTimeSent to time sent
    → of myMessage
  end tell

131

Code 7.8 This script will copy message information to a FileMaker database if the message contains keyword matches.

```
global myKeywordMatches
on run
    set myKeywords to {"Raza", "Chavez", "Latino"}
    set mySearchType to "or"
    set myIncludeSubject to true
    set myIncludeBody to true
    tell application "Claris Emailer"
        set myMessages to every message in folder "In Box"
        repeat with myMessage in myMessages
            set myText to ""
            set myKeywordMatches to ""
            if myIncludeBody then set myText to myText & the content of myMessage & return
            if myIncludeSubject then set myText to myText & the subject of myMessage
            set myFound to false
            considering case
                repeat with myKeyword in myKeywords
                    if myText contains myKeyword then
                        set myFound to true
                        set myKeywordMatches to myKeywordMatches & myKeyword & " "
                        if mySearchType = "or" then exit repeat
                    else
                        if mySearchType = "and" and myKeyword ≠ last item of myKeywords then
                            set myFound to false
                            exit repeat
                        end if
                    end if
                end repeat
            end considering
            if myFound then
                my processMail(myMessage)
            end if
        end repeat
    end tell
end run

on processMail(myMessage)
    tell application "Claris Emailer"
        set mySender to sender of myMessage
        set mySenderAddress to address of mySender
        set mySenderName to display name of mySender
        set mySubject to subject of myMessage
        set myContent to content of myMessage
        set myTimeSent to time sent of myMessage
        move myMessage to folder "Read Mail"
    end tell
    tell application "FileMaker Pro"
        tell database "Incoming Mail"
            set myNewRecord to (create new record)
            set cell "sender name" of myNewRecord to mySenderName
            set cell "sender address" of myNewRecord to mySenderAddress
            set cell "subject" of myNewRecord to mySubject
            set cell "content" of myNewRecord to myContent
            set cell "time sent" of myNewRecord to myTimeSent as text
        end tell
    end tell
end processMail
```

Next, we retrieve the sender address and name, subject, body, and send time of the message and store their values in variables. We'll use this data to populate our database.

4.
```
tell application "FileMaker Pro"
    tell database "Incoming Mail"
```
Now, we begin speaking to FileMaker Pro, immediately telling it that we want to speak only to the database Incoming Mail. You'll need to create this database in FileMaker Pro before using this script; the sidebar explains how.

5.
```
set myNewRecord to
    → (create new record)
```
Next we create a new record and store a reference to the new record in the variable myNewRecord.

6.
```
set cell "sender name" of
    → myNewRecord to mySenderName
set cell "sender address" of
    → myNewRecord to mySenderAddress
set cell "subject" of
    → myNewRecord to mySubject
set cell "content" of
    → myNewRecord to myContent
set cell "time sent" of
    → myNewRecord to myTimeSent as
    → text
    end tell
  end tell
end processMail
```
Finally, we have FileMaker Pro fill the fields of the new record with the data we captured from the mail message.

✔ Faster record creation in FileMaker

■ If you know that you created the fields in your database as listed in the sidebar, you can replace steps 5 and 6 with this code to make your script faster:

```
set myNewRecord to
    → (create new record with
    → data {mySenderName,
    → mySenderAddress,
    → mySubject,
    → myContent,
    → myTimeSent})
    end tell
  end tell
end processMail
```

■ FileMaker Pro processes the single event of creating a new record and populating that record's sequential fields with data much faster than processing the creation of a record and then a series of separate set commands.

Creating a mailing list with FileMaker Pro

Code 7.9 will loop through the currently found set of records in a database of mail messages, generating a new outgoing e-mail message with a subject and body defined by variables in our function `processMail`.

This script can be used to run a broadcast-only mailing list from Emailer. This would be useful if you had a contact database in FileMaker filled with many different kinds of people (vendors, friends, clients) and you had a message specifically tailored for one of these groups. With this script, you could find just the recipients you wanted in FileMaker and then run this script to send them all a message. **Figure 7.11** shows our FileMaker Pro database when the script is running.

To create a mailing list with FileMaker Pro:

1.
```
tell application "FileMaker Pro"
    tell document "Incoming Mail"
```
Here we begin talking to FileMaker Pro. We immediately let FileMaker know that we want to speak directly to the open database named Incoming Mail. By referencing it as a `document` object, we let FileMaker know that we only want to deal with the currently found set of records in the database. If we referenced it as `database "Incoming Mail"` then FileMaker would give us access to all records in the database.

2.
```
repeat with i from 1 to
→ number of records
set mySenderName to cell
→ "sender name" of record i
set mySenderAddress to cell
→ "sender address" of record i
```
We begin a loop through each database record in the current found set,

Code 7.9 This script will send mail to certain recipients based on the current found set of records in our sample FileMaker database.

```
code
on run
    tell application "FileMaker Pro"
        tell document "Incoming Mail"
            repeat with i from 1 to number of
            → records
                set mySenderName to cell
                → "sender name" of record i
                set mySenderAddress to cell
                → "sender address" of record i
                my processMail(mySenderName,
                → mySenderAddress)
            end repeat
        end tell
    end tell
end run


on processMail(mySenderName, mySenderAddress)
    tell application "Claris Emailer"
        set mySubject to
        → "Mailing List Announcement"
        set myBody to
        → "The new message text goes here!"
        make new outgoing message with properties
            {subject:mySubject,
            → content:myBody,
            → recipient:{{address:
            → {display name:mySenderName,
            → address:mySenderAddress},
            → recipient type:to recipient,
            → delivery status:unsent}}}
    end tell
end processMail
```

Figure 7.11 The outgoing message in Emailer's Out Box was just created by our script as it completed processing the first FileMaker Pro record in our database.

✔ Making this script work with Outlook Express

■ See the note for step 4 above to modify this script to work with Microsoft Outlook Express.

✔ More on FileMaker Pro

■ See Chapter 12 for more on scripting FileMaker Pro.

capturing the values of the fields for the name and e-mail address to send our message to.

3.
```
        my processMail
            → (mySenderName,
                → mySenderAddress)
        end repeat
    end tell
  end tell
end run
```

We then call our function processMail, passing it the name and address of our message recipient.

4.
```
on processMail(mySenderName,
    → mySenderAddress)
        tell application "Claris Emailer"
```

Our processMail function in this script is passed the values for name and e-mail address in the variables mySenderName and mySenderAddress. We then let AppleScript know that we want to speak to Emailer.

5.
```
        set mySubject to "Mailing
            → List Announcement"
        set myBody to "The new
            → message text goes here!"
```

We now define variables to hold the subject and message body for our outgoing message.

6.
```
    make new outgoing message
        → with properties ¬
            {subject:mySubject,
                → content:myBody,
                → recipient:{{address:{display
                → name:mySenderName,
                → address:mySenderAddress},
                → recipient type:to recipient,
                → delivery status:unsent}}}
    end tell
end processMail
```

We then tell Emailer to make a new outgoing message, ready to be sent.

SCRIPTING
EUDORA PRO

Figure 8.1 Eudora's dictionary entry for its message object.

Although Eudora has always had some AppleScript support, its dictionary is somewhat unique and has quirks that are noticeable if you compare these scripts with similar scripts for Emailer or Outlook.

When used in conjunction with FileMaker Pro, Eudora becomes an e-mail engine for generating mailing list databases and mining e-mail for data. Eudora's message class is a perfect analog to FileMaker's record object. By copying data from a message in Eudora into a record in FileMaker Pro, you can use your e-mail information to calculate statistics, summarize mail, or send mail back out. **Figure 8.1** shows Eudora's dictionary entry for its message object.

Scripting Eudora Pro

All the scripts that follow were designed and tested for Eudora Pro 4.0.2.

Most of these scripts do not work with other versions of Eudora.

Eudora Pro is published by Qualcomm Inc., which can be reached at http://www.eudora.com/.

Filing mail based on keywords

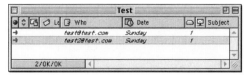

Figure 8.2 Eudora's Test message folder as it appears while the script is running.

Like **Code 7.3** in the last chapter, **Code 8.1** will move messages that contain specified search strings in their subjects and/or bodies to a mailbox named Test. **Figure 8.2** shows this mailbox as it appears while the script is running. Rather than allowing us to create a new message transparently as both Emailer and Outlook Express do, Eudora actually opens a new window for each new message, forcing us to close it before proceeding to avoid clutter.

To file mail based on keywords:

1. `global myKeywordMatches`

   We begin by defining the variable myKeywordMatches as global. A global variable allows our function and main program to both use its value.

2. `on run`
   ```
       set myKeywords to
   → {"help", "script"}
       set mySearchType to "or"
       set myIncludeSubject to true
       set myIncludeBody to true
   ```

   Next, we begin our on run handler and define variables to hold our search strings ("s" and "aaa"), the type of search to execute ("or"), and flags indicating whether to search the subject and/or body. These variables are named `myKeywords`, `mySearchType`, `myIncludeSubject`, and `myIncludeBody`, respectively.

3. ```
       tell application "Eudora Pro
   → 4.0.2"
   ```

   Here we begin talking to Eudora

4. ```
       repeat with i from
   → (number of messages in
   → mailbox "In" of mail
   → folder "") to 1 by -1
   ```

Code 8.1 This script moves messages that have the keywords in their bodies and/or subjects to a specific mailbox.

```
global myKeywordMatches
on run
    set myKeywords to {"help", "script"}
    set mySearchType to "or"
    set myIncludeSubject to true
    set myIncludeBody to true
    tell application "Eudora Pro 4.0.2"
        repeat with i from (number of messages
        → in mailbox "In" of mail folder "")
        → to 1 by -1
            set myText to ""
            set myKeywordMatches to ""
            set myMessage to body of message i
            → of mailbox "In" of mail folder ""
            set mySubject to subject of
            → message i of mailbox "In" of mail
            → folder ""
            if myIncludeBody then set myText to
            → myText & myMessage & return
            if myIncludeSubject then set myText
            → to myText & mySubject
            set myFound to false
            considering case
                repeat with myKeyword in
                → myKeywords
                    if myText contains myKeyword
                    → then
                        set myFound to true
                        set myKeywordMatches to
                        → myKeywordMatches &
                        → myKeyword & " "
                        if mySearchType = "or" then
                        → exit repeat
                    else
```

Code continues on next page

Code 8.1 *continued*

```
                  if mySearchType = "and" and
                → myKeyword ≠last item of
                → myKeywords then
                     set myFound to false
                     exit repeat
                  end if
               end if
            end repeat
         end considering
         if myFound then
            my processMail(i)
         end if
      end repeat
   end tell
end run

on processMail(myMessage)
   tell application "Eudora Pro 4.0.2"
      move (message myMessage of mailbox "In"
       → of mail folder "") to
         end of mailbox "Test" of mail
          → folder ""
   end tell
end processMail
```

Next, we loop through each message, starting with the last one and moving backward with the by -1 modifier. We do it this way so that our script can file each message away without disturbing the processing of subsequent messages in the queue.

5. `set myText to ""`

At the beginning our loop, we initialize the variable myText by placing nothing in it. For each search through we'll use this variable to store keywords we're trying to match.

6. `set myKeywordMatches to ""`

We also initialize the variable myKeywordMatches that we'll use to hold all of the matches found in the currently searched message.

7. `if myIncludeBody then set`
`→ myText to myText & the`
`→ content of myMessage &`
`→ return`

If the flag variable myIncludeBody is true, we'll add the body of the current message to the variable myText so that it is searched for matches below.

8. `if myIncludeSubject then`
`→ set myText to myText &`
`→ the subject of myMessage`

If the flag variable myIncludeSubject is true, we'll add the subject of the current message to our variable myText so that it is searched for matches below.

9. `set myFound to false`

Before we start looping through our keywords to test for matches, we need to initialize a variable, myFound, that we'll use to indicate whether any matches are found.

10.   `considering case`

Next, we let AppleScript know that we want it to perform all subsequent string comparisons with case sensitivity.

11.   `repeat with myKeyword`
            `→ in myKeywords`

Now we start to loop through our list.

12.   `if myText contains`
            `→ myKeyword then`

We test to see if our current keyword is found inside of myText.

13.   `set myFound to true`

If we find a keyword in myText, we first set our flag variable myFound to true.

14.   `set myKeywordMatches to`
            `→ myKeywordMatches & myKeyword`
            `→ & " "`

We add the found keyword to our variable x to track which matches are found for the current message.

15.   `if mySearchType =`
            `→ "or" then exit`
            `→ repeat`

Next, we check to see if our search is an "or" type search. If it is, we exit our loop. In our case, we set mySearchType to "or" in step 2. You could modify this script to conduct an "and" search by changing mySearchType.

16.   `else`
            `→ if mySearchType = "and"`
            `→ and myKeyword ≠ last item`
            `→ of myKeywords then`
            `    set myFound to false`
            `    exit repeat`
            `  end if`
            `end if`
                `end repeat`
                `end considering`

If our search is an "and" search and we haven't tested the last keyword yet, we clear our flag so that the searching continues, ensuring that all keywords are found.

17.
```
        if myFound then
            my processMail(i)
        end if
    end repeat
  end tell
end run
```

If we have a match, we call our function `processMail`, passing it the current message.

18.
```
on processMail(myMessage)
    tell application "Eudora Pro
    → 4.0.2"
        move (message myMessage of
        → mailbox "In" of mail
        → folder "") to ¬
            end of mailbox "Test" of
            → mail folder ""
    end tell
end processMail
```

Our function `processMail` receives a message reference in the variable `myMessage` and then tells Eudora to move the message to the mailbox named Test, putting it after all the other messages in the mailbox.

Sending replies based on keywords

Code 8.2 will send a reply to the sender of any incoming message that contains certain keywords. You could use this script to automatically send replies to spam mail solicitations by strategically searching for a set of keywords, e.g. "credit card offer," and then sending back a polite but terse cease-and-desist request. **Figure 8.3** shows what Eudora's Out mailbox looks like as the script is running.

To send replies based on keywords:

1. The on run handler of this script is covered in detail in steps 1 through 17 of the previous spread, *Filing mail based on keywords.*

2. ```
on processMail(myMessage)
   tell application "Eudora Pro
   → 4.0.2"
      set myNewMessage to (reply
      → (message myMessage of
      → mailbox "In" of mail folder
      → "") without quoting and
      → everyone)
```

   Our processMail function in this script begins by telling Eudora to create a new reply message using its unique reply command. This command returns a reference to the new message in the variable myNewMessage.

3. ```
      set myBody to body of
      → myNewMessage
```

   We set the variable myBody to the body text of the new message.

4. ```
      set myBody to myBody &
      → "Thanks for inquiring about "
      → & myKeywordMatches
```

   We then append to the variable myBody a note about which keywords were matched.

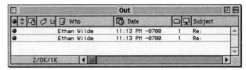

**Figure 8.3** What Eudora's Out mailbox looks like as the script is running.

**Code 8.2** This script replies to messages that contain the keywords.

```
code
global myKeywordMatches

on run
   set myKeywords to {"help", "script"}
   set mySearchType to "or"
   set myIncludeSubject to true
   set myIncludeBody to true
   tell application "Eudora Pro 4.0.2"
      repeat with i from (number of messages
      → in mailbox "In" of mail folder "")
      → to 1 by -1
         set myText to ""
         set myKeywordMatches to ""
         set myMessage to body of message i
         → of mailbox "In" of mail folder ""
         set mySubject to subject of message
         → i of mailbox "In" of mail
         → folder ""
         if myIncludeBody then set myText to
         → myText & myMessage & return
         if myIncludeSubject then set myText
         → to myText & mySubject
         set myFound to false
         considering case
            repeat with myKeyword in
            → myKeywords
               if myText contains myKeyword
               → then
                  set myFound to true
                  set myKeywordMatches to
                  → myKeywordMatches &
                  → myKeyword & " "
                  if mySearchType = "or" then
                  → exit repeat
               else
                  if mySearchType = "and" and
                  → myKeyword ≠ last item of
                  → myKeywords then
                     set myFound to false
```

Code continues on next page
```

Code 8.2 *continued*

```
                    exit repeat
                end if
            end if
        end repeat
    end considering
    if myFound then
        my processMail(i)
    end if
    end repeat
    end tell
end run

on processMail(myMessage)
    tell application "Eudora Pro 4.0.2"
        set myNewMessage to (reply (message
→ myMessage of mailbox "In" of mail
→ folder "") without quoting and
→ everyone)
        set myBody to body of myNewMessage
        set myBody to myBody & "Thanks for
→ inquiring about " & myKeywordMatches
        set body of myNewMessage to myBody
        save myNewMessage
        close myNewMessage
    end tell
end processMail
```

5. `set body of myNewMessage to myBody`

Now we're ready to change the body text of the new message to the string stored in our variable *myBody*.

6.
```
        save myNewMessage
        close myNewMessage
    end tell
end processMail
```

Finally, we have Eudora save the new message and close the message window that automatically opened with the `reply` command in step 2.

Forwarding mail based on keywords

Code 8.3 will forward any incoming message that contains the keywords. **Figure 8.4** shows how Eudora's Out mailbox looks as the script is running.

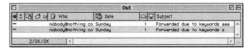

Figure 8.4 Eudora's Out mailbox as it appears when the script is running.

To forward mail based on keywords:

1. The on run handler of this script is covered in detail in steps 1 through 17 of the spread *Filing mail based on keywords* earlier in this chapter.

2. ```
on processMail(myMessage)
    tell application "Eudora Pro
    → 4.0.2"
        set myNewMessage to (forward
        → (message myMessage of
        → mailbox "In" of mail
        → folder ""))
```
   Our processMail function in this script begins by telling Eudora to create a new message that is a copy of the current message using the unique forward command.

3. ```
    set field "Subject" of
    → myNewMessage to "Forwarded due
    → to keywords " & myKeywordMatches
```
   We then set the subject of the new message to be a note about which keywords were matched.

4. ```
    set field "To" of myNewMessage
    → to "nobody@nothing.com"
```
   Now we set the recipient for the new outgoing message—in this case, nobody@nothing.com.

5. ```
        save myNewMessage
        close myNewMessage
    end tell
end processMail
```
   Finally, we have Eudora save the message and close the window that the forward command automatically created.

FORWARDING MAIL BASED ON KEYWORDS

Code 8.3 This script forwards messages that contain the keywords.

```
                              code
global myKeywordMatches
on run
   set myKeywords to {"help", "script"}
   set mySearchType to "or"
   set myIncludeSubject to true
   set myIncludeBody to true
   tell application "Eudora Pro 4.0.2"
      repeat with i from (number of messages in mailbox "In" of mail folder "") to 1 by -1
         set myText to ""
         set myKeywordMatches to ""
         set myMessage to body of message i of mailbox "In" of mail folder ""
         set mySubject to subject of message i of mailbox "In" of mail folder ""
         if myIncludeBody then set myText to myText & myMessage & return
         if myIncludeSubject then set myText to myText & mySubject
         set myFound to false
         considering case
            repeat with myKeyword in myKeywords
               if myText contains myKeyword then
                  set myFound to true
                  set myKeywordMatches to myKeywordMatches & myKeyword & " "
                  if mySearchType = "or" then exit repeat
               else
                  if mySearchType = "and" and myKeyword ≠ last item of myKeywords then
                     set myFound to false
                     exit repeat
                  end if
               end if
            end repeat
         end considering
         if myFound then
            my processMail(i)
         end if
      end repeat
   end tell
end run


on processMail(myMessage)
   tell application "Eudora Pro 4.0.2"
      set myNewMessage to (forward (message myMessage of mailbox "In" of mail folder ""))
      set field "Subject" of myNewMessage to "Forwarded due to keywords " & myKeywordMatches
      set field "To" of myNewMessage to "nobody@nothing.com"
      save myNewMessage
      close myNewMessage
   end tell
end processMail
```

Copying mail data to FileMaker Pro

Code 8.4 will copy data from any messages in the In mailbox that contain our keywords to a new record in a sample FileMaker database. This script can be used to transfer e-mail information to a database using sophisticated keyword searching of many mail messages. **Figure 8.5** shows what the FileMaker Pro database looks like as the script is running.

To copy mail data to FileMaker Pro:

1. The on run handler of this script is covered in detail in the spread *Filing mail based on keywords* in this chapter.

2. on processMail(myMessage)

```
tell application "Eudora Pro
→ 4.0.2"
    set mySender to sender of
    → message myMessage of
    → mailbox "In" of mail
    → folder ""
    set mySubject to subject of
    → message myMessage of
    → mailbox "In" of mail
    → folder ""
    set myContent to body of
    → message myMessage of
    → mailbox "In" of mail
    → folder ""
    set myTimeSent to message
    → date of message myMessage
    → of mailbox "In" of mail
    → folder ""
```

We begin our function by retrieving the sender address and name, subject, body, and send time of the message and storing their values in variables. We'll use this data to populate our database.

Figure 8.5 How our FileMaker Pro database looks as the script is running.

Code 8.4 This script will copy message information to a FileMaker database if the message contains keyword matches.

```
code
global myKeywordMatches
on run
    set myKeywords to {"help", "script"}
    set mySearchType to "or"
    set myIncludeSubject to true
    set myIncludeBody to true
    tell application "Eudora Pro 4.0.2"
        repeat with i from (number of messages
        → in mailbox "In" of mail folder "")
        → to 1 by -1
            set myText to ""
            set myKeywordMatches to ""
            set myMessage to body of message i
            → of mailbox "In" of mail folder ""
            set mySubject to subject of message
            → i of mailbox "In" of mail folder ""
            if myIncludeBody then set myText to
            → myText & myMessage & return
            if myIncludeSubject then set myText
            3→ to myText & mySubject
            set myFound to false
            considering case
                repeat with myKeyword in
                → myKeywords
                    if myText contains myKeyword
                    → then
                        set myFound to true
                        set myKeywordMatches to
                        → myKeywordMatches &
                        → myKeyword & " "
                        if mySearchType = "or" then
                        → exit repeat
                    else
                        if mySearchType = "and" and
                        → myKeyword ≠ last item of
                        → myKeywords then
                            set myFound to false
                            exit repeat
                        end if
                    end if
                end repeat
        end repeat
```

Code continues on next page

Code 8.4 *continued*

```
                 end considering
            if myFound then
                my processMail(i)
            end if
        end repeat
    end tell
end run
on processMail(myMessage)
    tell application "Eudora Pro 4.0.2"
        set mySender to sender of message
            → myMessage of mailbox "In" of mail
            → folder ""
        set mySubject to subject of message
            → myMessage of mailbox "In" of mail
            → folder ""
        set myContent to body of message
            → myMessage of mailbox "In" of mail
            → folder ""
        set myTimeSent to message date of
            → message myMessage of mailbox "In" of
            → mail folder ""
        move (message myMessage of mailbox "In"
            → of mail folder "") to ¬
            end of mailbox "Test" of mail
                → folder ""
    end tell
    tell application "FileMaker Pro"
        tell database "Incoming Mail"
            set myNewRecord to (create new
                → record)
            set cell "sender" of myNewRecord to
                → mySender
            set cell "subject" of myNewRecord to
                → mySubject
            set cell "content" of myNewRecord to
                → myContent
            set cell "time sent" of myNewRecord
                → to myTimeSent as text
        end tell
    end tell
end processMail
```

Creating a sample database

Before using this script, create a new
database in FileMaker Pro. Define the
following fields, using the "text" type
for each:

- sender name
- sender address
- subject
- content
- time sent

3.
```
        move (message myMessage of
        → mailbox "In" of mail folder
        → "") to ¬
    end of mailbox "Test" of
        → mail folder ""
    end tell
```
Next, we tell Eudora to move the message
so that it is the last message in a mailbox
named Test.

4.
```
    tell application "FileMaker Pro"
        tell database "Incoming Mail"
```
Now we begin speaking to FileMaker Pro,
immediately telling it that we want to
speak only to the database Incoming
Mail.(You'll need to create this database
in FileMaker Pro before using this script.)
We store a reference to the new record in
the variable myNewRecord.

5.
```
        set myNewRecord to (create
        → new record)
```
Next we create a new record and store a
reference to the new record in the variable myNewRecord.

6.
```
    set cell "sender" of
→ myNewRecord to mySender
        set cell "subject" of
→ myNewRecord to mySubject
        set cell "content" of
→ myNewRecord to myContent
        set cell "time sent" of
→ myNewRecord to myTimeSent as text
    end tell
    end tell
end processMail
```
Finally we have FileMaker Pro fill the
fields of the new record with the data we
captured from the mail message.

Creating a mailing list with FileMaker Pro

Code 8.5 will search through the currently found set of records in a database of mail messages, generating a new outgoing e-mail message for each with a subject and body defined by the variables in our function `processMail`. This script can be used to run a broadcast-only mailing list from Eudora. With this type of mailing list only you can send out messages. **Figure 8.6** shows our FileMaker Pro database as it appears when the script is running.

To create a mailing list with FileMaker Pro:

1.
```
tell application "FileMaker Pro"
    tell document "Incoming Mail"
```
As we did in the previous spread, we begin talking to FileMaker Pro, letting it know that we want to speak directly to the open database named Incoming Mail.

2.
```
repeat with i from 1 to
→ number of records
    set mySenderAddress to
    → cell "sender address"
    → of record i
```
We begin a loop through each database record in the current set, capturing the values of the field for the e-mail address to send our message to.

3.
```
        my processMail
            → (mySenderAddress)
    end repeat
    end tell
end tell
end run
```
We then call our function `processMail`, passing it the address for our message recipient.

Code 8.5 This script will send mail to certain recipients based on the current found set of records in our sample FileMaker database.

```
on run
    tell application "FileMaker Pro"
        tell document "Incoming Mail"
            repeat with i from 1 to number of
            →  records
                set mySenderAddress to cell
                → "sender address" of record i
                    my processMail
                        → (mySenderAddress)
            end repeat
        end tell
    end tell
end run


on processMail(mySender)
    tell application "Eudora Pro 4.0.2"
        set myNewMessage to
        → (make new message at end of mailbox
        → "Out" of mail folder "")
        set field "Subject" of myNewMessage to
        → "Mailing List Announcement"
        set field "To" of myNewMessage to →
        mySender
        set body of myNewMessage to "The new
        → message text goes here!"
        save myNewMessage
        close myNewMessage
    end tell
end processMail
```

Figure 8.6 Our FileMaker Pro database as it looks when the script is running.

4.
```
on processMail(mySender)
    tell application "Eudora Pro
    → 4.0.2"
        set myNewMessage to (make new
        → message at end of mailbox
        → "Out" of mail folder "")
```

Our processMail function in this script begins by telling Eudora to make a new outgoing message in the Out mailbox. Eudora returns a reference to the new message in the variable myNewMessage.

5.
```
        set field "Subject" of
        → myNewMessage to "Mailing List
        → Announcement"
        set body of myNewMessage to
        →"The new message text goes here!"
```

We now set the subject and message body for our outgoing message.

6.
```
        set field "To" of
        → myNewMessage to mySender
```

Next, we set the recipient for our outgoing message to the value passed to our function in the variable mySender.

7.
```
        save myNewMessage
        close myNewMessage
    end tell
end processMail
```

Finally, we save the message and close the window that Eudora automatically opened with the make new message command.

FETCH AND ANARCHIE FOR FTP

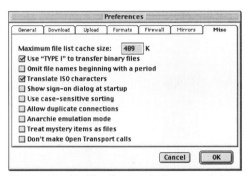

Figure 9.1 Fetch's Miscellaneous Preferences window with "show sign-on" disabled.

Fetch is a fully recordable and scriptable FTP client application. With it we will get and send files, list directories, and synchronize remote directories with local folders.

Anarchie does everything Fetch does and more. With Anarchie Pro 3.0, we can even retrieve files and whole sites from HTTP servers (Web servers).

Both Fetch and Anarchie offer complete AppleScript dictionaries. Fetch includes partial support for Anarchie's AppleScript dictionary along with its own commands, and is fully recordable. To see fully formed object-model code appear before your eyes, try recording some of your own actions in Fetch. Before you start scripting, make sure to review your application preferences. To enable scripts to launch Fetch without your intervention, be sure to disable the automatic sign-on dialog box. Look in Fetch's Miscellaneous Preferences window to disable this default option. **Figure 9.1** shows Fetch's Miscellaneous Preferences window with this option disabled.

Sending a file via FTP

Code 9.1 uploads files to a remote server. To send a file from your local filesystem to a remote server via FTP, simply set the variables inside of the `on open` handler and drag and drop files onto the script application's icon.

Figure 9.2 shows a transfer window in Fetch immediately after a user has dragged and dropped the file `default.gif` onto our saved script application. Note that the file has been uploaded and appears in the remote FTP server's directory.

To send a file via FTP:

1.
```
on open myUploadItem
    set myUser to "john"
    set myPassword to "xxx"
    set myHost to "ftp.trope.com"
    set myDirectory to "public_html"
```
We begin by storing the file passed by drag and drop in `myUploadItem` and setting variables for username, password, hostname, and directory. We could have used dialog boxes to set these variables, so the script would be able to log onto any server, but to simplify matters we are going to hard-code them into our script.

2.
```
set myURL to "ftp://" & myUser &
→ ":" & myPassword & "@" & myHost
→ & "/" & myDirectory
```
Next we assemble an FTP URL out of the variables we just defined.

3.
```
with timeout of 300 seconds
    tell application "Fetch 3.0.3"
```
Now we begin speaking to Fetch inside of a `with timeout` statement. This statement instructs AppleScript to wait 300 seconds for the code contained within it to execute before continuing. We do this in case Fetch fails to make a connection to the server. If, after five minutes, Fetch

Code 9.1 This script uploads items dropped on its application icon.

```
on open myUploadItem
    set myUser to "john"
    set myPassword to "xxx"
    set myHost to "ftp.trope.com"
    set myDirectory to "public_html"
    set myURL to "ftp://" & myUser & ":"
    → & myPassword & "@" & myHost & "/"
    → & myDirectory
    with timeout of 300 seconds
        tell application "Fetch 3.0.3"
            set myBinPref to the add bin suffix
            set the add bin suffix to false
            put into url myURL item myUploadItem
            → text format Raw Data binary
            → format Raw Data
            set the add bin suffix to myBinPref
            quit
        end tell
    end timeout
end open
```

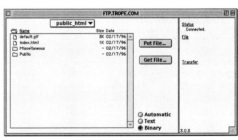

Figure 9.2 A transfer window in Fetch immediately after a user has dragged and dropped the file `default.gif` onto our saved script application.

Scripting Fetch

All the scripts that follow were designed and tested for Fetch 3.0.3.

Fetch is licensed free of charge to users closely affiliated with educational or non-profit charitable organizations. All others may obtain an individual license for $25.

Fetch was written by Jim Matthews and is published by Dartmouth College, which can be reached at `http://`
→ `www.dartmouth.edu/pages/softdev/`.

Scripting Anarchie

All the scripts that follow were designed and tested for Anarchie Pro 3.0.

Anarchie is shareware. A single copy costs $35.

Anarchie Pro 3.0 was written by Peter N. Lewis and is published by Stairways Software, who can be reached at http://www.stairways.com/.

Making it work with Anarchie

To make this script work with Anarchie Pro 3.0, replace steps 2 through 6 of the code above with the following:

```
with timeout of 300 seconds
    tell application "Anarchie Pro"
        store myUploadItem host
        → myHost path myDirectory
        → user myUser password
        → myPassword with binary
        quit
    end tell
end timeout
end open
```

cannot make a connection, the script will fail.

4.
```
        set myBinPref to the add
        → bin suffix
        set the add bin suffix to
        → false
```

Now we save the current preference setting for adding a MacBinary .bin suffix to uploaded files and then set the preference to false. We change this setting to ensure that our file is uploaded as raw data without any MacBinary II encoding. You should change this setting to true only if you are uploading Mac files that another Mac user will need to download via FTP. The MacBinary II format preserves the data and resource forks of a Mac file, as well as its creator and file type information.

5.
```
        put into url myURL item
        → myUploadItem text
        → format Raw Data binary
        → format Raw Data
```

Then we send the file via FTP to the server as a raw data file. If this is not a file for a Web site or other non-Mac use, we can use the MacBinaryII format.

6.
```
        set the add bin suffix to
        → myBinPref
        quit
    end tell
end timeout
end open
```

Finally, we restore the .bin suffix preference setting and end the script.

✔ Modifying this script

■ You can easily modify this script to upload multiple folders full of files, or even test file names for matches to decide whether to upload them or not. Code 4.5 in Chapter 4 illustrates how your script can move through a folder full of files and work with each file individually.

Retrieving a file via FTP

Code 9.2 retrieves a file—specifically, the current readme from the official Fetch Web site—from a remote server to your local filesystem via FTP.

To retrieve a file via FTP:

1. `set myUser to "anonymous"`
`set myPassword to`
`→ "name@domain.com"`
`set myHost to "ftp.dartmouth.edu"`
`set myDirectory to`
`→ "/pub/software/mac/"`
`set myFile to "README"`

We begin by hard-coding the variables we will need for username, password, hostname, directory, and the file to get.

2. `set myURL to "ftp://"`
`→ & myUser & ":"`
`→ & myPassword & "@"`
`→ & myHost & "/" & myDirectory`

As before, we assemble an FTP URL based on our newly defined variables.

3. `set myFolder to (choose folder)`

Now we prompt the user to choose a folder in which to save the retrieved file.

4. `tell application "Fetch 3.0.3"`
`    activate`
`    open url myURL`
`    copy remote file myFile to`
`    → beginning of myFolder`
`    close transfer window 1`
`end tell`

Finally, we open an FTP connection to the appropriate host and directory and get the file specified, saving it in the folder myFolder.

Code 9.2 This script retrieves the current readme file from the Fetch Web site.

```
set myUser to "anonymous"
set myPassword to "name@domain.com"
set myHost to "ftp.dartmouth.edu"
set myDirectory to "/pub/software/mac/"
set myFile to "README"
set myURL to "ftp://" & myUser & ":"
→ & myPassword & "@" & myHost & "/"
→ & myDirectory
set myFolder to (choose folder)
tell application "Fetch 3.0.3"
    activate
    open url myURL
    copy remote file myFile to beginning of
    → myFolder
    close transfer window 1
end tell
```

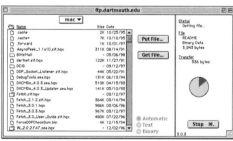

Figure 9.3 A new transfer window in Fetch as it is actively getting the readme file from the official Fetch Web site at Dartmouth.

Making it work with Anarchie

To make this script work with Anarchie Pro 3.0, replace step 4 above with the following code:

```
set myFolder to myFolder as string
tell application "Anarchie Pro"
    fetch alias (myFolder & myFile)
    → host myHost path (myDirectory
    → & myFile) user myUser password
myPassword with binary
end tell
```

Code 9.3 This script returns a directory listing with item names in the list myItemNames and item types in the list myItemTypes.

```
                    code
set myDirectory to
→ "ftp://ftp.dartmouth.edu/pub/mac"

set {myItemNames, myItemTypes} to
→ listDirectory(myDirectory)

on listDirectory(myDirectory)

    tell application "Fetch 3.0.3"

        set myIgnoreCache to ignore cache

        set ignore cache to true

        open url myDirectory

        set view order of transfer window 1 to
        → byName

        set itemCount to count transfer window
        → 1 each remote item

        set myItemNames to {}

        set myItemTypes to {}

repeat with itemIndex from 1 to → itemCount

            set curItemName to (name of remote
            → item itemIndex of transfer
            → window 1)

            set myItemNames to myItemNames &
            → curItemName

            set curItemType to (item type of
            → remote item itemIndex of transfer
            → window 1)

            set myItemTypes to myItemTypes &
            → curItemType

        end repeat

        close transfer window 1 saving no

        set ignore cache to myIgnoreCache

    end tell

    return {myItemNames, myItemTypes}

end listDirectory
```

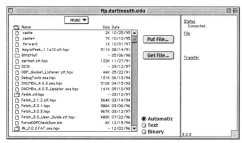

Figure 9.4 A new transfer window in Fetch with the directory listing showing as the script is running.

Retrieving a directory listing via FTP

Why would you want a directory listing, you ask? Well, let's suppose you want to check a specific server periodically to see if a certain file, like a new beta version of software, is available yet. With **Code 9.3** as a basis, you could write a script to get the directory listing and then test for the existence of a specific file name. If it exists, you could then use the code from the previous spread to retrieve it. **Figure 9.4** shows a new transfer window in Fetch with the directory listing displayed as the script is running.

To retrieve a directory listing via FTP:

1. set myDirectory to
   → "ftp://ftp.dartmouth.edu/pub/mac"

   We begin by setting the directory name for which we'll return the listing. You can set this URL to anything you like.

2. set {myItemNames, myItemTypes} to
   → listDirectory(myDirectory)

   Next, we call the function listDirectory, passing it the directory name we want to get a listing for in the variable myDirectory. We should receive two lists back: myItemNames contains names of items, and myItemTypes contains types of items in the directory.

3. on listDirectory(myDirectory)
       tell application "Fetch 3.0.3"
           set myIgnoreCache to ignore
           → cache
           set ignore cache to true

   Here we define our function listDirectory to list the FTP directory passed in the variable myDirectory. We begin talking to Fetch and store the "ignore file cache" setting before changing it to true. We change this setting to

RETRIEVING A DIRECTORY LISTING VIA FTP

155

make sure Fetch is not giving us a directory listing that it cached locally from an old access, but instead is giving us a new directory listing from the remote server itself.

4.
```
open url myDirectory
set view order of transfer
→ window 1 to byName
set itemCount to count transfer
→ window 1 each remote item
```

Now we open the directory in Fetch, view it by name, and get the count of all items in the directory.

5.
```
set myItemNames to {}
set myItemTypes to {}
```

Next, we initialize two list variables, one to hold item names and one to hold the item types. For more information on variables, see page 15 in Chapter 3.

6.
```
repeat with itemIndex from 1
→ to itemCount
```

Now we begin a loop to go through each item.

7.
```
set curItemName to
→ (name of remote item
→ itemIndex of transfer
→ window 1)
```

We set curItemName to the file name of the current item in our loop.

8.
```
set myItemNames to
→ myItemNames & curItemName
```

We then append the file name stored in curItemName to the end of our list of file names, myItemNames.

9.
```
set curItemType to
→ (item type of remote
→ item itemIndex of
→ transfer window 1)
```

We set curItemType to the file type of the current item in our loop.

10.
```
        set myItemTypes to
     → myItemTypes &
        → curItemType
    end repeat
```

We then append the file type stored in curItemType to the end of our list of file types, myItemTypes.

11.
```
        close transfer window 1
        → saving no
        set ignore cache to
        → myIgnoreCache
    end tell
```

Then we close the FTP window in Fetch and restore the "ignore file cache" setting.

12.
```
        return {myItemNames,
     → myItemTypes}
    end listDirectory
```

Finally, our function returns the list of item names and list of item types to the line of the script that called the function in the first place.

Making it work with Anarchie

Anarchie can get an FTP server's directory listing in a single command, but the results must be saved in a text file for later use. This code will save our directory listing into a file named by the user:

```
set myfile to new file
tell application "Anarchie Pro"
   list myfile host
   → "ftp.dartmouth.edu" path
   → "/pub/mac" user "anonymous"
   → password "name@domain.com"
end tell
```

Updating a remote directory via FTP with Fetch

Code 9.4 will compare the contents of a local folder with a remote directory via FTP. Any new or updated files in the local directory will be copied to the remote server. **Figure 9.5** shows a new transfer window in Fetch with a file being uploaded as this script is running.

To update a remote directory via FTP:

1. `set myURL to`
   → `"ftp://user:password@www.`
   → `trope.com/Public/"`
   `set myFolder to (choose folder)`
   → `as string`

   We begin by setting the FTP URL for the remote directory and prompting the user for the name of the local folder to compare it with.

2. `tell application "Fetch 3.0.3"`
        `set myEncodedNames to encode`
        → `names`
        `set myTextFormat to default`
        → `upload text format`
        `set myBinaryFormat to default`
        → `upload binary format`
        `set myIgnoreCache to ignore`
        → `cache`
        `set encode names to false`
        `set default upload text format`
        → `to text`
        `set default upload binary format`
   → `to Raw Data`
        `set ignore cache to true`

   Next, we begin talking to Fetch, getting and saving preference settings for upload formats, name encoding, and whether to ignore the file cache. Then we change those settings. We change the encode names setting so that file names don't

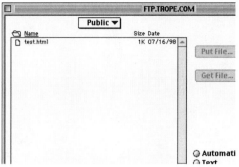

Figure 9.5 A new transfer window in Fetch with a file being uploaded as this script is running.

Code 9.4 This script compares a local folder with a remote directory and copies new or updated local files to the remote directory.

```
set myURL to "ftp://user:password@
→ www.trope.com/Public/"
set myFolder to (choose folder) as string

tell application "Fetch 3.0.3"
    set myEncodedNames to encode names
    set myTextFormat to default upload text
    → format
    set myBinaryFormat to default upload
    → binary format
    set myIgnoreCache to ignore cache
    set encode names to false
    set default upload text format to text
    set default upload binary format to Raw
    → Data
    set ignore cache to true
    with timeout of 300 seconds
        open url myURL
    end timeout
end tell
tell application "Finder"
    set myFolderItems to list folder alias
    → myFolder without invisibles
    repeat with x in myFolderItems
        try
            tell application "Fetch 3.0.3" to
            → set myRemoteDate to modification
            → date of remote item x of transfer
            → window 1
            set myExistFlag to true
```

Code continues on next page

Code 9.4 *continued*

```
                      code
      on error
         set myExistFlag to false
      end try
      if kind of alias (myFolder & x) is not
   → "folder" then
         if myExistFlag then
            set myLocalDate to modification
         → date of alias (sourceFolder & x)
            set myUploadFlag to
         → (myRemoteDate < myLocalDate)
         else
            set myUploadFlag to true
         end if
         if myUploadFlag then
            with timeout of 300 seconds
               tell application "Fetch 3.0.3"
            → to put into transfer window
            → 1 item alias (myFolder & x)
            end timeout
         end if
      end if
   end repeat
end tell

tell application "Fetch 3.0.3"
   set encode names to myEncodedNames
   set default upload text format to
   → myTextFormat
   set default upload binary format to
   → myBinaryFormat
   set ignore cache to myIgnoreCache
end tell
```

get encoded as they're uploaded. We change the `default upload text format` setting so that any text files are uploaded as plain text. We change the `default upload binary format` setting so that any non-text files are uploaded as raw data. We change the `ignore cache` setting so that Fetch doesn't use its own local cache when comparing file names and dates.

3.
```
      with timeout of 300 seconds
         open url myURL
      end timeout
   end tell
```
Now we have Fetch open the directory within a 300 second timeout. If it takes Fetch more than 300 seconds, the script will fail.

4.
```
   tell application "Finder"
      set myFolderItems to list folder
   → alias myFolder without
   → invisibles
      repeat with x in myFolderItems
```
Once the directory is opened in Fetch, we talk to the Finder, storing the list of items in our local folder in the variable `myFolderItems`. By adding the qualifier `without invisibles`, we omit any hidden files from our list. We begin a loop through each item.

5.
```
      try
         tell application
      → "Fetch 3.0.3" to set
      → myRemoteDate to
      → modification date of
      → remote item x of
      → transfer window 1
         set myExistFlag to true
      on error
         set myExistFlag to false
      end try
```
Now we have Fetch try to get the file date of an item in the remote directory with

the same name as the current local item in the loop. If we get an error, the item doesn't exist in the remote directory. If the item exists, we set the flag variable myExistFlag to true; otherwise we set myExistFlag to false.

6.
```
    if kind of alias
→ (myFolder & x) is not
→ "folder" then
```
Now we check to make sure our local item isn't a folder.

7.
```
        if myExistFlag then
```
If the local item isn't a folder, we check our variable myExistFlag to see if an item with the same name exists in the remote directory.

8.
```
            set myLocalDate to
→ modification date of
→ alias (sourceFolder
→ & x)
```
Now we set the variable myLocalDate to the date of our local file.

9.
```
            set myUploadFlag to
→ (myRemoteDate <
→ myLocalDate)
        else
            set myUploadFlag to true
        end if
```
We're ready to compare the local file date with the remote file date and store the results (true or false) in the flag variable myUploadFlag to indicate whether we'll upload the file later. If there's no remote item with that name, we set the flag variable myUploadFlag to true as well.

10.
```
        if myUploadFlag then
            with timeout of 300
→ seconds
                tell application
→ "Fetch 3.0.3" to
→ put into transfer
```

```
                          → window 1 item
                          → alias (myFolder
                          → & x)
                     end timeout
                 end if
             end if
         end repeat
     end tell
```

If the upload flag myUploadFlag is true, we tell Fetch to copy the local file to the remote directory (which is still open in the frontmost transfer window, transfer window 1) within a 300 second timeout before continuing the repeat loop.

11.
```
    tell application "Fetch 3.0.3"
        set encode names to
        → myEncodedNames
        set default upload text format
        → to myTextFormat
        set default upload binary
        → format to myBinaryFormat
        set ignore cache to
        → myIgnoreCache
    end tell
```

Finally, we restore the preference settings we changed at the beginning of the script.

Retrieving a file via HTTP with Anarchie

Anarchie speaks more than FTP (File Transfer Protocol). It can also talk to Web servers in their native HTTP (Hypertext Transfer Protocol). **Code 9.5** will retrieve the source code file for Apple's home page, located at www.apple.com, and store it on your local hard drive. **Figure 9.6** shows the results of running **Code 9.5** from the Script Editor.

To retrieve a Web file via HTTP:

1. `set myfile to (path to me as`
   `→ string) & " Temp File"`

   We start by storing a file path to a new temporary file that we'll have Anarchie create in a moment. This file will be named the same as our script application plus the string `Temp File` and be saved in the same folder as our script application. If you run this from the Script Editor, the temporary file will be stored in the folder containing the Script Editor.

2. `tell application "Anarchie Pro"`
   `    webfetch alias myfile url`
   `    → "http://www.apple.com/"`
   `end tell`

   Now we have Anarchie retrieve the file from the server defined by the URL http://www.apple.com/ and store it in a new file defined by `myfile`.

3. `set myfileref to (open for access`
   `→ alias myfile)`

   Next, we open the text file saved by Anarchie in `myfile` and store the reference to our open file in the variable `myfileref`.

4. `set myHTML to (read myfileref)`
   Then we get all of the text in the file and store it in the variable `myHTML`.

5. `close access myfileref`
   Finally, we close the file.

Script 9.5 This script retrieves the source code for Apple's home page.

```
                      code
set myfile to (path to me as string) &
→ "Temp File"
tell application "Anarchie Pro"
   webfetch alias myfile url
   → "http://www.apple.com/"
end tell
set myfileref to (open for access alias
→ myfile)
set myHTML to (read myfileref)
close access myfileref
```

Figure 9.6 Partial results of our script, as shown in the Event Log in the Script Editor.

Code 9.6 This script retrieves an entire site's files and directory structure, saving everything to the local hard drive in the folder chosen by the user.

```
                     code
set myFolder to (choose folder with prompt
→ "Folder to save web files:")

tell application "Anarchie Pro"

    getwebsite myFolder url
    → "http://www.apple.com/"

end tell
```

Figure 9.7 The AppleScript dictionary entry for Anarchie Pro 3.0's getwebsite command.

Retrieving an entire site's files via HTTP with Anarchie

With Anarchie's getwebsite command, it is possible to systematically gather an entire Web site's collections of files and directories for local use. This script, **Code 9.6**, retrieves an entire site's files and directory structure. It might be used in conjunction with the browser-based Web page printing scripts found in Chapter 6 to print an entire site's Web pages on a regular basis for archival purposes. **Figure 9.7** shows the powerful getwebsite command definition from Anarchie Pro 3.0's AppleScript dictionary.

To retrieve an entire Web site:

1. `set myFolder to (choose folder`
   `→ with prompt "Folder to save web`
   `→ files:")`

   We start by prompting the user for a folder to save the Web site's files and directories into. We store this reference in the variable myFolder.

2. `tell application "Anarchie Pro"`
   `    getwebsite myFolder url`
   `    → "http://www.apple.com/"`
   `end tell`

   Next, we have Anarchie retrieve the files and directories at the desired URL. In this example, we are retrieving Apple's Web site. To adapt this script for your own use, substitute the appropriate URL for http://www.apple.com/.

DataComet
for Telnet

Figure 10.1 DataComet's AppleScript dictionary showing some of its unique commands like execute and targetwindow.

DataComet opens a bridge enabling AppleScripts to reach out and control UNIX systems via telnet. For instance, you might use DataComet to retrieve administrative text files from a UNIX server and modify them in your script before copying them back to the server. Then you could run administrative command-line programs on the UNIX server to control every aspect of the machine.

DataComet's AppleScript dictionary is unique and improving from version to version. Still, however, many essential operations can only be performed by sending complex macro string codes to DataComet. This hindrance is best overcome by writing many small handlers with simple descriptive names to execute the obscure codes. This way your code can call obviously named functions instead of sending unintelligible string codes.

Figure 10.1 shows DataComet's unique AppleScript dictionary.

Reading a UNIX passwd file or restarting a UNIX server

Code 10.1 uses the UNIX shell command cat to display the system's passwd file to the standard output. Our function returns the standard output to the variable myResult.

Figure 10.2 shows the contents of the passwd file returned in the Script Editor's Event Log window.

To read a UNIX passwd file:

1. ```
global myHostPrompt
global myHostName
global myLinesUsed
```

   We begin by initializing some global variables shared by our main program and the functions.

2. ```
on run
    set myHostName to "192.0.0.1"
    set myUserID to "root"
    set myPassword to "xxx"
    set myHostPrompt to "#"
    set myLinesUsed to 2
```

   Next, in our on run handler, we set our variables to control the session. These variables include: myHostName for the name of the host we want to connect to, myUserID for the name of the user we want to connect as, myPassword for the user's password, myHostPrompt for the prompt character used by this server (we need this to test for the readiness of the server). Finally, myLinesUsed is used by code below to decide what part of the UNIX server's standard output to return after completing a command.

3. ```
tell application "dataComet4.5.2B"
    geturl "telnet://" & myHostName
```

   Now we have DataComet open a telnet connection to the host.

**Figure 10.2** The Event Log window shows the contents of our server's passwd file after the script has run in the Script Editor.

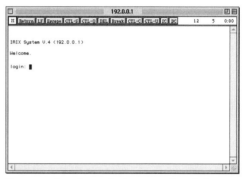

**Figure 10.3** DataComet displays a session window with our server's login screen as our script executes the geturl command in step 3.

## Scripting DataComet

All the scripts that follow were designed and tested for DataComet 4.5.2b.

Most of these scripts do not work with older versions of DataComet.

DataComet is shareware. A single-user license is $20.

DataComet is published by DataBeast Software, which can be reached at http://www.databeast.com/.
```

Code 10.1 This script returns the UNIX server passwd file to the variable myResult.

```
code
global myHostPrompt
global myHostName
global myLinesUsed

on run
    set myHostName to "192.0.0.1"
    set myUserID to "root"
    set myPassword to "xxx"
    set myHostPrompt to "#"
    set myLinesUsed to 2

    tell application "dataComet4.5.2B"
        geturl "telnet://" & myHostName
        targetwindow
        execute "!Z\\255:!D\\001"
        execute myUserID& return
        execute "!Z\\255:!D\\001"
        execute myPassword & return
    end tell

    waitprompt(myHostPrompt)
    set myResult to
    ↦ (sendcommand("cat /etc/passwd"))
    tell application "dataComet4.5.2B"
        send "logout" & return
        repeat
            if (status) contains "Closed" then
            ↦ exit repeat
        end repeat
        try
            with timeout of 5 seconds
                execute "!\\001\\150"
            end timeout
        on error
        end try
    end tell
end run

on sendcommand(myCommand)
    tell application "dataComet4.5.2B"
        send myCommand & return
    end tell
```

Code continues on next page

4. `targetwindow`

We use `targetwindow` (which is a DataComet command) to specify our new telnet window as the recipient of the subsequent statements.

5. `execute "!Z\\255:!D\\001"`
`execute myUserID& return`
`execute "!Z\\255:!D\\001"`
`execute myPassword & return`
`end tell`

Then we use `execute` to send our username and password as strings to the server. The line `execute "!Z\\255:!D\\001"` causes DataComet to wait for a prompt before sending each string.

6. `waitprompt(myHostPrompt)`

Finally, we are connected. We now use our function defined below, `waitprompt`, to wait for a new prompt to appear on the server.

7. `set myResult to (sendcommand`
`↦ ("cat /etc/passwd"))`

Once we know the server is ready to receive a command, we use our function `sendcommand` to send the UNIX `cat` command. Our function, defined below, returns the UNIX server's standard output. We store this returned value in `myResult`.

8. `tell application "dataComet4.5.2B"`
`send "logout" & return`

Now we tell DataComet to send a UNIX `logout` command to the host.

9. `if (status) contains "Closed"`

This line tells AppleScript to wait until the session is closed. We put this test into a repeat loop to wait for DataComet to let us know that the previous command has been sent. When DataComet's property `status` contains the string `Closed`, we know that the previous command was sent.

10.
```
    with timeout of 5 seconds
        execute "!\\001\\150"
    end timeout
```
Then we use the **execute** statement to send DataComet a special macro character sequence, `"!\\001\\150"`, that tells DataComet to trigger the Quit menu item in the File menu. These macro strings are explained in detail in DataComet's documentation.

11.
```
on sendcommand(myCommand)
    tell application
    → "dataComet4.5.2B"
        send myCommand & return
    end tell
```
Our function **sendcommand** receives a string from the code calling it and stores it in a variable named **myCommand**. The function sends the string **myCommand** to the host.

12.
```
    waitprompt(myHostPrompt)
```
We use our function **waitprompt** to wait for a new prompt to appear on the server.

13.
```
    tell application
    → "dataComet4.5.2B"
        execute "!EA"
        copy
```
Next, we send DataComet a special macro character string, `"!EA"`, to select the current telnet session window's text. Then we **copy** the text to the result.

14.
```
        set myScreen to the result
```
Now we set the variable **myScreen** to the **result**, which contains the server's standard output, thanks to the line above.

Code 10.1 *continued*

```
    waitprompt(myHostPrompt)
    tell application "dataComet4.5.2B"
        execute "!EA"
        copy
        set myScreen to the result
        set myCurrentScreen to paragraphs
        → (myLinesUsed + 1) through ¬
            ((count of paragraphs in myScreen)
            → - 2) of myScreen
        set myResult to ""
        repeat with myLine in myCurrentScreen
            set myResult to myResult &
            → (myLine as text) & return as text
        end repeat
    end tell
    set myLinesUsed to (count of paragraphs in
    → myScreen)
    return myResult
end sendcommand


on waitprompt(myHostPrompt)
    tell application "dataComet4.5.2B"
        execute "!Z\\255" & myHostPrompt &
        → "!D\\000"
        set waiting to false
        repeat until waiting is true
            if (status) contains "Waiting" then
                set waiting to true
            end if
        end repeat
    end tell
end waitprompt
```

15.
```
        set myCurrentScreen to
    → paragraphs (myLinesUsed
    → + 1) through ¬
        ((count of paragraphs in
        → myScreen) - 2) of
        → myScreen
```
Now we store specific lines of the text returned by the server in the list variable myCurrentScreen. The particular lines to pick are defined by the global variable myLinesUsed, which we set at the beginning of our script. The value we set it to, 2, was chosen by trial-and-error testing.

16.
```
        set myResult to ""
```
We then initialize a variable, myResult, to hold a string version of myCurrentScreen.

17.
```
        repeat with myLine in
        → myCurrentScreen
            set myResult to myResult
            → & (myLine as text)
            → & return as text
        end repeat
    end tell
```
Here we loop through each item in myCurrentScreen, appending the item as text along with a return character to myResult.

18.
```
    set myLinesUsed to (count of
    → paragraphs in myScreen)
        return myResult
    end sendcommand
```
Finally, we update the global myLinesUsed to reflect the new text in the standard output.

19.
```
    on waitprompt(myHostPrompt)
        tell application
        → "dataComet4.5.2B"
            execute "!Z\\255" &
            → myHostPrompt & "!D\\000"
```
Our function waitprompt keeps DataComet waiting for new prompt

from the UNIX server. This indicates that the server is ready to receive a new command. Using `execute` we send a special macro character string to DataComet, telling it to wait for the host prompt character, defined above in the global `myHostPrompt`, to be returned from the UNIX server.

20.   `set waiting to false`

Once we've sent the above line, we need to monitor DataComet to see when it's finished waiting for the host prompt character to appear. So here we initialize a flag variable `waiting` that we'll use to test DataComet's `status` property below.

21.
```
        repeat until waiting is true
            if (status) contains
        → "Waiting" then
                set waiting to true
            end if
        end repeat
    end tell
end waitprompt
```

Here we loop, continuously testing the application's `status` property. Once the prompt has appeared, `status` will contain the string `Waiting`.

✔ Changing this script to restart a UNIX server

■ By simply changing the command we send to the server in step 7 above, we can restart the entire server. Replace the code in step 7 with: `set myResult to (sendcommand("shutdown -i6 -y"))` This statement sends the server the shell command `shutdown` with the attributes `-i6 -y` to restart the machine to its default multi-user state and restart without any prompting. Most UNIX machines will respond to this syntax for the shutdown command.

Figure 10.4 Our session window in DataComet displays the results of our login sequence as the execute commands in step 5 are run.

Adding mail aliases to a UNIX server

Code 10.2 uses the UNIX shell commands `cp`, `echo`, `cat`, and `newaliases` to add a user to `sendmail`'s aliases file and then have `sendmail` reload it. The detailed step-by-step analysis of this script can be found under the listing for **Code 10.1**, steps 1 through 21. The big change here is that we're replacing step 7 in **Code 10.1** with our new steps below. These new steps are the code we use to work directly with `sendmail`.

Figure 10.4 shows the session in progress while the script is running with the server host prompt ready for a command.

To add a mail alias to a UNIX server:

1. `set myResult to (sendcommand`
  `→ ("cp /etc/aliases`
  `→ /etc/aliases.bak"))`

Once we have made a telnet connection to our server, as we did in **Code 10.1**, we send the UNIX command `cp` to back up the existing aliases file.

2. `set myNewAlias to`
  `→ "test:test@test.com"`
  `set myResult to (sendcommand`
  `→ ("echo '" & myNewAlias & "'`
  `→ /etc/aliases.new"))`

Then we define our new alias in the variable `myNewAlias` before we send the UNIX command `echo` to print the new mail user line to a new text file.

3. `set myResult to (sendcommand`
  `→ ("cat /etc/aliases /etc/`
  `→ aliases.new >/etc/aliases"))`

Now we send the UNIX command `cat` to concatenate the original aliases file with the new text file and we save this concatenated version over the original.

Code 10.2 This script adds a new user to the server's mail aliases file and has the server reload it.

```
                              code
global myHostPrompt
global myHostName
global myLinesUsed

on run
    set myHostName to "192.0.0.1"
    set myUserID to "root"
    set myPassword to "xxx"
    set myHostPrompt to "#"
    set myLinesUsed to 2

    tell application "dataComet4.5.2B"
        geturl "telnet://" & myHostName
        targetwindow
        execute "!Z\\255:!D\\001"
        execute myUserID& return
        execute "!Z\\255:!D\\001"
        execute myPassword & return
    end tell

    waitprompt(myHostPrompt)
    set myResult to (sendcommand("cp /etc/aliases /etc/aliases.bak"))
    set myNewAlias to "test:test@test.com"
    set myResult to (sendcommand("echo '" & myNewAlias & "' /etc/aliases.new"))
    set myResult to (sendcommand("cat /etc/aliases /etc/aliases.new >/etc/aliases"))
    set myResult to (sendcommand("newaliases"))
    tell application "dataComet4.5.2B"
        send "logout" & return
        repeat
            if (status) contains "Closed" then exit repeat
        end repeat
        try
            with timeout of 5 seconds
                execute "!\\001\\150"
            end timeout
        on error
        end try
    end tell
end run

on sendcommand(myCommand)
    tell application "dataComet4.5.2B"
```

Code continues on next page

4. `set myResult to`
`(sendcommand("newaliases"))`

Finally, we send the UNIX command
`newaliases` to have sendmail reload the
aliases file.

Code 10.2 *continued*

```
                              code
     send myCommand & return
   end tell
   waitprompt(myHostPrompt)
   tell application "dataComet4.5.2B"
      execute "!EA"
      copy
      set myScreen to the result
      set myCurrentScreen to paragraphs (myLinesUsed + 1) through
         ((count of paragraphs in myScreen) - 2) of myScreen
      set myResult to ""
      repeat with myLine in myCurrentScreen
         set myResult to myResult & (myLine as text) & return as text
      end repeat
   end tell
   set myLinesUsed to (count of paragraphs in myScreen)
   return myResult
end sendcommand
on waitprompt(myHostPrompt)
   tell application "dataComet4.5.2B"
      execute "!Z\\255" & myHostPrompt & "!D\\000"
      set waiting to false
      repeat until waiting is true
         if (status) contains "Waiting" then
            set waiting to true
         end if
      end repeat
   end tell
end waitprompt
```

Retrieving an environment variable from a UNIX server

Code 10.3 uses the UNIX shell command print env to return the server's environment variables. It uses the name prompted from the user at the beginning to return the value of the desired environment variable. Detailed step-by-step analysis of this script can be found in steps 1 through 21 of **Code 10.1**.

Figure 10.5 shows the session in progress while the script is running.

Figure 10.5 At the end of our script's execution, it displays a dialog with the value of the requested environment variable from the server, in this case, we see the value for our server's TZ (time zone) variable.

To retrieve an environment variable from a UNIX server:

1. set myEnvVariable to text returned
→ of (display dialog
→ "ENV Variable:" default answer
→ "TZ")

This line prompts the user for the name of an environmental variable, and stores the result in the variable myEnvVariable.

2. set myResult to
→ sendcommand("printenv")

Once we have a telnet connection established, as we did in **Code 10.1**, we send the UNIX command print env and capture the standard output in the variable myResult.

3. repeat with i from 1 to number of
→ paragraphs of myResult
    if paragraph i of myResult
    → starts with myEnvVariable
    → then

The term paragraphs here checks for the newline character, which lets us loop through the lines of the returned input, looking for one that starts with the desired environment variable name (the one the user entered in step 1).

RETRIEVING AN ENVIRONMENT VARIABLE

Code 10.3 This script returns the user-requested server environment variable's value.

```
                                    code
global myHostPrompt
global myHostName
global myLinesUsed

on run
   set myEnvVariable to text returned of (display dialog "ENV Variable:" default answer "TZ")
   set myHostName to "192.0.0.1"
   set myUserID to "root"
   set myPassword to "xxx"
   set myHostPrompt to "#"
   set myNewAlias to "test:test@test.com"
   set myLinesUsed to 2

   tell application "dataComet4.5.2B"
      geturl "telnet://" & myHostName
      targetwindow
      execute "!Z\\255:!D\\001"
      execute myUserID& return
      execute "!Z\\255:!D\\001"
      execute myPassword & return
   end tell

   waitprompt(myHostPrompt)
   set myResult to sendcommand("printenv")
   tell application "dataComet4.5.2B"
      send "logout" & return
      repeat
         if (status) contains "Closed" then exit repeat
      end repeat
      try
         with timeout of 5 seconds
            execute "!\\001\\150"
         end timeout
      on error
      end try
   end tell
   repeat with i from 1 to number of paragraphs of myResult
if paragraph i of myResult starts with myEnvVariable then
         set myEnvValue to characters ((offset of "=" in (paragraph i of myResult)) + 1) thru
         ⇢ (length of paragraph i of myResult) of ¬
            paragraph i of myResult as string
         exit repeat
      end if
```

Code continues on next page

4.
```
set myEnvValue to characters
→ ((offset of "=" in (paragraph i
→ of myResult)) + 1) thru (length
→ of paragraph i of myResult) of
→ paragraph i of myResult as string
exit repeat
end if
end repeat
```

When we find the right line, we use `offset` to determine the first character position after the equals sign in the returned text stored in `myResult`. By selecting just the characters after the equals sign, we set `myEnvValue` to the value of the server environment variable.

5. `display dialog myEnvValue`

Finally, we display a dialog with the value of the server environment variable the user asked for.

Code 10.3 *continued*

```
            code
    end repeat
    display dialog myEnvValue
end run

on sendcommand(myCommand)
    tell application "dataComet4.5.2B"
        send myCommand & return
    end tell
    waitprompt(myHostPrompt)
    tell application "dataComet4.5.2B"
        execute "!EA"
        copy
        set myScreen to the result
        set myCurrentScreen to paragraphs
        → (myLinesUsed + 1) through ¬
            ((count of paragraphs in myScreen)
            → - 2) of myScreen
        set myResult to ""
        repeat with myLine in myCurrentScreen
            set myResult to myResult &
            → (myLine as text) & return as text
        end repeat
    end tell
    set myLinesUsed to
    → (count of paragraphs in myScreen)
    return myResult
end sendcommand
on waitprompt(myHostPrompt)
    tell application "dataComet4.5.2B"
        execute "!Z\\255" & myHostPrompt &
        → "!D\\000"
        set waiting to false
        repeat until waiting is true
            if (status) contains "Waiting" then
                set waiting to true
            end if
        end repeat
    end tell
end waitprompt
```

Figure 10.6 This DataComet session shows an active Script Daemon telnet session in which we have retrieved the names of all running processes on our remote Mac using `get name of every process` with the Finder.

Telnet to your Mac with Script Daemon

Nothing like winding up with a 180-degree turn! Script Daemon is a background application that runs on your Mac without any visible windows. It lets you telnet into your own Mac using your owner name and password and send AppleScripts that are executed immediately! Amazing. And it works....

This great application might be very useful for anyone who's traveling and needs to launch applications or manage a server remotely.

Figure 10.6 shows a Script Daemon telnet session logged into a Mac.

Scripting with Script Daemon

Script Daemon 1.0.1 shouldn't be confused with the Netscape plug-in ScriptDemon from Royal Software.

Script Daemon is freeware.

Script Daemon is written by Peter N. Lewis and published by Stairways Software, which can be reached at `http://www.stairways.com/`.

TELNET TO YOUR MAC WITH SCRIPT DAEMON

BUILDING CGIs

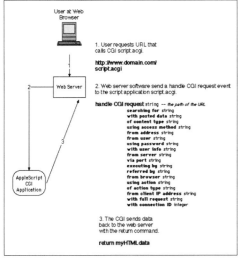

User at Web
Browser

1. User requests URL that
calls CGI script.acgi.

**http://www.domain.com/
script.acgi**

Web Server

2. Web server software send a handle CGI request event
to the script application script.acgi.

handle CGI request string -- *the path of the URL*
    searching for string
    with posted data string
    of content type string
    using access method string
    from address string
    from user string
    using password string
    with user info string
    from server string
    via port string
    executing by string
    referred by string
    from browser string
    using action string
    of action type string
    from client IP address string
    with full request string
    with connection ID integer

AppleScript
CGI
Application

3. The CGI sends data
back to the web server
with the return command.

return myHTML data

Figure 11.1 This diagram shows the exchange of
information between a web server application, like
WebSTAR, and an AppleScript CGI. When a user
requests a URL that calls the CGI, the web server
sends the CGI application a `handle CGI request`
event. Along with this event, the server sends all
server variables and form data to the CGI. The event
triggers the on `handle CGI request` handler in the
CGI script, which runs and then returns a string for the
web server to display as an HTML page with its
`return` command.

CGI... ICG... GCI... GIC... do we care where
this strange acronym came from? We do.

The mysteries of its parent words hold the
key to understanding how these Web-
enabled scripts work. "Common gateway
interface" is the phrase that was coined to
describe the manner in which local scripts
on a server receive data from an Internet
client and return results at the end of their
execution. A group of standards describes
the way CGIs communicate on each platform.
On UNIX, script and server sometimes share
data via environment variables. On the Mac,
the natural avenue for CGIs is Apple Events,
which makes AppleScript a natural choice
for handling the passing of data.

CGIs on the Mac are often AppleScript script
applications or FaceSpan applications. Most
Mac Web servers, including WebSTAR and
Apple's built-in Personal Web Sharing, are set
up out of the box to support the `.acgi` and
`.cgi` file suffixes to run AppleScript applications that support the standard CGI event
handler we're about to meet.

Mac OS 8.5 and CGIs

A standard event to allow AppleScripts to communicate with Web servers has existed for some time. This event was previously known as on «event WWWΩsdoc». It lacked an English equivalent until OS 8.5 arrived. AppleScript 1.3.x gives us a simple and complete on handle CGI request handler. AppleScript automatically returns server variables to any on handle CGI request handler.

With this new handler plus the improvements to speed and language you'll see how easy CGI scripting is in PPC-native AppleScript 1.3.x.

✔ FIFO: First In, First Out

■ FaceSpan is often used in creating AppleScript CGIs to take advantage of its built-in FIFO (first in first out) capabilities. When multiple CGI calls are sent to a normal script application, the last person to call the application gets their results first (this is called LIFO, or last in first out). This order of execution isn't desirable in a CGI environment, so it's often worthwhile to save your CGI script applications as FaceSpan stand-alone applications to get FIFO performance.

✔ Saving your CGI

■ Save your script as a stay-open application, never showing the startup dialog. When choosing between file suffixes, .acgi is most often is right choice over .cgi. Why? The a in .acgi stands for "asychronous," meaning that the web server will continue to work on other tasks while waiting for the CGI to return results. If you use the .cgi suffix for your CGI, the web server will wait for your CGI to get back to it before doing anything else! Not usually a good thing.

Figure 11.2 The dictionary entry for handle CGI request in OS 8.5's standard additions dictionary, showing all of the values it returns.

✔ Eventually you'll need Encode URL and Decode URL

■ Once you write a CGI, you'll quickly discover that you need to convert encoded text from the Web. You have probably seen strings like %20 in the location field of your browser before. This encoding, %20, stands for a space character, which would otherwise not transmit properly. Other %XX codes exist for all non-alphanumeric ASCII characters. See *Submitting form data from Interent Explorer* in Chapter 6 for Encode URL in action.

■ Encode URL adds the statement encode URL, which takes a standard string as an argument and returns the string encoded in the URL %XX scheme so that extended ASCII characters are properly transmitted over the Web. As you might suspect, decode URL does the opposite.

Mac OS 8.5 and CGIs

All the scripts that follow were designed and tested for Mac OS 8.5.

Most of these scripts do not work with older versions of the Mac OS.

Code 11.1 Parsing the URL reply string and returning a form value in HTML results.

```
                        code
on handle CGI request myURL

    searching for mySearchArgs

    set myArgList to (tokenize mySearchArgs
    → with delimiters {"&", "="})

    set mySearchValue to
    → (offset in list myArgList of "name"
    → with returning next item)

    set crlf to  (ASCII character 13) &
    → (ASCII character 10)

    set myHTML to "HTTP/1.0 200 OK" & crlf &
    → "Server: MacHTTP/2.0" & crlf &
    → "MIME-Version: 1.0" & crlf &
    → "Content-type: text/html" & crlf & crlf

        set myHTML to myHTML &
        → "<HTML><BODY><P>Your name is " &
        → mySearchValue & "</BODY></HTML>"

    return myHTML

end handle CGI request
```

Figure 11.3 Our browser displays the results of our CGI, script.acgi. In this case, the user had entered the text "John Doe" into the "name" field in the preceeding form before submitting it. Since the form used a GET method to send the form data, the data appears encoded in the URL as shown in the browser's Go To field.

Understanding GET data

All data that goes to your AppleScript CGI application for processing comes from a Web client, and is submitted to the server using either the GET or POST methods. Forms submitted using the GET method will generate their name-value pairs and add them to the end of the submitted URL. For example, when you submit an HTML form with user-entered data of "John Doe" in the field named "name", the URL sent to the server will have the values of the form filed encoded into it like this: http://www.domain.com/
→ script.acgi?name=John%20Doe.

Figure 11.3 shows the results returned for this **Code 11.1** as a CGI.

To parse the URL reply string:

1. on handle CGI request myURL
         searching for mySearchArgs

   We begin our CGI handler by putting the searching for property into our variable mySearchArgs. searching for contains the reply string from the URL. The reply string value is all of the text that follows the question mark in a GET URL.

2. set myArgList to
       → (tokenize mySearchArgs with
       → delimiters {"&", "="})

   ACME Script Widgets adds the statement tokenize, which returns a list from a string given list item delimiters, in this case the ampersand and the equals sign. We convert the string mySearchArgs into a series of items in a list, following the format: {name, value}.

3. set mySearchValue to
       → (offset in list myArgList of
       → "name" with returning next item)

   ACME Script Widgets also adds the statement offset in list. Now we retrieve the value for the field "name" using `offset in list` with the modifier `returning next item` to give us the item in the list right after "name," where its value is stored.

4. `set crlf to (ASCII character 13)`
   `→ & (ASCII character 10)`

   For convenience and prettier code, we store the line break character sequence needed in our HTML data header in a variable, `crlf`. These two characters, a return (13) and a line break (10), comprise the standard HTML line break string.

5. `set myHTML to`
   `→ "HTTP/1.0 200 OK" & crlf &`
   `→ "Server: MacHTTP/2.0" & crlf &`
   `→ "MIME-Version: 1.0" & crlf &`
   `→ "Content-type: text/html" & crlf`
   `→ & crlf`

   We initialize a variable for our returned data with the CGI header to let the server know we're returning text as HTML.

6. `set myHTML to myHTML &`
   `→ "<HTML><BODY><P>Your name is " &`
   `→ mySearchValue & "</BODY></HTML>"`

   Next we add our results string to our variable by adding the value of the form field "name" to the user.

7. `return myHTML`
   `end handle CGI request`

   Finally, we return the text to our Web server in the variable myHTML.

8. To make your AppleScript work as a CGI, you must save the script as an application. It is best to save your application so that it stays open. By staying open, your CGI script application will run faster, since it won't have to be launched every time it's called.

Scripting with Encode URL and Decode URL

The scripting additions Encode URL and Decode URL are freeware. They can be found at `http://www2.starnine.com/ → extendingwebstar/osax/`.

Both additions were written by Chuck Shotton and published by BIAP Systems, Inc., which can be reached at `http://www.biap.com/`.

GET versus POST

The HTTP protocol defines two different ways for Web forms to return form data to the server. The HTML tag `<FORM METHOD="POST" ACTION="script.acgi">` determines the method used for a form.

With `METHOD="GET"`, all field data is appended to the end of the URL that the `ACTION` tag defines. This field data, also known as the reply string, is appended to the URL with a question mark indicating its start. Each field name and value are paired and separated by an equals sign. Each pair is separated by an ampersand. `GET` limits the length of form data and lets the user see the form data passed in their browser.

With `METHOD="POST"`, all field data is put into a packet, called the post data, by the user's browser and sent along to the URL that the `ACTION` tag defines. With `POST`, form data can be much longer and is hidden from the user when it is submitted.

9. Name your application `script.acgi` and move it into the same folder as WebSTAR, or whichever folder is the designated CGI folder for your web server software.

10. Try sending your web server the URL `http://www.domain.com/script.acgi?` → `name=John%20Doe`, substituting your server's hostname for `www.domain.com` to test your new AppleScript CGI!

✔ Doing it without ACME Script Widgets

■ **Code 11.2** shows how to tokenize data and get offsets in lists using functions instead of a scripting addition!

Scripting with ACME Script Widgets

This script requires the scripting addition ACME Script Widgets. You must have ACME Script Widgets installed in your Scripting Additions folder for this script to work.

ACME Script Widgets is shareware. It costs $29 for a single-user license.

ACME Script Widgets is published by ACME Technologies, which can be reached at `http://www.acmetech.com/`.

Parsing form POST data

Any forms submitted using the POST method will generate their name-value pairs as part of the post data of the reply. The post data is the data entered by the user into a form that has its METHOD tag set to "POST".

The post data sent back to the URL contains `name=John%20Doe` when the user has entered "John Doe" into the name field of the form. **Figure 11.4** shows the results returned for this script as a CGI, with the user's entered form data, "John Doe", embedded into the returned HTML by our CGI.

This time, we will create our own functions to handle the tasks of tokenizing (or separating the string into a list of items) the returned post data and finding the offset in a list of items of a specific string. This way, we don't need the ACME Script Widgets scripting addition for this script!

To parse form data:

1. `on handle CGI request myURL`
      `with posted data mySearchArgs`

We begin our CGI handler by capturing the post data value using `with posted data` and storing the value in `mySearchArgs`. AppleScript automatically returns many server variables to any `on handle CGI request` handler. Here we're only concerned with `posted data`, since it holds the form's post data.

2. `set myArgList to`
   → `goTokenize(mySearchArgs,`
   → `{"&", "="})`

As before, we convert the string into a series of items in a list, following the format: {name, value}. This time we use our own function, `goTokenize`, defined below to do what as ACME Script Widgets did in the previous script.

Figure 11.4 Our browser displays the results of our CGI, `script.acgi`. In this case, the user had entered the text "John Doe" into the "name" field in the preceeding form before submitting it.

Making an HTML page to call your new CGI

Make a new document in a text editor like BBEdit or SimpleText and type in the following:

```
<HTML><HEAD></HEAD><BODY>
<FORM METHOD="GET" ACTION=
→ "script.acgi">
<INPUT TYPE=TEXT NAME="name">
<INPUT TYPE=SUBMIT></BODY></HTML>
```

Now save the file with the name "form.html" in the same web server directory as your CGI. Then point your Web browser to `http://www.domain.com/` → `form.html`, where `www.domain.com` is your server's host name.

Code 11.2 Parsing the post data and returning a form value in HTML results.

```
                       code
on handle CGI request myURL
   with posted data mySearchArgs
   set myArgList to goTokenize(mySearchArgs,
   → {"&", "="})
   set mySearchValue to
   → goOffsetInList(myArgList, "name")
   set crlf to  (ASCII character 13) & (ASCII
   → character 10)
   set myHTML to "HTTP/1.0 200 OK" & crlf &
   → "Server: MacHTTP/2.0" & crlf &
   → "MIME-Version: 1.0" & crlf &
   → "Content-type: text/html" & crlf & crlf
      set myHTML to myHTML &
      → "<HTML><BODY><P>Your name is " &
      → mySearchValue & "</BODY></HTML>"
return myHTML
end handle CGI request


on goTokenize(incomingData, incomingDelimits)
   set incomingDataitems to characters of
   → incomingData as list
   set outgoingList to {}
   set currentData to ""
   repeat with incomingItem in
   → incomingDataitems
      set myFlag to false
      repeat with incomingDelimit in
      → incomingDelimits
         if incomingItem = incomingDelimit
         → then
            set myFlag to true
            exit repeat
         end if
      end repeat
      if myFlag then
         set outgoingList to outgoingList &
         → currentData
         set currentData to ""
      else
         set currentData to currentData &
         → incomingItem
      end if
   end repeat
   set outgoingList to outgoingList &
   → currentData
   return outgoingList
end goTokenize
```

Code continues on next page

3. `set mySearchValue to`
`→ goOffsetInList(myArgList, "name")`

Now we retrieve the value for the field "name" using our own function, `goOffsetInList`, to give us the item following "name," where its value is stored.

4. `set crlf to  (ASCII character 13) &`
`→ (ASCII character 10)`

For convenience and prettier code, we store the line break character sequence needed in our HTML data header in a variable, `crlf`. These two characters, a return (13) and a line break (10), comprise the standard HTML line break string.

5. `set myHTML to "HTTP/1.0 200 OK" &`
`→ crlf & "Server: MacHTTP/2.0" &`
`→ crlf & "MIME-Version: 1.0" &`
`→ crlf & "Content-type: text/html" &`
`→ crlf & crlf`

We initialize a variable, `myHTML`, for our returned data with the CGI header to let the server know we're returning text as HTML.

6. `set myHTML to myHTML &`
`→ "<HTML><BODY><P>Your name is`
`→ " & mySearchValue &`
`→ "</BODY></HTML>"`

Next we add to `myHTML` our variable `mySearchValue` which holds the "name" field's value.

7. `return myHTML`
`end handle CGI request`

Finally, we return the text to our Web server in the variable `myHTML`.

8. `on goTokenize(incomingData,`
`→ incomingDelimits)`

Our function `goTokenize` receives two values when called: `incomingData` to hold the string to be tokenized, and `incomingDelimits` to hold the characters where the string should be broken into separate items.

9. `set incomingDataitems to`
`→ characters of incomingData`
`→ as list`

We first convert the string `incomingData` into a list, `incomingDataitems`, in which each item equals a single character.

10. `set outgoingList to {}`
`set currentData to ""`

Then we initialize two variables. We will use `outgoingList` to build the final list to return at the end of the function, and `currentData` will hold the string of each item as it is assembled in the loops below.

11. `repeat with incomingItem in`
`→ incomingDataitems`

We start to loop through each character in the incoming string.

12. `set myFlag to false`
`repeat with incomingDelimit`
`→ in incomingDelimits`

Here we clear the flag variable `myFlag` that we'll use to indicate when a delimiter is found in the loop that cycles through each delimiter in `incomingDelimits`.

13. `if incomingItem =`
`→ incomingDelimit then`
`set myFlag to true`
`exit repeat`
`end if`
`end repeat`

While looping through each delimiter, we test the current character `incomingItem` to see if it matches the delimiter. If it does, we set the flag `myFlag` to true and exit the loop.

Code 11.2 *continued*

```
on goOffsetInList(incomingList,
→ incomingItem)
    set outgoingPosition to 0
    set outgoingItem to ""
    repeat with i from 1 to number of items in
    → incomingList
        set incomingListItem to item i of
        → incomingList
        if contents of incomingItem = contents
        → of incomingListItem then
            set outgoingPosition to i
            exit repeat
        end if
    end repeat
try
    if outgoingPosition>0 then set
    → outgoingItem to item
    → (outgoingPosition+1) of incomingList
on error
end try
    return outgoingItem
end goOffsetInList
```

PARSING FORM POST DATA

14.
```
    if myFlag then
        set outgoingList to
        ⇢ outgoingList &
        ⇢ currentData
        set currentData to ""
    else
        set currentData to
        ⇢ currentData &
        ⇢ incomingItem
    end if
  end repeat
  set outgoingList to outgoingList &
  ⇢ currentData
```

Once we've tested the current character in `incomingItem` against all of the delimiters, we check to see if it matched any of them by looking at `myFlag`. If there is a match, we add the string built up in `currentData` to our list `outgoingList`. Otherwise, we simply append the current character `i` to the end of `currentData`. Once the loop is over, we add the remaining characters left to our list.

15.
```
    return outgoingList
  end goTokenize
```

With the loop completed, we're ready to return the list of tokenized items.

16.
```
on goOffsetInList(incomingList,
⇢ incomingItem)
```

Our function `goOffsetInList` receives two values when called: `incomingList` holds the list to be searched for the matching item `incomingItem`. This function replaces the `offset in list` command from ACME Script Widgets.

17.
```
    set outgoingPosition to 0
    set outgoingItem to ""
```

We start by clearing the variables we'll use to hold the position for an item that matches `incomingItem` and the value of the item right after the match.

18.
```
    repeat with i from 1 to number
    → of items in incomingList
        set incomingListItem to item
        → i of incomingList
        if contents of incomingItem
        → = contents of
        → incomingListItem then
            set outgoingPosition to i
            exit repeat
        end if
    end repeat
```

Now we loop through each item in the list incomingList, checking its contents for a match with the contents of incomingItem. If a match is found, we set outgoingPosition to the matching item's position and exit the loop.

19.
```
try
    if outgoingPosition>0 then set
    → outgoingItem to item
    → (outgoingPosition+1) of
incomingList
on error
end try
    return outgoingItem
end goOffsetInList
```

Finally, we see if a match was found by checking the value of outgoingPosition. If a match was found, we try to copy the value of the item right after the matching one to outgoingItem. Then we return the value.

20. Move your CGI application into the same folder as WebSTAR or whichever folder is the designated CGI folder for your web server software.

21. The URL for your CGI when it is in your server's root folder should be something like http://www.domain.com/ → script.acgi, where www.domain.com is your server's host name and script.acgi is the name of your script application. The actual URL depends on how your webserver is configured.

✔ Tip

■ To make your AppleScript work as a CGI, you must save the script as an application. It is best to save your application so that it stays open. By staying open, your CGI script application will run faster, since it won't have to be launched every time it's called.

Code 11.3 This script captures server variables and returns some of the values to the user as HTML.

```
on handle CGI request myURL
    of content type myContentType
    using access method myAccessMethod
    from user myUser
    using password myPassword
    referred by myReferrer
    from browser myBrowser
    from client IP address myAddress
    set crlf to  (ASCII character 13) &
    ⇢ (ASCII character 10)
set myHTML to "HTTP/1.0 200 OK" & crlf &
⇢ "Server: MacHTTP/2.0" & crlf &
⇢ "MIME-Version: 1.0" & crlf &
⇢ "Content-type: text/html" & crlf & crlf
    set myHTML to myHTML &
    ⇢ "<HTML><BODY><P>Your browser is " &
    ⇢ myBrowser
    set myHTML to myHTML & "<P>Referred to by
    ⇢ " & myReferrer & "</BODY></HTML>"
    return myHTML
end handle CGI request
```

Figure 11.5 Our browser displays the results of our CGI, `script.acgi`. This CGI returns the values of 2 server variables, browser type and referrer in the resulting HTML page shown. Here, we can see the user was using Netscape 4.04 on a PowerMac and came from the URL `http://www.somewhere.com/index.html`.

Scripting with ACME Script Widgets

This script requires the scripting addition ACME Script Widgets. See page 183.

Parsing server variables

Server variables offer untold power for customizing CGI results. Information like username, password, referrer URL, browser type, and client address are all delivered to the script by the server when you use the `handle CGI request` handler. This script (**Code 11.3**) shows how to get those values from the server and put them into variables you can use throughout a script. **Figure 11.5** shows the results of this script run as a CGI.

To parse server variables:

1. on handle CGI request myURL
       of content type myContentType
       using access method
       ⇢ myAccessMethod
       from user myUser
       using password myPassword
       referred by myReferrer
       from browser myBrowser
       from client IP address myAddress

   We begin our CGI handler by storing the content type of the data returned from a submitted form in myContentType, the access method of the form (either GET or POST) in myAccessMethod, the username of the client who sent the form in myUser, the user's password in myPassword, the referrer URL (or URL of the submitted form) in myReferrer, the client's browser type in myBrowser, and the client address in myAddress.

2. The remainder of the script simply prints out the variables we have found and sends them in a Web page back to the client, as we did in the previous spreads in this chapter. Of course, you will probably want to make more elaborate scripts that do some more stuff with these values, and we'll show you a few examples of that later in the book.

Returning content via redirection

Sometimes, rather than creating a large block of data to return from a CGI, the most efficient thing to do is to send the user to another URL as the result of the CGI, or even to run another CGI script.

We do this with URL redirection, which can be done in the CGI header, but in **Code 11.4** we'll do it simply by using an HTML META tag. **Figure 11.6** shows the browser results of this script run as a CGI with the form field "url" containing the value www.apple.com.

To return content via redirection:

1. We begin our CGI handler by capturing the post data value using with posted data and storing the value in mySearchArgs, as discussed in *Parsing form data* in this chapter.

2. set quote to ascii character 34

   For convenience, we store a quote character in the variable named quote so our code below can easily incorporate quotes into strings.

3. set myHTML to myHTML &
   → "<HTML><HEAD><META HTTP-EQUIV=
   → REFRESH CONTENT="&quote&"0;
   → URL=http://"&mySearchValue&quote&"
   → >"

   Next we add an HTML META tag to force the browser to redirect to the URL passed by the form field "url" in the post data and stored in the variable mySearchValue.

4. set myHTML to myHTML &
   → "</HEAD><BODY></BODY></HTML>"

   Then we add closing tags to the HTML.

Code 11.4 This script uses an HTML META tag to redirect the user to the URL passed in the form field "url".

```
on handle CGI request myURL
    with posted data mySearchArgs
    set myArgList to
    → (tokenize mySearchArgs with delimiters
    → {"&", "="})
    set mySearchValue to
    → (offset in list myArgList of "url" with
    → returning next item)
    set crlf to  (ASCII character 13) &
    → (ASCII character 10)
set myHTML to "HTTP/1.0 200 OK" & crlf &
→ "Server: MacHTTP/2.0" & crlf &
→ "MIME-Version: 1.0" & crlf &
→ "Content-type: text/html" & crlf & crlf
    set quote to ascii character 34
        set myHTML to myHTML &
        → "<HTML><HEAD><META HTTP-EQUIV=
        → REFRESH CONTENT="&quote&"0;
        → URL=http:// "&mySearchValue&quote&">"
        set myHTML to myHTML &
        → "</HEAD><BODY></BODY></HTML>"
return myHTML
end handle CGI request
```

Scripting with ACME Script Widgets

This script requires the scripting addition ACME Script Widgets. See page 183.

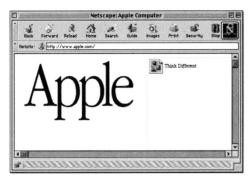

Figure 11.6 If we enter the value "www.apple.com" into the form field "url" that we send to our CGI, we'll end up being redirected to http://www.apple.com, as shown here.

5. `return myHTML`
   `end handle CGI request`
   Finally, we return the text to our Web server in the variable myHTML.

   Once again, save your script as an application and place it in the cgi folder of your web server as we have throughout this chapter.

✔ Doing it without ACME Script Widgets

■ **Code 11.2** shows how to tokenize data and get offsets in lists using functions instead of a scripting addition.

Returning content from other scriptable applications

Code 11.5 uses Finger to do a `whois` query on the InterNIC's domain name database to check on the status of a domain name passed by the calling form's field named "domain." The InterNIC holds the registry of domain names worldwide. This script will let you check on the availability of any domain name quickly. **Figure 11.7** shows the browser results for the domain name apple.com. You can use this script to finger any UNIX system!

This script illustrates the principle of integrating the features and capabilities of high-level AppleScriptable applications with CGIs.

To return whois query results from the InterNIC using Finger 1.5:

1. on handle CGI request myURL
        searching for mySearchArgs

We begin our CGI handler by capturing the reply string value with `searching for` and storing the value in mySearchArgs.

2. set myArgList to
   → (tokenize mySearchArgs with
   → delimiters {"&", "="})

Next, we convert the string into a series of items in a list, following the format: {name, value}.

3. set myDomainName to
   → (offset in list myArgList of
   → "domain" with returning next item)

Now we retrieve the value for the field "domain" using `offset in list` to give us the item following "domain," where its value is stored.

Code 11.5 This script queries the InterNIC whois server for domain name status and returns results in an HTML page.

```
on handle CGI request myURL
    searching for mySearchArgs
    set myArgList to (tokenize mySearchArgs
    → with delimiters {"&", "="})
    set myDomainName to
    → (offset in list myArgList of "domain"
    → with returning next item)
    tell application "Finger"
    set myResults to fetchurl
    → ("whois://rs.internic.net/"&myDomainName
    → as string)
    end tell

    set crlf to  (ASCII character 13) &
    → (ASCII character 10)
set myHTML to "HTTP/1.0 200 OK" & crlf &
→ "Server: MacHTTP/2.0" & crlf &
→ "MIME-Version: 1.0" & crlf &
→ "Content-type: text/html" & crlf & crlf
    set myHTML to myHTML &
    → "<HTML><BODY><P>InterNIC results: "
    set myHTML to myHTML &
    → (ACME replace return with "<BR>"&return
    → in myResults) & "</BODY></HTML>"
return myHTML
end handle CGI request
```

Scripting with ACME Script Widgets

This script requires the scripting addition ACME Script Widgets. See page 183.

Figure 11.7 If we enter the value "apple.com" into the form field "domain" that we send to our CGI, we'll end up getting the InterNIC domain record for Apple Computer's primary domain name, as shown here.

Scripting Finger

This script was designed and tested for Finger 1.5.

Finger is shareware. It costs $10.

Finger is written by Peter N. Lewis and is published by Stairways Software, which can be reached at `http://www.stairways.com/`.

4.
```
tell application "Finger"
    set myResults to fetchurl
    → ("whois://rs.internic.net/
    → "&myDomainName as string)
end tell
```
Next we get Finger to retrieve the results of a `whois` query to the InterNIC for the domain name passed in the variable `myDomainName`.

5.
```
set crlf to  (ASCII character 13) &
→ (ASCII character 10)
set myHTML to "HTTP/1.0 200 OK" &
→ crlf & "Server: MacHTTP/2.0" &
→ crlf & "MIME-Version: 1.0" &
→ crlf & "Content-type: text/html" &
→ crlf & crlf
```
We initialize a variable for our returned data with the CGI header to let the server know we're returning text as HTML.

6.
```
set myHTML to myHTML &
→ "<HTML><BODY><P>InterNIC
→ results: "
set myHTML to myHTML &
→ (ACME replace return with
→ "<BR>"&return in myResults) &
→ "</BODY></HTML>"
```
We add the InterNIC results to our variable myHTML, using ACME Script Widgets' ACME replace statement to substitute HTML breaks for Return characters. We do this to preserve paragraph breaks in the HTML so that it looks the same as the text received from the InterNIC server.

7.
```
return myHTML
end handle CGI request
```
Finally, we return the text to our Web server in the variable myHTML.

Sending partial replies with WebSTAR

WebSTAR supports extended communication between CGIs and itself with partial replies. With a partial reply, a CGI can begin returning data to the user before completing its operations. This technique, demonstrated in **Code 11.6**, offers users a sense of improved performance and keeps them occupied while we do some more work.

Figure 11.8 shows the browser results before the final data has been returned.

To send partial CGI replies with WebSTAR:

1. `on handle CGI request myURL`
    `searching for mySearchArgs`
    `with connection ID  myConnection`

We begin our CGI handler by capturing the reply string value with `searching for` and storing the value in `mySearchArgs`. We also store the unique ID for this connection with the server in `myConnection`. This unique ID is generated by the Web server software. We'll use it later to let WebSTAR know which connection to associate with the parts of our reply we'll send back.

2. `set myHTML to myHTML &`
    `→ "<HTML><BODY><P>InterNIC search`
    `→ in progress... <BR>"`

Once we have parsed the form data, as described in *Parsing form data* in this chapter, we go on to put some HTML together to let the user know things are happening.

3. `tell application "WebSTAR"`
    `send partial myHTML connection`
    `→ myConnection with more`
    `end tell`

Code 11.6 This script uses `send partial` to return partial results to WebSTAR before completing its execution.

```
on handle CGI request myURL
    searching for mySearchArgs
    with connection ID  myConnection
    set myArgList to (tokenize mySearchArgs
    → with delimiters {"&", "="})
    set myDomainName to
    → (offset in list myArgList of "domain"
    → with returning next item)
    set crlf to  (ASCII character 13) &
    → (ASCII character 10)
set myHTML to "HTTP/1.0 200 OK" & crlf &
→ "Server: MacHTTP/2.0" & crlf &
→ "MIME-Version: 1.0" & crlf &
→ "Content-type: text/html" & crlf & crlf
    set myHTML to myHTML &
    → "<HTML><BODY><P>InterNIC search in
    → progress... <BR>"
tell application "WebSTAR"
    send partial myHTML connection
    → myConnection with more
end tell
tell application "Finger"
    set myResults to fetchurl
    → ("whois://rs.internic.net/"&myDomainName
    → as string)
end tell
    set myHTML to (ACME replace return with
    → "<BR>"&return in myResults) &
    → "</BODY></HTML>" as string
return myHTML
end handle CGI request
```

Scripting with ACME Script Widgets

This script requires the scripting addition ACME Script Widgets. See page 183.

Figure 11.8 Using a partial reply, our CGI has sent back part of its results already, while it waits for the InterNIC to return more data that the CGI will return. In this way, we give the user some feedback while conducting the InterNIC search which can take some time.

Here we do a send partial to WebSTAR, returning HTML with the connection ID of our connection so WebSTAR knows which connection to associate the data with. We include the modifier with more to let WebSTAR know that more data is coming later and the connection shouldn't be closed.

4. tell application "Finger"
        set myResults to fetchurl
            → ("whois://rs.internic.net/
            → "&myDomainName as string)
    end tell

Next we use Finger to retrieve the results of a whois query to the InterNIC for the domain name passed in the variable myDomainName.

5. set myHTML to (ACME replace return
        → with "<BR>"&return in myResults)
        → & "</BODY></HTML>" as string

Now we use ACME Script Widgets' ACME replace statement to put HTML line breaks into the results instead of Return characters. We do this to preserve paragraph breaks in the HTML so that it looks the same as the text received from the InterNIC server.

6. return myHTML
    end handle CGI request

Finally, we return the text to our Web server in the variable myHTML.

Scripting WebSTAR

These scripts were designed and tested for WebSTAR 3.0.1.

WebSTAR is published by StarNine Technologies, who can be reached at http://www.starnine.com/.

SENDING PARTIAL REPLIES WITH WEBSTAR

Creating protected realms and users in WebSTAR

Our final script for this chapter, **Code 11.7**, demonstrates the creation and addition of password-protected directories, or *realms*, for WebSTAR. These settings will generate HTTP authentication prompts on the user's end when they access URLs that contain the realm's match string.

Figure 11.9 shows WebSTAR's password dialog with our new realm and user added.

To add a protected realm and user to WebSTAR:

1. ```
   set myRealm to "ADMINAREA"
   set myMatchString to "CLIENT-ADMIN"
   set myUser to "john"
   set myPassword to "test"
   ```

   We begin by setting some variables for our new realm, myRealm, its match string, myMatchString, and our user and password (myUser and myPassword).

2. ```
   tell application "WebSTAR"
   ```

   Now we're ready to talk to WebSTAR.

3. ```
   set myExistingRealms to realms
   ```

   We retrieve WebSTAR's current realm list using the application's property realms and store it in the variable myExistingRealms.

4. ```
   if myExistingRealms does not
   → contain (myRealm & return) then
       set realms to realms &
       → "REALM " & myMatchString
       → & " " & myRealm & return as
       → string
   end if
   ```

   Now we check to make sure the new realm myRealm doesn't already exist before adding it.

Code 11.7 This script adds a realm and user to WebSTAR.

```
┌─────────────── code ───────────────┐
    set myRealm to "ADMINAREA"

    set myMatchString to "CLIENT-ADMIN"

    set myUser to "john"

    set myPassword to "test"

tell application "WebSTAR"

    set myExistingRealms to realms

    if myExistingRealms does not contain
    → (myRealm & return) then

        set realms to realms & "REALM " &
        → myMatchString & " " & myRealm &
        → return as string

    end if

    set myExistingUsers to validate user
    → myUser password myPassword realm myRealm

    if myExistingUsers is false then

        add user myUser password myPassword
        → realm myRealm

    end if

end tell
```

Figure 11.9 After our script has added a new realm with a user and password, WebSTAR's Passwords window shows the new username, realm and password.

5. `set myExistingUsers to validate`
   `→ user myUser password myPassword`
   `→ realm myRealm`

Then we check to see if the user and password already exist for the realm.

6. `if myExistingUsers is false then`
   `    add user myUser password`
   `    → myPassword realm myRealm`
   `end if`
   `end tell`

If the user's not already defined, we create it with its password and realm association.

FILEMAKER PRO FOR HTML

FileMaker, Inc's (formerly Claris') FileMaker Pro was one of the first scriptable applications and is still one of the most useful. The very complete dictionary obeys the object model for syntax quite well, making it very powerful and easy to script.

Scripting FileMaker Pro as a data repository in conjunction with other applications is perhaps the most prevalent and productive use of AppleScript for the Internet. In this chapter, we'll explore the concept of creating a content database, with a simple event calendar example. In their most complete form, content databases can become all-encompassing entities that store an entire Web site's text as well as its graphics.

✔ CGI Tip

- FileMaker's built-in server, Tango for FileMaker from Everyware, or Lasso from Blue World Communications are faster Web connections to your FileMaker Pro database than an AppleScript CGI.

Scripting FileMaker Pro

For all of the following scripts that use FileMaker, we will refer to a single simple database, "Test Database," that we will create right now. It will be modeled as a simple event calendar database.

To get ready for the following AppleScripts for FileMaker:

1. Launch FileMaker Pro on your computer.

2. Choose New... from the File menu.

3. Click on the radio button labeled "Create a new empty file..." in the New Database window that appears. Now click the OK button. You'll be prompted to name and save your new database.

4. In the Define Fields window that appears, define some fields for the database as shown in **Figure 12.1**: "event title," "event description," "event location," and "event date." Be sure to create "event date" as a field of type date. Click the Done button when you're finished.

5. Now populate the database with at least a couple of records. **Figure 12.2** shows two records with sample data in them. The scripts that follow are written assuming that these records exist in the sample database.

6. We're ready to proceed with our scripts!

Figure 12.1 The Define Fields window with the sample database's fields already defined.

Figure 12.2 The sample database in FileMaker, shown with the two records you'll need to use the scripts that follow.

Scripting FileMaker Pro

All the scripts that follow were designed and tested for FileMaker Pro version 4.0v1.

These scripts should also work with version 3.x of FileMaker Pro.

FileMaker Pro is published by FileMaker, Inc., which can be reached at http://www.filemaker.com/.

Code 12.1 This script finds records in FileMaker Pro that meet the criteria defined in the show statement.

```
tell application "FileMaker Pro"
    activate
show (every record of database
→ "Test Database" whose cell "event date" >
→ "01/01/99")
    display dialog (count of records in
    → document "Test Database")
end tell
```

Figure 12.3 FileMaker Pro displays the found set of records in our sample database after our script has run.

Syntax issue: dealing with the found set of records versus all records

One peculiarity of FileMaker Pro that deserves special attention is that you need to specify whether you want to address only records in the current found set or all of the records in the database. Use the object *database* when you want to deal with all records. Use the object *document* when you want to deal only with the records in the current found set.

document records in current found set

database all records in database

Try changing *document* in line 3 of Code 12.1 to database to see the difference!

Finding records in a content database

What's more natural to do with a database than trying to find something contained within it? A script gives you some very powerful options for finding things, since you can search for values stored in variables and conduct custom searches conditionally, depending on different settings and states that AppleScript can read, like the current date.

Our first script (**Code 12.1**) finds records in our database that have values in the event date field greater than January 1st, 1999, or 1/1/99. You can run this script from the Script Editor window directly. You might open the Event Log window to see what goes on behind the scenes between AppleScript and FileMaker while the script is running. **Figure 12.3** shows what the database window in FileMaker will look like once we've run our find script.

To find some records in a content database:

1. `tell application "FileMaker Pro"`
   `activate`

   First, we need to let AppleScript know which application we want to speak to.

2. `show (every record of database`
   `→ "Test Database" whose cell`
   `→ "event date" > "01/01/99")`

   Now we tell FileMaker to find, or show, all of the records in the database that have values greater than January 1, 1999 in their event date field.

3. `display dialog (count of records`
   `→ in document "Test Database")`
   `end tell`

   Next we generate a dialog that displays the number of records FileMaker found.

Sorting the records in a content database

There are many reasons to want to sort your database, especially if your script is going to manipulate data from the database. Perhaps you'll want to take existing data and order it alphabetically or by date so that you can write a HTML file with everything in proper order.

Sometimes you may even want to sort your data by more than one field. You can do this very easily with FileMaker by using nested `sort` commands. FileMaker also makes it easy for you to reverse the order of your sort by using the modifier `in order descending`.

Code 12.2 will sort our database in descending order by date. You might try adding an `activate` command right after the `tell` so that you can watch FileMaker in action as the script is running. **Figure 12.4** shows our database in FileMaker, nicely sorted.

To sort the records in a content database:

1. `tell application "FileMaker Pro"`

   First, we need to let AppleScript know which application we want to speak to.

2. `show every record in database`
   `→ "Test Database"`

   Next, we ask FileMaker to find all records in the database so that our sort will apply to every record.

3. `sort database "Test Database"`
   `→ by field "event date" in order`
   `→ descending`
   `end tell`

   Finally, we get down to the matter at hand and sort our database's records. If we omit the `in order descending` modifier, FileMaker will default to sorting in ascending order.

Code 12.2 Sorting all of the records in a FileMaker Pro database.

```
tell application "FileMaker Pro"
    show every record in database
    → "Test Database"
    sort database "Test Database" by field
    → "event date" in order descending
end tell
```

Figure 12.4 FileMaker Pro displays the records in our database, nicely sorted after our sort script has run.

Different tricks for different scripts

There is another way to get data from FileMaker besides requesting one field, or cell, at a time, which can be slow.

If asked, FileMaker will return an entire record's data as a list, for example:

`set myList to record 1 of database "Test Database"`

However, you will then need a way of knowing which field is first and so on. If you know the order of the fields, then this isn't a problem.

Code 12.3 This script retrieves data from a FileMaker Pro database.

```
                    code
tell application "FileMaker Pro"
    show every record in database
    → "Test Database"
    sort database "Test Database" by field
    → "event date" in order descending
    set myInfo to ""
    repeat with i from 1 to count of records
    → in database "Test Database"
        set myInfo to myInfo & cell
        → "event title" of record i of
        → database "Test Database"
        set myInfo to myInfo &
        → "(" & cell "event date" of record i
        → of database "Test Database" & ")"
        → & return
    end repeat
    display dialog myInfo
end tell
```

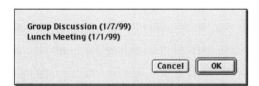

Figure 12.5 The dialog displayed by our script, showing the title and date for the two records in our database in the specified sort order.

Getting data from a record in a content database

Manipulating databases is all fine and dandy, but don't we really just want to get some data out of them to play with? Well, getting data out is just as easy as finding and sorting thanks to FileMaker's exquisite implementation of AppleScript.

We've seen how to find with show and sort with sort. Any guesses for a command to retrieve data? How about get? Who would have guessed?

In this quick script (**Code 12.3**) we'll expand on our sort script by including a repeat loop to traverse all records in the database in sort order and extract some data from their fields to display in a dialog. Of course, more exciting things like creating folders full of HTML files are not such a big step from here. But we'll save those tricks for another spread, *Merging data with templates to create HTML files*. **Figure 12.5** shows the product of our handiwork here, a lovely dialog populated with bits of sorted data.

To get data from a record in a content database:

1. set myInfo to ""

   After we have gotten and sorted the data as we covered in the previous spread, *Sorting records in a content database*, we need to create a string variable to hold the data that we'll request from FileMaker and eventually display. So first we initialize the variable myInfo by setting it to a null string.

2. repeat with i from 1 to count of
   → records in database
   → "Test Database"

   Our script begins its repeat loop here, filling the variable i with the next record incrementally from 1 to the number of records in our database.

3. `set myInfo to myInfo & cell`
   `→ "event title" of record i of`
   `→ database "Test Database"`

Hidden in this line of code is our first request to get data from FileMaker. The `set` command tells FileMaker to return the value of the cell from record number i.

4. `set myInfo to myInfo &`
   `→ "(" & cell "event date" of`
   `→ record i of database`
   `→ "Test Database" & ")" & return`

Again we retrieve another field of data from record i and add it to our variable `myInfo`.

5. `end repeat`

This statement closes our repeat loop and lets AppleScript know that it should increment the variable i and, if i is still less than or equal to the number of records, it can move its execution back up to the line after `repeat`.

6. `display dialog myInfo`
   `end tell`

Now we're ready to have AppleScript display the results of our loop by showing us the value stored in our variable `myInfo`.

Code 12.4 This script creates a new record in FileMaker and populates it with data.

```
                    code
tell application "FileMaker Pro"
   create record at end of database
   → "Test Database"
   set cell "event title" of last record of
   → database "Test Database" to
   → "New Meeting"
   set cell "event date" of last record of
   → database "Test Database" to "2/1/99"
end tell
```

Figure 12.6 Our database in FileMaker with its new record.

✔ Tips

■ If you know that you created the fields in Test Database in the order listed at the beginning of this chapter ("event title" first and "event date" fourth), you can replace steps 2 and 3 with this code to make your script faster:

```
create new record with data
→ {"New Meeting", "", "", "2/1/99"}
end tell
```

■ FileMaker Pro processes the single event of creating a new record much faster than the multiple events of creating a record and responding to a series of separate set commands.

Creating a new record in a content database

Now that we're masters at commanding FileMaker to find, sort, and give us existing data in our database, we'll want to teach it to add records to our database and populate them with fresh data (see **Code 12.4**). Then, our palette of basic FileMaker Pro tricks will be complete.

Figure 12.6 shows the database window in FileMaker with its new record once the script has run.

To create a new record in a database:

1. `tell application "FileMaker Pro"`

   As always, we need to let AppleScript know which application we want to speak to.

2. `create record at end of database`
   `→ "Test Database"`

   Now we ask FileMaker to create a new record at the end of the database.

3. `set cell "event title" of last`
   `→record of database "Test Database"`
   `to "New Meeting"`
   `set cell "event date" of last`
   `→record of database "Test Database"`
   `to "2/1/99"`
   `end tell`

   Next, we set the values in two of the fields of the new record, which we know is the last record in the database since we asked FileMaker to create it at the end of the database.

Merging data with templates to create HTML files

Perhaps the most powerful use of FileMaker for content production is creating HTML files by combining FileMaker data with template files. **Code 12.5** very gracefully works with any FileMaker database currently open. It searches a template file for database field names enclosed by number signs (#) and replaces them with the actual data from that field.

Figure 12.7 shows our template HTML file as viewed in Netscape, with database field name placeholder tags enclosed in number signs.

Figure 12.7 Our template HTML file as viewed in Netscape.

Code 12.5 This script merges FileMaker data with a template to produce HTML files.

```
set myTemplateFile to (choose file with prompt "Select HTML template:")
if (myTemplateFile as string) ends with ".html" then
    set myFileRef to (open for access myTemplateFile)
    set myTemplate to read myFileRef
    close access myFileRef
    tell application "FileMaker Pro"
        set myFields to name of every cell of layout 0
        set myRecordNumber to number of records
    end tell
    repeat with x from 1 to myRecordNumber
        set myHTML to myTemplate
        tell application "FileMaker Pro"
            set myCells to cellValue of every cell of record x of layout 0
        end tell
        repeat with myField in myFields
            set mySearch to ("#" & myField & "#") as string
            set myCell to item (offset in list myFields of myField) of myCells
            set myHTML to (ACME replace mySearch in myHTML with myCell)
        end repeat
        set myHTMLFile to (ACME replace ".html" in (myTemplateFile as string) with (x & ".html" as
        → string))
        set myFileRef to (open for access file myHTMLFile with write permission)
        write myHTML to myFileRef
        close access myFileRef
    end repeat
end if
```

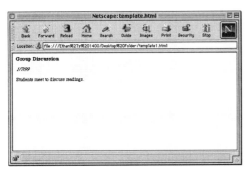

Figure 12.8 One of the HTML files produced by our script, showing field name tags replaced with actual data.

Making an HTML template file

You can make a template file in any text editor: SimpleText, BBEdit, Word, or any other program capable of saving a text-only file.

You can also create one in a visual HTML editor even more quickly than in a text editor.

1. In the text editor of your choosing, make a new file.

2. Create a set of minimal HTML tags, with a database field placeholder:

   `< HTML> < HEAD>`
   `< TITLE> Page Name</TITLE>`
   `< /HEAD>`
   `< BODY>`
   `< P> Data appears here: #event`
   `→ title#.`
   `< /BODY> < /HTML>`

3. Save your template file with a .html extension.

Figure 12.8 shows one of the HTML files produced by our script, with field name tags replaced with actual data.

To merge data with templates to create HTML files:

1. `set myTemplateFile to`
   `→ (choose file with prompt`
   `→ "Select HTML template:")`
   `if (myTemplateFile as string)`
   `→ ends with ".html" then`

   We begin by prompting the user to select a template HTML file. We test the file name to make sure it ends in .html before proceeding.

2. `set myFileRef to (open for`
   `→ access myTemplateFile)`
   `set myTemplate to read myFileRef`
   `close access myFileRef`

   Next, we load the contents of the template file into the variable myTemplate.

3. `tell application "FileMaker Pro"`
   `   set myFields to name of every`
   `→ cell of layout 0`
   `   set myRecordNumber to number`
   `→ of records`
   `end tell`

   Now we retrieve a list of the field names for the current database from FileMaker, as well as the number of records in the database.

4. `repeat with x from 1 to`
   `→ myRecordNumber`
   `   set myHTML to myTemplate`
   `   tell application "FileMaker`
   `→ Pro"`
   `      set myCells to cellValue`
   `→ of every cell of record`
   `→ x of layout 0`
   `   end tell`

   Here we begin a loop through each record of the database, initializing a variable to hold this record's HTML by loading the template contents into it. Next, we retrieve a list of all values for the fields of the current record.

5.
```
    repeat with myField in
  → myFields
      set mySearch to ("#" &
      → myField & "#") as string
```

Next, we loop through each field name in our list of fields. We set the variable `mySearch` to be our search string by adding number signs to the field name .

6. `set myCell to item (offset in list → myFields of myField) of myCells`

Now we retrieve the value from our database's field by looking for the position of the field name in the list of field names, called `myFields`. We use that same offset position to look up the value of the field in the list of field values in `myCells`. These two lists match up with each other, creating a name-value pair scheme across two lists.

7.
```
    set myHTML to
    → (ACME replace mySearch
    → in myHTML with myCell)
  end repeat
```

Finally, we use ACME Script Widgets' statement `ACME replace` to substitute the value of the current field for the placeholder text.

8.
```
    set myHTMLFile to
    → (ACME replace ".html" in
    → (myTemplateFile as string)
    → with (x & ".html" as string))
    set myFileRef to
    → (open for access file
    → myHTMLFile with write
    → permission)
    write myHTML to myFileRef
    close access myFileRef
  end repeat
end if
```

Once we've completed the loop through each field in the current record, we build our new HTML file name by adding the record number before the `.html` suffix.

Scripting with ACME Script Widgets

This script requires the scripting addition ACME Script Widgets. You must have ACME Script Widgets installed in your Scripting Additions folder for this script to work.

ACME Script Widgets adds the `offset in list` statement, which finds matches in lists, and the `acme replace` statement, a very useful string find-and-replace command.

ACME Script Widgets is shareware. It costs $29 for a single-user license.

ACME Script Widgets is published by ACME Technologies, which can be reached at `http://www.acmetech.com/`.

MICROSOFT WORD FOR HTML 13

Microsoft Word is one of the most ubiquitous applications around. Most everyone uses it and has their own opinions about it. Word has supported AppleScript for some time now, and Word 98 is no exception.

Word 98 is recordable, which places it in a small and exclusive group of applications, and offers us a solution to figuring out how to control Word with AppleScript. Got a trick you'd like to script? Simply perform the operations manually in Word while recording and you'll get executable AppleScript!

Since Microsoft has integrated Visual Basic for Applications into its product line, Word 98 uses this as its underlying scripting engine. The AppleScript support is still extensive, but some functions need to be written in VBA code. Word 98 supports this through the implementation of the do Visual Basic statement. While this is somewhat of an obstacle to simple scripting, Word 98 helps us out by being a recordable application.

Scripting Microsoft Word

All the scripts that follow were designed and tested for Word 98 only.

Since Word 98 really uses Visual Basic for Applications, the following scripts are not beautiful, but still quite powerful and functional.

Word 98 is published by Microsoft Corporation, which can be reached at http://www.microsoft.com/.

Screen shots reprinted by permission of Microsoft Corporation. Word 98 is a registered trademark of Microsoft Corporation.

Recording a script to modify type styles

We'll begin our AppleScripting of Word 98 by recording our actions in the application using the Script Editor's record mode. While doing this, we'll create a script that finds all bold text and makes it italic as well, as shown in **Code 13.1**.

Before we begin, it's a good idea to familiarize yourself with the steps below, since any mistakes you make while recording will be recorded as well.

To record a script in Microsoft Word 98:

1. Begin by launching Word 98 on your computer and creating a new window. Type in some text and style a few words as bold.

2. Now switch to the Script Editor and make a new script. Then click on the Record button in your new script's window.

3. Switch back to Word and choose Replace... from the Edit menu. Click on the More button and choose Any Character from the Special pull-down. Now choose Font... from the Format pull-down menu and select Bold from the Font Style list. Finally, tab to the Replace with field and choose Find What Text from the Special pull-down. Again choose Font... from the Format pull-down and select Italic from the Font Style list. When you're done, the window should look like **Figure 13.1**. Whew!

4. Now click the Replace All button. Your document should look like **Figure 13.2**.

Code 13.1 The fruits of our first script recording effort, which, thanks to Word 98, look very un-AppleScriptlike.

```
tell application "Microsoft Word"
    activate
    do Visual Basic
    → "    Selection.Find.ClearFormatting"
    do Visual Basic
    → "    Selection.Find.Font.Bold = True"
    do Visual Basic
    → "    Selection.Find.Replacement.
    → ClearFormatting"
    do Visual Basic
    → "    Selection.Find.Replacement.Font.
    →    Italic = True"
    do Visual Basic "    With Selection.Find
        .Text = \"^?\"
        .Replacement.Text = \"^&\"
        .Forward = True
        .Wrap = wdFindContinue
        .Format = True
        .MatchCase = False
        .MatchWholeWord = False
        .MatchWildcards = False
        .MatchSoundsLike = False
        .MatchAllWordForms = False
    End With"
    do Visual Basic "    Selection.Find.Execute
    → Replace:=wdReplaceAll"
end tell
```

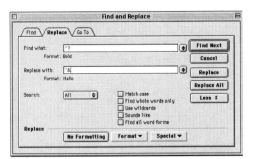

Figure 13.1 This Find and Replace window in Word 98 has been set up to find all bold characters and make them italic as well.

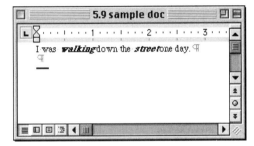

Figure 13.2 Our sample Word 98 document after the find-and-replace operation is complete.

5. Switch back to the Script Editor and click the Stop button. You should see some magical code appear in your window with lots of do Visual Basic statements in it.

6. Save your new script and thank your Mac for speaking AppleScript most of the time instead of VBA.

Modifying a recorded script for batch processing

In the previous section, we performed the simple and elegant act of recording a script in the Script Editor and were rewarded with the awful-looking syntax of Visual Basic for Applications (VBA), thanks to the double-edged sword of Word 98.

Now, we'll modify this script to create an AppleScript that will batch process folders of Word 98 documents and change styles as requested by the user (see **Code 13.2**).

To modify a recorded script for batch processing:

1. `on open myFolder`

   We begin by defining an on open handler to receive a reference in the variable myFolder to the folder dropped onto our script application from the Finder.

2. ```
   set findStyle to the button
   → returned of (display dialog
   → "Select a style to find" buttons
   → {"Bold", "Italic", "Cancel"}
   → default button "Cancel")
   set replaceStyle to the button
   → returned of (display dialog
   → "Select a style to add" buttons
   → {"Bold", "Italic", "Cancel"}
   → default button "Cancel")
   ```

   Next we prompt the user with a dialog for a style to find, either bold or italic, and store the choice in the variable findStyle. We then prompt the user for a style to replace the original with and store it in the variable replaceStyle.

3. ```
   tell application "Finder"
      set myFolderContents to list
      → folder myFolder without
      → invisibles
   ```

Code 13.2 A batch processing script for Word 98 that allows the user to choose which styles to search for and modify.

```
code
on open myFolder
   set findStyle to the button returned of
   → (display dialog "Select a style to find"
   → buttons {"Bold", "Italic", "Cancel"}
   → default button "Cancel")
   set replaceStyle to the button returned of
   (display dialog "Select a style to add"
   → buttons {"Bold", "Italic", "Cancel"}
   → default button "Cancel")
   tell application "Finder"
      set myFolderContents to list folder
      → myFolder without invisibles
      repeat with i in myFolderContents
         if kind of alias (myFolder & i as
         → text) is not "folder" then
            goReplace((myFolder & i as text),
            → findStyle, replaceStyle) of me
         end if
      end repeat
   end tell
end open


on goReplace(myFile, findStyle, replaceStyle)
   tell application "Microsoft Word"
      activate
      open myFile
      do Visual Basic "   Selection.Find.
      → ClearFormatting"
      do Visual Basic "   Selection.Find.
      → Font." & findStyle & " = True"
      do Visual Basic "   Selection.Find.
      → Replacement.ClearFormatting"
      do Visual Basic "   Selection.Find.
      → Replacement.Font." & replaceStyle &
      → " = True"
      do Visual Basic "   With Selection.Find
      .Text = \"^?\"
      .Replacement.Text = \"^&\"
      .Forward = True
      .Wrap = wdFindContinue
      .Format = True
      .MatchCase = False
      .MatchWholeWord = False
      .MatchWildcards = False
```

Code continues on next page

212

Code 13.2 *continued*

```
         .MatchSoundsLike = False
         .MatchAllWordForms = False
      End With"
      do Visual Basic "   Selection.Find.
      → Execute Replace:=wdReplaceAll"
      close front window saving yes saving in
      → myFile
   end tell
end goReplace
```

```
   repeat with i in myFolderContents
      if kind of alias (myFolder & i
      → as text) is not "folder" then
         goReplace((myFolder & i as
         → text), findStyle,
         → replaceStyle) of me
      end if
   end repeat
   end tell
end open
```

Now we're ready to get the list of items in the folder from the Finder, store the list in myFolderContents, and loop through the items, calling our function goReplace for each item.

4. on goReplace(myFile, findStyle,
→ replaceStyle)

Here we define our function goReplace and tell AppleScript that it takes three arguments.

5. tell application "Microsoft Word"
      activate
      open myFile

Now we let AppleScript know that we want to talk to Word and we tell Word to come to the front and open the file referred to by myFile.

6. do Visual Basic
→ " Selection.Find.ClearFormatting"

We send instructions to Word with the do Visual Basic statement followed by a Visual Basic command contained in quotes. In this case, we clear all formatting for the find string in the Find and Replace window.

7. do Visual Basic "
→ Selection.Find.Font." &
→ findStyle & " = True"

While not elegant-looking, this statement demonstrates how we can customize the VBA command sent by inserting variables into the string passed. In this

213

case, we pass the string from the variable findStyle as the style to be found.

8. do Visual Basic
→ "   Selection.Find.Replacement.
→ ClearFormatting"

Now we tell Word via VBA to clear all formatting for the replace string.

9. do Visual Basic
→ "   Selection.Find.Replacement.
→ Font." & replaceStyle & " = True"

Again we use a variable, replaceStyle, to customize our VBA command to Word, this time setting the style for the replace string.

10. do Visual Basic
→ "   With Selection.Find

    …

End With"
do Visual Basic
→ "   Selection.Find.Execute
→ Replace:=wdReplaceAll"

These two lines pass VBA commands to Word tell it to find any character and replace it with the same character, just styled differently, while also setting all other parameters for the find-and-replace operation. Without the magic of AppleScript recording, figuring out the syntax for this operation would be difficult, to say the least.

11. close front window saving yes
→ saving in myFile
end tell
end goReplace

Now we're ready to ask Word to close the document window and save it over the existing file referred to by myFile.

Figure 13.3 The new script in the Script Editor.

✔ Don't type all of this script

■ Make sure you've followed the instructions in *Recording a script to modify type styles* to record the majority of this script, which should look like **Figure 13.3**. Once your script looks correct in the Script Editor, save it as an application.

MODIFYING FOR BATCH PROCESSING

Batch exporting Word documents as HTML

One of the new and powerful features of Word 98 is its ability to save regular Word documents as HTML files.

We'll build on this feature with **Code 13.3** to make it possible to batch process entire folders of Word documents into HTML and save them in a separate directory.

Code 13.3 This script will process an entire folder of Word documents, converting them to HTML and saving them in a user-selected destination folder.

```
on open myFolder
    set myHTMLFolder to (choose folder with prompt "Select folder to save HTML into:")
    tell application "Finder"
        set myFolderContents to list folder myFolder without invisibles
        repeat with i in myFolderContents
            if kind of alias (myFolder & i as text) is not "folder" then
                saveHTML(myFolder, i as text, myHTMLFolder) of me
            end if
        end repeat
    end tell
end open


on saveHTML(myFolder, myFile, myHTMLFolder)
    set quote to ASCII character 34
    set myHTMLfilename to myHTMLFolder & myFile & ".html"
    tell application "Microsoft Word"
        activate
        open (myFolder & myFile as text)
        do Visual Basic "   ActiveDocument.SaveAs FileName:=" & quote & myHTMLfilename & quote & ",
        → FileFormat:=100,   _
        LockComments:=False, Password:=\"\", AddToRecentFiles:=True, WritePassword _
        :=\"\", ReadOnlyRecommended:=False, EmbedTrueTypeFonts:=False,   _
        SaveNativePictureFormat:=False, SaveFormsData:=False, SaveAsAOCELetter:= _
        False"
        close front window saving no
    end tell
end saveHTML
```

To batch export Word documents as HTML:

1. `set myHTMLFolder to (choose folder`
`→ with prompt "Select folder to`
`→ save HTML into:")`

We prompt the user to select the folder where they want the HTML files produced to be saved and store a reference to that folder in the variable myHTMLFolder.

2. `tell application "Finder"`

Now we let AppleScript know that we want to talk to the Finder.

3. `set myFolderContents to list folder`
`→ myFolder without invisibles`

We get a list of all items in our folder myFolder and store that list in myFolderContents.

4. `repeat with i in myFolderContents`

Then we begin a repeat loop, moving through the list of items in myFolderContents and loading each one into i.

5. `if kind of alias (myFolder & i as`
`→ text) is not "folder" then`
`    saveHTML(myFolder, i as text,`
`    → myHTMLFolder) of me`
`end if`
`end repeat`
`end tell`
`end open`

Finally, we test the kind of each item. If the item isn't a folder we pass it, along with its folder and the destination folder, to our function saveHTML.

6. `on saveHTML(myFolder, myFile,`
`→ myHTMLFolder)`

Here we define our function saveHTML as having three parameters: myFolder (the source folder), myFile (the source file name), and myHTMLFolder (the destination folder).

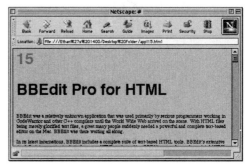

Figure 13.4 An HTML file produced by our script, as shown in Netscape.

7. `set quote to ASCII character 34`

Now we define a string variable, `quote`, to hold a quotation mark character.

8. `set myHTMLfilename to`
`→ myHTMLFolder & myFile & ".html"`

We set our variable `myHTMLfilename` to the full path for our destination file.

9. `tell application "Microsoft Word"`
`    activate`

Now we're ready to begin speaking to Word, bringing it to the front first of all.

10. `open (myFolder & myFile as text)`

We have Word open our source file.

11. `do Visual Basic`
`→ "    ActiveDocument.SaveAs`
`→ FileName:=" & quote &`
`→ myHTMLfilename & quote & ",`
`→ FileFormat:=100, _`
`LockComments:=False,`
`→ Password:=\"\",`
`→ AddToRecentFiles:=True,`
`→ WritePassword:=\"\",`
`→ ReadOnlyRecommended:=False,`
`→ EmbedTrueTypeFonts:=False, _`
`SaveNativePictureFormat:=False,`
`→ SaveFormsData:=False,`
`→ SaveAsAOCELetter:= _`
`        False"`

We pass Word this complicated Visual Basic command to have it save the current document as HTML (apparently FileFormat 100; this command was figured out the easy way—by recording the action of saving a document as HTML!) and specify the destination file with its full pathname contained in quotes in `myHTMLfilename`.

12. `close front window saving no`
`end tell`
`end saveHTML`

And finally we close the document window.

CYBERSTUDIO 14
FOR HTML

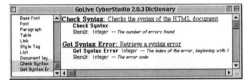

Figure 14.1 CyberStudio has some unique error-checking statements in its AppleScript dictionary.

GoLive CyberStudio is the only visual HTML editor that supports AppleScript in any meaningful way. Luckily, CyberStudio also happens to be a very sophisticated editor with impressive capabilities.

In this chapter, we'll look at controlling CyberStudio with AppleScript in order to globally modify text, fonts, and styles, add hypertext links to every occurrence of a string, do error checking, and convert selections to HTML tables. There are many more tasks that could be scripted in CyberStudio, so be sure to explore its AppleScript dictionary for possibilities.

CyberStudio's AppleScript dictionary includes a unique HTML extensions suite with statements like `style`, `heading`, `font`, `table`, `link`, and `list` that can be used to add tags around the current selection of HTML source code in CyberStudio.

`Check Syntax` and `Get Syntax Error` make it possible to perform sophisticated HTML error logging as well as checking and correction. **Figure 14.1** shows CyberStudio's dictionary entries for error checking.

Scripting GoLive CyberStudio

All the scripts that follow were designed and tested for CyberStudio 3.1.1.

These scripts should also work with version 2.x and 3.x of CyberStudio.

CyberStudio is published by GoLive Systems, Inc. which can be reached at `http://www.golive.com/`.

Modifying, styling, and hyperlinking text

With CyberStudio's `replace` command, it's easy to search a document for a matching string and replace it with new text, or to modify the string's HTML tags for font, size, and style. Both the `replace` and `find` statements match the current selection. This script (**Code 14.1**) replaces every instance of "Company" with "Company©" and then sets the new text's HTML tags for font, size, and style. **Figure 14.2** shows the Web page after the script has run.

To modify text, fonts, and styles for a search string:

1. `tell application "GoLive`
   `→ CyberStudio 3.1.1"`

   We begin by letting AppleScript know that we want to talk to CyberStudio.

2. `    set noneFlag to true`
   `    Go to Character 1`

   Next, we initialize a flag variable to test for successful replacements in the loop below. We also move the insertion point to the beginning of the document.

3. `    repeat until not noneFlag`

   Now we start a loop that runs until we stop having successful replacements, i.e. until the variable `noneFlag` that we're using below to check on the success of the replace is `false`.

4. `        set noneFlag to`
   `            → (Replace "Company" Using`
   `            → "Company&copy;")`

   Here we try to replace our search string with new text. CyberStudio returns a boolean value to indicate whether the string was found and replaced; this value is stored in the variable we set in step 1. Each time through the loop, each line of

Code 14.1 This script performs a search and replace, modifying the new text by adding a font face and size tag along with styles.

```
                    code
tell application "GoLive CyberStudio 3.1.1"
    set noneFlag to true
    Go to Character 1
    repeat until not noneFlag
        set noneFlag to (Replace "Company"
        → Using "Company&copy;")
        Font "Courier" Size 2
        Style {Bold, Italic}
    end repeat
end tell
```

Figure 14.2 The HTML page after the script has run, showing the modified text styles.

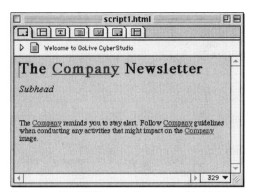

Figure 14.3 The HTML page after we've added linking to our script, showing the hyperlinked text.

text will be checked for our replacement string, and this variable will be set.

5.
```
        Font "Courier" Size 2
        Style {Bold, Italic}
    end repeat
end tell
```

Now we change the font, size, and style tags for the new text, and close up our repeat loop.

✔ Modify this script to also create hyperlinks

■ To hyperlink every occurrence of "Company" to the URL http://www.company.com/, add this line of code to the beginning of step 5:
```
Link "http://www.company.com/".
```

Figure 14.3 shows the Web page after hyperlinks have been added.

Logging errors for a folder of HTML files

CyberStudio has sophisticated HTML code error-checking. It also has AppleScript statements that allow your script to access these error-checking capabilities. This script (**Code 14.2**) uses these statements, Check Syntax and Get Syntax Error, to build a text file log of every HTML error in a folder full of HTML files. **Figure 14.4** shows the log file generated by a run of this script.

To log all errors for a folder of HTML files:

1. `set myFolder to (choose folder`
   `→ with prompt "Folder to log`
   `→ errors for:")`
   `set myNewFile to (new file)`

   We begin by prompting the user for a folder of HTML files to test, along with a log file name and folder location. If a file with the name given for the log file already exists, the statement `new file` will ask the user if they want to replace the existing file.

2. `set myFileRef to (open for access`
   `→ myNewFile with write permission)`
   `write "CyberStudio HTML Error Log`
   `→ for" & return to myFileRef`
   `write (myFolder as string) & return`
   `→ to myFileRef`

   Next, we open the new log file with write permission and write a header message to it including the path to the folder we're testing.

3. `set myFolderContents to list`
   `→ folder myFolder without`
   `→ invisibles`

   Now we retrieve a list of all files contained in the folder and store it in the variable myFolderContents.

Figure 14.4 The log file generated by a run of this script.

Code 14.2 This script generates a text file log of all HTML errors in a folder full of HTML files.

```
set myFolder to (choose folder with prompt
→ "Folder to log errors for:")
set myNewFile to (new file)
set myFileRef to (open for access myNewFile
→ with write permission)
write "CyberStudio HTML Error Log for" &
→ return to myFileRef
write (myFolder as string) & return to
→ myFileRef
set myFolderContents to list folder myFolder
→ without invisibles
tell application "GoLive CyberStudio 3.1.1"
    repeat with myFile in myFolderContents
        Open (myFolder & myFile as string)
        set myErrorCount to (Check Syntax)
        if myErrorCount > 0 then
            repeat with i from 1 to myErrorCount
                set myErrorCode to (Get Syntax
                → Error i)
                set myStatus to Status Line of
                → Document 1
                set mySelection to Selection of
                → Document 1
                set myLine to Line Index of
                → Document 1
                set myColumn to Column Index of
                → Document 1
                set myContents to (Contents of
                → Selection of Document 1)
                set myLength to number of
                → Characters in myContents
                Select Characters (myColumn -
                → myLength) thru (myColumn + 1)
                → of Line (myLine)
                set myActualSelection to (Contents
                → of Selection of Document 1)
```

Code continues on next page

Code 14.2 *continued*

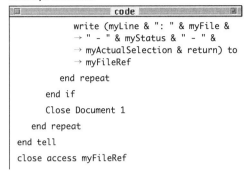

```
        write (myLine & ": " & myFile &
        → " - " & myStatus & " - " &
        → myActualSelection & return) to
        → myFileRef
      end repeat
    end if
    Close Document 1
  end repeat
end tell
close access myFileRef
```

4. `tell application`
`→ "GoLive CyberStudio 3.1.1"`
`  repeat with myFile in`
`  → myFolderContents`

Then we begin talking to CyberStudio and start a repeat loop through each file in the folder. Each time through the loop, the variable myFile will be set to the next item in the list myFolderContents.

5. `    Open (myFolder & myFile as`
`    → string)`

We have CyberStudio open the current file in the loop.

6. `    set myErrorCount to (Check`
`    → Syntax)`

The CyberStudio function Check Syntax returns the number of HTML syntax errors in the current open document; we store this number in myErrorCount.

7. `    if myErrorCount > 0 then`
`      repeat with i from 1 to`
`      → myErrorCount`

If we have any errors, we start a loop to collect some details about each error.

8. `      set myErrorCode to`
`      → (Get Syntax Error i)`
`      set myStatus to Status`
`      → Line of Document 1`
`      set mySelection to`
`      → Selection of Document 1`
`      set myLine to Line`
`      → Index of Document 1`
`      set myColumn to Column`
`      → Index of Document 1`
`      set myContents to`
`      → (Contents of Selection`
`      → of Document 1)`
`      set myLength to number`
`      → of Characters in myContents`

We collect a bunch of details for each error: the error code, an error description from CyberStudio's status line, and the position and length of the selected error.

9.
```
        Select Characters
        → (myColumn - myLength)
        → thru (myColumn + 1)
        → of Line (myLine)
        set myActualSelection
        → to (Contents of Selection
        → of Document 1)
```

Next, we adjust the selection to include tag brackets and store the selected string in myActualSelection.

10.
```
        write (myLine & ": "
        → & myFile & " - "
        → & myStatus & " - "
        → & myActualSelection
        → & return) to myFileRef
    end repeat
end if
```

Here we write a line to our log file. Each error found gets its own line in the log since we include a return character on the end of the string we write. Each line in the log contains the line number and file name for the found error, along with the description of the error and the code that generated the error.

11.
```
        Close Document 1
    end repeat
end tell
close access myFileRef
```

We close the document window once we've looped through every error in the current document. Once we've looped though all files in the folder, we close the log file and end our script.

Code 14.3 This script imports a tab-delimited file into the current document and converts it into a table.

```
                        code
set myTableFile to (choose file with prompt
 → "Tab-delimited file to import as table:")
tell application "GoLive CyberStudio 3.1.1"
    Find "#TABLE#"
    Insert file myTableFile
    Table Separator tab
end tell
```

Figure 14.5 The source code for our open document.

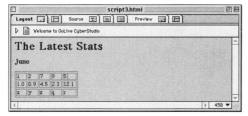

Figure 14.6 The document as it appears once our data has been imported and formatted.

Importing a tab-delimited file as a table

Excel, FileMaker, Word, and other programs can format their information for export with tabs separating the columns of data (this is known as a *tab-delimited file*). The script shown in **Code 14.3** has CyberStudio search an open document for a special tag, #TABLE#. It replaces this string with tabular data from a user-selected tab-delimited file and then converts the data to an HTML table. **Figure 14.5** shows the source code for our sample document. **Figure 14.6** shows the document after our data has been imported and formatted.

To import a tab-delimited file as a table:

1. `set myTableFile to (choose file → with prompt "Tab-delimited file → to import as table:")`

We begin by prompting the user to select a file to import as a table using the `choose file` operator.

2. `tell application → "GoLive CyberStudio 3.1.1" Find "#TABLE#"`

Next, we begin speaking to CyberStudio and have it find the special placeholder (#TABLE#) that indicates the insertion location for our new table. Note that the #TABLE# placeholder should be on its own line without any leading white space.

3. `Insert file myTableFile`

Now that CyberStudio has located and selected the special tag, we replace it with the contents of the user-selected file.

4. `Table Separator tab end tell`

Finally, we have CyberStudio convert the new data to a table, using the tab character as the delimiter between columns.

225

Converting styled text in the clipboard to HTML

This spread is not specific to CyberStudio, but CyberStudio is a useful place to take advantage of a great scripting addition called ClipboardToHTML by Donald Olsen. In **Code 14.4**, we'll copy styled text from a field in a FileMaker Pro database into the clipboard. From there, we'll use ClipboardToHTML to convert the clipboard's contents to HTML. Then, we'll paste the text into the current document in CyberStudio. This script could be expanded to insert styled text from many FileMaker records into a series of Web pages. **Figure 14.7** shows the styled text in our FileMaker database. **Figure 14.8** shows the results in CyberStudio's preview mode of running our script. The styles from our FileMaker text are preserved in the HTML!

To convert styled text from FileMaker Pro into HTML and paste it into CyberStudio:

1. ```
tell application "FileMaker Pro"
    activate
    go to cell "body text" of the
    → current record
```

   We begin by bringing FileMaker Pro to the front and selecting the text of our field named "body text." We must configure this field in FileMaker to select the entire contents of the field on entry so the go to command will select the entire field's contents.

2. ```
    copy
end tell
```

   Now we copy the selected text to the clipboard.

3. ```
tell application
    → "GoLive CyberStudio 3.1.1"
```

   Next, we begin talking to CyberStudio. We will call the scripting addition in the next

**Code 14.4** This script inserts styled text from a FileMaker Pro database field into a CyberStudio document, converting styles to HTML tags.

```
tell application "FileMaker Pro"
    activate
    go to cell "body text" of the current
    → record
    copy
end tell


tell application "GoLive CyberStudio 3.1.1"
    set myHTML to (convert the clipboard to
    → html returns as paragraphs true ¬
        underlines as raw HTML false ¬
        returning html to clipboard false ¬
        replacing bullets with "-")
    Activate Window 1
    Insert text myHTML
end tell
```

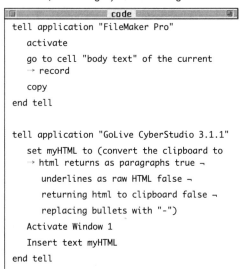

Figure 14.7 The styled text in our FileMaker database.

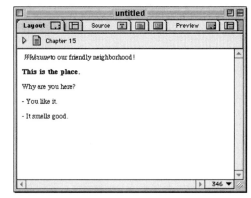

Figure 14.8 The results of running our script, shown in CyberStudio's preview mode.

CONVERTING STYLED TEXT TO HTML
```

line, but we need to switch applications first so that the clipboard gets properly updated. This is due to the fact that the Mac OS only updates the clipboard's contents when switching applications.

4.  ```
    set myHTML to (convert the
    ⇢ clipboard to html returns as
    ⇢ paragraphs true ¬
        underlines as raw HTML false ¬
        returning html to clipboard
        ⇢ false ¬
        replacing bullets with "-")
    ```
    Now we set our variable myHTML to the results of the convert the clipboard to HTML command made available by our scripting addition. We set the parameter returns as paragraphs to true to have the conversion change return characters to <P> tags. (We could also have set the returns as line breaks parameter to true to have the conversion change return characters to <BR> tags.) We also set underlines as raw HTML to false so that underlined text is not left alone and assumed to be raw HTML. If you want to include HTML tags in your styled text, however, setting this parameter to true will preserve any underlined HTML tags in the source text. We set the returning html to clipboard parameter to false to keep the conversion from putting its results in the clipboard. We set the replacing bullets parameter to replace bullet characters (Option-8) with dashes.

5.  ```
    Activate Window 1
        Insert text myHTML
    end tell
    ```
    Finally, we have CyberStudio insert the text stored in myHTML into the current document at the current insertion point.

✔ Tip

■ You can get details about all these parameters and what they do by consulting the documentation that comes with ClipboardToHTML.

Scripting with ClipboardToHTML

This script requires the scripting addition ClipboardToHTML. You must have ClipboardToHTML installed in your Scripting Additions folder for this script to work.

ClipboardToHTML adds the convert the clipboard to html command, which returns HTML-tag-encoded text of the clipboard's contents when the clipboard holds styled text.

ClipboardToHTML is freeware.

ClipboardToHTML is written by Donald Olsen.

CONVERTING STYLED TEXT TO HTML

QuarkXPress
for HTML and Images

The fact that QuarkXPress is AppleScriptable and has a very complete and useful dictionary may be one of the biggest reasons that AppleScript remains so popular and indispensable. Numerous publishing professionals have developed truly amazing AppleScripts that make Quark sit up, roll over, and beg.

In this chapter, we'll leave the desktop publishing depths of Quark scripting for others, and instead focus on some Internet-related uses for scripting QuarkXPress. We'll use Quark to create nicely formatted pages of HTML source code, useful for documenting a Web site. We'll also batch export pages as EPS images useful for rasterization in Photoshop. Finally, we'll batch export all text in a document for repurposing.

Scripting QuarkXPress

Quark's AppleScript dictionary is one of the most complete available for any application. Entire documents can be created from scratch via scripting.

Our Quark scripts will operate on the frontmost currently open document. Before we begin scripting with QuarkXPress, you'll need to create a new document and set it up to work with our first script. The steps below describe how to do this.

To get ready for the following AppleScript for XPress:

1. Launch Quark and create a new document by choosing New from the File menu (**Figure 15.1**).

2. Quark will display a dialog box to set the attributes of your new document, as shown in **Figure 15.2**. Make sure the Automatic Text Box checkbox is selected. Then click the OK button.

3. Save your new empty document. Be sure to leave it open. Now you're ready to script Quark!

Figure 15.1 Creating a new document in QuarkXPress.

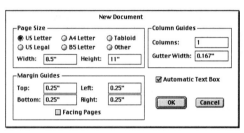

Figure 15.2 Setting the attributes of your new Quark document.

Scripting QuarkXPress

All the scripts that follow were designed and tested for QuarkXPress 3.31.

These scripts should also work with version 4 of XPress.

QuarkXPress is published by Quark, Inc., which can be reached at http://www.quark.com/.

SCRIPTING QUARKXPRESS

Figure 15.3 A view of some sample HTML as formatted by our script in Quark.

Importing and formatting HTML source code

QuarkXPress has very powerful text manipulation abilities, including the ability to selectively format paragraphs, words, and characters. One use of this feature is to create nicely formatted HTML source code that you can use to document your special HTML or JavaScript scripting techniques!

This script (**Code 15.1**) will prompt the user to select an HTML file to import and then proceed to style all HTML tags while leaving the rest of the text alone. **Figure 15.3** shows the results of running this script on a sample HTML file.

Code 15.1 This script will import an HTML file selected by the user into Quark and apply uniform styles to all HTML tags contained in the text.

```
set myFile to (choose file "Select an HTML file:")
set myFileRef to (open for access myFile)
set myFileContents to (read myFileRef)
close access myFileRef

tell application "QuarkXPress™"
   activate
   tell story 1 of text box 1 of page 1 of document 1
      set contents of it to myFileContents
      set font to "Times"
      set size of every word to 12
      set tagFlag to false
      set tagEndFlag to true
      repeat with i from 1 to count of characters
         if character i is equal to "<" then
            set tagFlag to true
            set tagEndFlag to false
         else
            if character i is equal to ">" then set tagEndFlag to true
         end if
         if tagFlag then
            set style of character i to bold
            set font of character i to "Helvetica"
            if tagEndFlag then set tagFlag to false
         end if
      end repeat
   end tell
end tell
```

To import and format HTML source code:

1. ```
set myFile to (choose file "Select
→ an HTML file:")
```
   First we prompt the user to select an HTML file to bring into Quark and store a reference to the file in the variable myFile.

2. ```
set myFileRef to (open for access
→  myFile)
```
   Next, we tell AppleScript to open the file and store the returned file reference number in the variable myFileRef.

3. ```
set myFileContents to
→ (read myFileRef)
```
   Now we read the entire file contents into the variable myFileContents.

4. ```
close access myFileRef
```
   Then we tell AppleScript to close the file referred to by myFileRef.

5. ```
tell application "QuarkXPress™"
    activate
```
   Now we tell Quark to come to the front.

6. ```
tell story 1 of text box 1 of
→ page 1 of document 1
```
   Using Quark's extensive dictionary support, we hone in on the target of our commands by directly addressing the story of our document.

7. ```
set contents of it to
→ myFileContents
set font to "Times"
set size of every word to 12
```
   Next we set the contents of the story to myFileContents and also set the font and point size of the whole story. Because we are inside a tell statement directed to the store object on the first page (see step 6), we can access the properties of the story by referencing the constant it,
```

which holds a reference to the current target of the tell statement.

8.
```
set tagFlag to false
set tagEndFlag to true
```
We're now ready to initialize our script's variables. We'll use these variables to keep track of whether we're looking at an HTML tag in the story or not.

9.
```
repeat with i from 1 to count of
→ characters
```
Now we'll loop through all characters in the story.

10.
```
if character i is equal to "<" then
    set tagFlag to true
    set tagEndFlag to false
```
We test the current character to see if it's an opening HTML tag, "<". If it is, we set our variables accordingly to make sure the code below restyles this character and all following characters properly.

11.
```
else
    if character i is equal to ">"
    → then set tagEndFlag to true
end if
```
If the current character isn't an opening tag, "<", is it a closing one, ">"? If so, we set our variable to make sure this last tag character is still properly styled, but subsequent characters are not.

12.
```
if tagFlag then
    set style of character i to bold
    set font of character i to
    → "Helvetica"
    if tagEndFlag then set tagFlag
    → to false
```
This final if... then statement styles the current character if and only if the code in step 6 has found that an HTML tag has started and set the tagFlag variable to true.

✔ Having Quark make a new document

■ To have Quark automatically create a new document, rather than rely on our example document, add this line to end of step 5, right after activate:

make new document at beginning

Exporting all pages in a document as EPS files

There are times when you find yourself facing a seemingly insurmountable task, like creating EPS files from a 100-plus-page Quark document for later conversion to individual Web graphics. Just such a task.

We'll start to chip away at this waste of our good time with **Code 15.2** that exports every page in the currently open Quark document as an EPS file to a folder of the user's choosing. These EPS files can then be batch processed in a program like Adobe Photoshop or Macromedia FreeHand. **Figure 15.4** shows a Finder window with the fruits of our script's processing a small (three-page) Quark document.

To export all pages in a document as EPS files:

1. ```
set myFolder to (choose folder with
→ prompt "Select a folder to save
→ EPS files in:")
```
   We begin by prompting our user for a folder destination for the EPS files produced.

2. ```
tell application "QuarkXPress™"
    activate
```
   Now we're ready to speak with Quark.

3. ```
repeat with i from 1 to count of
→ pages in document 1
```
   We'll loop through each page in the current document with this repeat.

4. ```
tell document 1
    save page i in (myFolder & i as
    → text) EPS format "Mac Color"
    → EPS data "binary EPS"
```
   For each page in the current document, we tell Quark to save the page as a binary Macintosh color EPS file. To help identify the files, we name each file with the current page number i.

Code 15.2 This script will save each page in the currently open Quark document as a separate EPS file.

```
set myFolder to (choose folder with prompt
→ "Select a folder to save EPS files in:")
tell application "QuarkXPress™"
    activate
    repeat with i from 1 to count of pages in
    → document 1
        tell document 1
            save page i in (myFolder & i as
            → text) EPS format "Mac Color" EPS
            → data "binary EPS"
        end tell
    end repeat
end tell
```

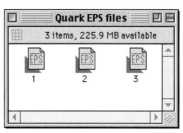

Figure 15.4 A Finder window displaying the three new EPS files that our script produced by processing a three-page Quark document.

Code 15.3 This script saves all text in the current document as plain text.

```
                  code
set myFolder to (choose folder with prompt
→ "Select a folder to save text into:")
tell application "QuarkXPress™"
   activate
   repeat with i from 1 to count of stories
of document 1
      save story i of document 1 in
      → (myFolder & i as text)
   end repeat
end tell
```

Code 15.4. This script saves all text in the current document with XPress Tags.

```
                  code
set myFolder to (choose folder with prompt
→ "Select a folder to save text into:")
tell application "QuarkXPress™"
   activate
   repeat with i from 1 to count of stories
   → of document 1
      save story i of document 1 in
      → (myFolder & i as text) as "TEXT"
   end repeat
end tell
```

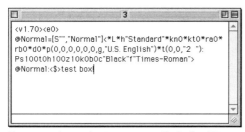

```
                  3
<v1.70><e0>
@Normal=[S"","Normal"]<*L"h"Standard"*kn0*kt0*ra0*
rb0*d0*p(0,0,0,0,0,0,g,"U.S. English")*t(0,0,"2  "):
Ps100t0h100z10k0b0c"Black"f"Times-Roman">
@Normal:<$>test box|
```

Figure 15.5 A sample story exported including XPress Tags.

✔ Tip

- A more elaborate script might manipulate the exported text with included tags in BBEdit to produce formatted HTML from these text files.

Exporting all text from a document

These scripts export each story in the current Quark document to a new text file in a user-selected folder. **Code 15.3** saves each story as plain text, while **Code 15.4** has Quark save each story with XPress Tags. **Figure 15.5** shows what a sample story exported with XPress Tags by **Code 15.4** looks like.

To export all text from a document:

1. ```
   set myFolder to (choose folder with
   → prompt "Select a folder to save
   → EPS files in:")
   ```
   We begin by prompting the user to select a destination folder for our text files.

2. ```
   tell application "QuarkXPress™"
      activate
   ```
   Next we tell Quark to come to the front.

3. ```
   repeat with i from 1 to count of
   → stories of document 1
      save story i of document 1 in
      → (myFolder & i as text)
   end repeat
   end tell
   ```
   Now we begin our repeat loop, continuing through each story in the current document and saving each to our destination folder as text only, without XPress Tags

4. ```
   .save story i of document 1 in
   → (myFolder & i as text) as "TEXT"
   ```
   Code 16.4 is identical to **16.3**, except for one key change in the save statement. In **16.4**, we specify to Quark that we want to save each file as "TEXT". By specifying "TEXT" as the file type, we tell Quark that we want each story saved as text including XPress Tags. If you omit the file type specification, the text will be exported as plain text.

CLIP2GIF AND GIFBUILDER FOR IMAGES

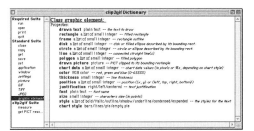

Figure 16.1 The dictionary entry for clip2gif's graphic element object class.

clip2gif? If you're not already a diehard AppleScripter, you probably haven't heard of this application before. clip2gif is the freeware Swiss Army knife of scriptable bitmap graphics applications. It can open and save TIFF, PICT, GIF, and JPEG images. With it, you can script the creation of lines, polygons, rectangles, circles, text, and four types of charts—pretty amazing for freeware.

Along with clip2gif, the generous Swiss programmer Yves Piguet has also given the world GifBuilder, which scripts the creation of animated GIF files for use on the World Wide Web.

clip2gif's **save** statement has one extremely important and deep object known as **drawing**. The **drawing** object is composed of a big list of graphic elements, each with its own subproperties.

Figure 16.1 shows clip2gif's dictionary entry for its graphic element object class.

Scripting clip2gif and GifBuilder

All the scripts that follow were designed and tested for clip2gif 0.7.2 and GifBuilder 0.5.

clip2gif and GifBuilder are freeware.

clip2gif and GifBuilder are published by Yves Piguet, who can be reached at
`http://iawww.epfl.ch/Staff/Yves.`
`▸ Piguet/clip2gif-home/`.

Creating and exporting graphical text in clip2gif

Your script has total control of font, size, color, and justification, thanks to clip2gif's complete AppleScript dictionary.

The script shown in **Code 16.1** creates some graphical text in clip2gif and exports it as a GIF file. **Figure 16.2** shows the drawing window in clip2gif after our script has created drawn text.

To create and export graphical text with clip2gif:

1. ```
   save {200, 100} in window drawing
   → {{drawn text:"Graphical text is
   → easy with clip2gif.",
   → position:{0, 0, 200, 100},
   → font:"Helvetica",
   → justification:center,
   → style:{bold, italic},
   → size:20, color:{65535, 0, 0}}}
   ```

   Here we send clip2gif one very long and powerful statement that instructs it to create a new window 200 x 200 pixels in size with a drawing in it. This drawing is defined as a record with properties that we set as follows: drawn text is the text to display; position (top, left, bottom, right) defines the coordinates to draw the text into; and font, justification, style, size, and color (red, green, blue) all define attributes of the drawn text.

2. ```
   save window 1 as GIF in file
   → (myFolder & "text.gif" as text)
   → scale 50 depth 8 with dithering
   → without transparency
   ```

   We then have clip2gif save our new drawing window as an 8-bit non-transparent GIF with dithering.

3. ```
   close window 1
   end tell
   ```

   Finally, we end our conversation.

Code 16.1 This script creates graphical text in clip2gif and exports it as a GIF.

```
                    code
set myFolder to (choose folder with prompt
→ "Select folder to save image:")
tell application "clip2gif"
    save {200, 100} in window drawing ¬
        {{drawn text:"Graphical text is easy
        → with clip2gif.", position:{0, 0,
        → 200, 100}, font:"Helvetica",
        → justification:center, style:{bold,
        → italic}, size:20, color:{65535, 0,
        → 0}}}
    save window 1 as GIF in file (myFolder &
        → "text.gif" as text) scale 50 depth 8
        → with dithering without transparency
    close window 1
end tell
```

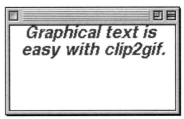

Figure 16.2 Drawn text in a new drawing window in clip2gif.

✔ Tip

■ The one thing that is difficult to do with clip2gif is create antialiased text. This requires an additional scripting trick we'll cover here in step 3. The trick is to draw the text at twice the desired size and then scale it to 50%, antialiasing the graphic by reducing it. When doing this, you need to remember to draw the text twice as big as you want it to be in its final size.
```

Code 16.2 This script creates a filled pie chart with four segments in a new window; each segment is assigned its own value and color.

```
code
tell application "clip2gif"
    activate
    set color1 to {0, 32768, 0}
    set color2 to {50000, 0, 0}
    set color3 to {32768, 65535, 0}
    set color4 to {0, 0, 65535}
    save {200, 200} in window drawing ¬
        {{chart data:{50, color1, 125, color2,
        ¬ 200, color3, 25, color4},
        ¬ chart style:pie, position:
        ¬ {0, 0, 200, 200}}}
end tell
```

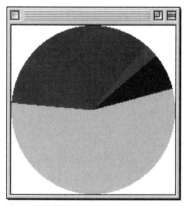

Figure 16.3 The drawing window that Code 16.2 generates.

Creating graphical charts

Creating graphical charts in clip2gif is very easy if you have a data set to use. Your script can specify one of four different chart types: lines, bars, filled pies and empty pies.

In **Code 16.2**, we'll create a filled pie chart, since it's the most impressive of the four choices. **Figure 16.3** shows the results of our script, a new drawing window with a color pie chart.

To create graphical charts with clip2gif:

1. `tell application "clip2gif"`
   `activate`

   We begin by letting AppleScript know we want to speak with clip2gif.

2. `set color1 to {0, 32768, 0}`
   `set color2 to {50000, 0, 0}`
   `set color3 to {32768, 65535, 0}`
   `set color4 to {0, 0, 65535}`

   We define four variables to hold color properties in list form {red, green, blue}. Each channel of color can hold a value from 0 to 65535. For example, color4, which is set to {0,0,65535}, is maximum blue.

3. `save {200, 200} in window drawing`
   `{{chart data:{50, color1, 125,`
   `→ color2, 200, color3, 25,`
   `→ color4}, chart style:pie,`
   `→ position:{0, 0, 200, 200}}}`
   `end tell`

   Now we're ready to send a single powerful `save` command to clip2gif that generates a new window 200 x 200 pixels in size with a pie chart comprised of four segments. Notice in the `chart data` subrecord how we define each segment of the pie with its value and color? This is all we need to do, so we end our conversation with clip2gif.

CREATING GRAPHICAL CHARTS

239

Converting images to GIFs with adaptive palettes

clip2gif was born to convert images to GIF files. It can open PICT, TIFF, or JPEG files or access images on the clipboard and then save them as GIF files with interlacing, transparency, and color palettes of any depth up to 8 bits.

Code 16.3 demonstrates how to easily convert images using clip2gif to pick the best palette. For a more elaborate use of a custom palette defined in the script, see **Code 16.4**.

To convert files to GIF format with adaptive palettes:

1. `set myFile to (choose file with`
   `→ prompt "Select PICT/TIFF/JPEG to`
   `→ convert:")`
   `tell application "clip2gif"`

   We prompt the user to select an image file to convert and store a reference to the file in the variable `myFile`.

2. `save myFile as GIF in file (myFile`
   `→ & ".gif" as text) ¬`
   `depth 8 colors palette input colors`
   `→ scale 100 with interlacing`
   `→ without transparency`
   `end tell`

   Here we send clip2gif a command to open the file referred to by `myFile` and re-save it as a GIF with the same name plus the suffix `.gif`, using an 8-bit (`depth 8 colors`) adaptive color palette with interlacing and no transparency.

Code 16.3 Converting image files to GIFs is easy with clip2gif and AppleScript.

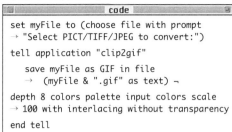

```
set myFile to (choose file with prompt
 → "Select PICT/TIFF/JPEG to convert:")
tell application "clip2gif"
   save myFile as GIF in file
    → (myFile & ".gif" as text) ¬
depth 8 colors palette input colors scale
 → 100 with interlacing without transparency
end tell
```

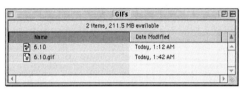

Figure 16.4 Icons for our original file and new GIF file in the Finder.

Controlling the Color Palette

The most complicated aspect of exporting an image as a GIF from clip2gif is controlling the color palette. clip2gif offers four options for defining your GIF's color palette:

◆ System colors (uses Apple's 256-color System colors)

◆ Gray shades (uses 4, 8, 16, or 256 shades of gray depending on the depth setting)

◆ Input colors, also known as the adaptive palette (clip2gif will attempt to create the best palette it can for the image at hand)

◆ A custom palette defined by a list of colors, with each color defined by the sublist {red, green, blue}

Code 16.4 This script builds the Web-safe color palette and then converts a user-selected file to a GIF using this palette.

```
                       code
set myFile to (choose file with prompt
→ "Select PICT/TIFF/JPEG to convert:")
set myColorPalette to {}
repeat with myRed from 0 to 5
    repeat with myGreen from 0 to 5
        repeat with myBlue from 0 to 5
            set myColorPalette to myColorPalette
            → & {{myRed * 13107, myGreen *
            → 13107, myBlue * 13107}} as list
        end repeat
    end repeat
end repeat
tell application "clip2gif"
    save myFile as GIF in file (myFile &
    → ".gif" as text) colors palette
    → myColorPalette depth 8 with interlacing
    → without transparency
end tell
```

Converting images to GIFs with the Web-safe palette

clip2gif's GIF conversion function can be very powerful if you define your own palette, especially if you are trying to create graphics that only use the 216 Web-safe colors, sometimes known as the Netscape palette.

To define your own palette, you must specify it as a list of {red, green, blue} values ranging from 0 to 65535. At first, it might seem like an onerous task to define all 216 colors in the Web palette within your script. However, all 216 colors follow a very simple mathematical rule that makes it easy to build the palette-defining list on the fly within a script. The rule is as follows: Each channel (red, green, and blue) has six fixed values (0%, 20%, 40%, 60%, 80% and 100%). On the scale of 0 to 65535, these percentages work out to be increments of 65535 divided by 5, or 13107.

Our fancy Web-safe GIF converting script (**Code 16.4**) builds this table in three nested repeat loops. **Figure 16.5** shows how the converted GIF is forced into the Web safe palette.

To convert files to GIF format with the Web-safe palette:

1. `set myColorPalette to {}`

   We initialize a variable `myColorPalette` as an empty list variable.

2. `repeat with myRed from 0 to 5`
   `    repeat with myGreen from 0 to 5`
   `        repeat with myBlue from 0 to 5`

   Now we're ready to create our three repeat loops, one for each color channel, nested inside of each other.

3. `set myColorPalette to`
    → `myColorPalette & {{myRed * 13107,`
    → `myGreen * 13107, myBlue * 13107}}`
    → `as list`
`end repeat`
    `end repeat`
`end repeat`

For each iteration of the loops, we store a list of the form {red, green, blue} within the overall list that defines our palette.

4. `tell application "clip2gif"`
`save myFile as GIF in file`
    → `(myFile & ".gif" as text)`
    → `colors palette myColorPalette`
    → `depth 8 scale 100 with interlacing`
    → `without transparency`
`end tell`

Our single statement to clip2gif instructs it to open the file referred to by `myFile` and resave it as an 8-bit (256-color) interlaced GIF using our Web-safe color palette with a 100% scale and no transparency.

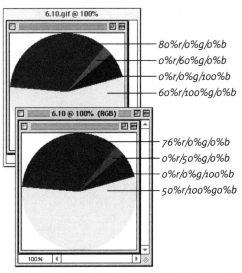

Figure 16.5 A comparison between the original PICT file with its color values and the Web-safe GIF after conversion by Code 16.4.

CONVERTING IMAGES TO GIFS

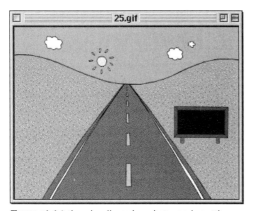

Figure 16.6 A thumbnail produced at a scale setting of 50%.

Making interlaced framed GIF images

Our last exercise with clip2gif gives us a drag-and-drop script application that will process an entire folder of images in any format clip2gif can open (TIFF, PICT, JPEG, or GIF) and save copies as scaled and interlaced GIFs with a 1-pixel black frame around each image.

This script, shown in **Code 16.5**, can be used to quickly produce thumbnails of images for a Web page. **Figure 16.6** shows a thumbnail produced at a scale setting of 50%.

Code 16.5 This script can be used to quickly produce thumbnails of images saved as GIFs for use on a Web page.

```
on run
    set myFolder to (choose folder with prompt "Select folder to create thumbnails from:")
    makeThumb(myFolder)
end run


on open myFolder
    makeThumb(myFolder)
end open


on makeThumb(myFolder)
    set myThumbFolder to (choose folder with prompt "Select folder to save thumbnails to:")
    set myScale to text returned of (display dialog "Set scale:" default answer "50")
    set myFolderList to list folder myFolder without invisibles
    tell application "clip2gif"
        repeat with myFile in myFolderList
            set mySize to measure file (myFolder & myFile as text)
            save file (myFolder & myFile as text) as GIF in file (myThumbFolder & myFile & ".gif" as
            → text) ¬
                colors palette input colors drawing {{frame:{0, 0, (item 1 of mySize)*(myscale/100),
                → (item 2 of mySize)*(myscale/100)}}} ¬
                depth 8 scale myScale with interlacing without transparency
        end repeat
    end tell
end makeThumb
```

To make interlaced framed GIF images with clip2gif:

1. `on run`

In this case we begin by covering our bases with an `on run` handler in case the user double-clicks the script application instead of dropping a folder onto it.

2. `set myFolder to (choose folder with`
`→ prompt "Select folder to create`
`→ thumbnails from:")`

We prompt the use to select a folder and store a reference to the folder in `myFolder`.

3. `makeThumb(myFolder)`
`end run`

Now we call our handler `makeThumb`, passing it the reference for our folder.

4. `on open myFolder`
`    makeThumb(myFolder)`
`end open`

Here we define our `on open` handler to receive the reference to the folder dropped on the script application's icon in the Finder. We then pass this reference, stored in `myFolder`, to our function `makeThumb`.

5. `on makeThumb(myFolder)`

We begin our function by defining any parameters it will receive. In this case, `myFolder` receives the folder reference passed to it by one of the handlers above.

6. `set myThumbFolder to (choose`
`→ folder with prompt "Select folder`
`→ to save thumbnails to:")`

Now we prompt the user to select a destination folder and store it in `myThumbFolder`.

7. `set myScale to text returned of`
`→ (display dialog "Set scale:"`
`→ default answer "50")`

Then we prompt the user to enter a scale value for the thumbnailing process and store it in `myScale`.

8. ```
set myFolderList to list folder
→ myFolder without invisibles
```
We get the list of items in the folder `myFolder`.

9. ```
tell application "clip2gif"
```
Now we let AppleScript know we want to talk to clip2gif.

10. ```
repeat with myFile in myFolderList
```
After switching to clip2gif, we begin our repeat loop to cycle through all the items contained in `myFolderList`.

11. ```
set mySize to measure file
→ (myFolder & myFile as text)
```
Here we ask clip2gif to return the dimensions of the current file as a item pair {width, height} and store this in `mySize`.

12. ```
save file (myFolder & myFile as
→ text) as GIF in file
→ (myThumbFolder & myFile & ".gif"
→ as text) ¬
colors palette input colors drawing
→ {{frame:{0, 0, (item 1 of mySize)
→ *(myscale/100), (item 2 of mySize)
→ *(myscale/100)}}} ¬
depth 8 scale myScale with
→ interlacing without transparency
end repeat
end tell
end makeThumb
```
Finally, we're ready to issue the big command to clip2gif to save a copy of our current file as an interlaced, non-transparent 8-bit GIF with an adaptive palette. We save it to a new file in the destination folder `myThumbFolder` with the suffix `.gif`. We also sneak in a quick frame sized to the current image using the `drawing` record.

## ✔ Make it drag and drop!

■ This script can be run from the Script Editor, but to make it an easy-to-use drag-and-drop application, it should be saved as an application with the Never Show Startup Screen option selected. See Chapter 3 for details on ways of saving scripts.
```

Creating animated GIFs of moving text

GifBuilder can be scripted to create new GIF animations from scratch as long as you have images to supply as individual frames of the animation. The source for these images could be saved files in a folder or graphics copied onto the clipboard from any scriptable graphics application. We'll take the latter approach in this script (**Code 16.6**), where we'll use clip2gif to create graphics on the fly, store them as pictures in a variable, and pass them to GifBuilder, where we'll create a frame at a time.

✔ Look at the Event Log this time

■ Try running this script from the Script Editor with the Event Log window open and watch how AppleScript handles picture data in a variable without even so much as a hiccup.

Code 16.6 This script automatically produces an animated GIF of flying text using both clip2gif and GifBuilder.

```
set myFolder to (choose folder with prompt "Save animation in:")
tell application "GifBuilder"
   new
   set background color to {65535, 65335, 65535}
   set depth to 8
   set loop to 0
   set interlacing to false
   set dithering to false
   repeat with i from 1 to 10
      tell application "clip2gif"
         set myImage to (save {100, 100} in picture drawing ¬
            {{drawn text:"Hi!", position:{i * 10, 50}, font:"Helvetica", size:36, color:{0, 65535,
            ⇥ 0}}})
      end tell
      make new frame at end with data {contents:myImage, transparency:no, disposal method:restore
      ⇥ to background, interframe delay:10}
   end repeat
   save in file (myFolder & "animation.gif" as text)
end tell
```

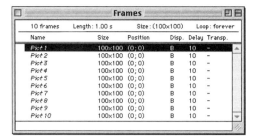

Figure 16.7 The Frames window in GifBuilder as it appears after our script has run.

Figure 16.8 The Preview window in GifBuilder with our first frame in place.

Figure 16.7 shows the Frames window in GifBuilder after our script has run. **Figure 16.8** shows the Preview window in GifBuilder with our first frame in place.

To automatically construct an animated GIF with GifBuilder:

1. `tell application "GifBuilder"`

We begin speaking to GifBuilder.

2. `new`

We first tell GifBuilder to create a new, empty animation sequence.

3. `set background color to`
`→ {65535, 65335, 65535}`
`set depth to 8`
`set loop to 0`
`set interlacing to false`
`set dithering to false`

Next we set some global properties like image background color (white), color depth (8-bit), looping (forever), interlacing (none), and dithering (none).

4. `repeat with i from 1 to 10`

Now we're ready to begin our repeat loop.

5. `tell application "clip2gif"`

We let AppleScript know that we'd like to talk to clip2gif.

6. `set myImage to (save {100, 100}`
`→ in picture drawing`
`{{drawn text:"Hi!",`
`→ position:{i * 10, 50},`
`→ font:"Helvetica", size:36,`
`→ color:{0, 65535, 0}}})`
`end tell`

With the `set` statement, we have clip2gif store the result of the `save` command (a graphic with text in it) into the variable `myImage`. Then we conclude our conversation with clip2gif. Within the drawing record, we create text and position the x coordinate of the text at a multiple of our variable i to move it.

CREATING ANIMATED GIFS OF MOVING TEXT

247

7.
```
make new frame at end with data
→ {contents:myImage,
→ transparency:no,
→ disposal method:restore to
→ background,
→ interframe delay:10}
end repeat
```

We then ask GifBuilder to create a new frame at the end of the current sequence using the picture stored in myImage with the specified frame properties. Our image data that is stored in myImage is passed to the contents property. We set the transparency to no for an opaque frame. We set the frame's disposal method (when the next frame is drawn) to return to the background and finally we set the frame's display time delay to 10/100ths of a second. Then we continue our repeat loop.

8.
```
save in file (myFolder &
→ "animation.gif" as text)
end tell
```

Finally, once the loop is over, we have GifBuilder save the animated GIF in a file named animation.gif in the folder myFolder.

✔ Moving text in different ways

- By modifying the settings for the variable i in step 6 you can change the way the text moves within the animation. For example, change position:{i * 10, 50} to position:{i * 10, i * 5} to make the text object move diagonally.

IMAGES WITH PHOTOSHOP AND PHOTOSCRIPTER

17

Figure 17.1 PhotoScripter's Photoshop dictionary entries for file formats.

When this book was started it was difficult to get impressive results with scripts for Photoshop. Armed only with the `do script` command to trigger actions that I had to create manually, I was not having dazzling success with my Photoshop scripting efforts. Then a new plug-in for Photoshop called PhotoScripter appeared.

PhotoScripter makes the world's most popular and powerful image editing software, Adobe Photoshop 5.0, fully AppleScript-aware. And the AppleScript it speaks thanks to PhotoScripter is clear and coherent, relying on an elegant and intuitive object model.

Figure 17.1 shows PhotoScripter's dictionary entries for file formats.

✔ Unit types, OS 8.5, and PhotoScripter

■ PhotoScripter is the first third-party implementation of the new unit types of AppleScript in OS 8.5. PhotoScripter lets you specify unit types using the coercion operator `as`. For example:

```
set selection to {0 as pixels,
→ 0 as pixels, 100 as pixels,
→ 100 as pixels}
```

Scripting Photoshop with PhotoScripter

All the scripts that follow were designed and tested for Adobe Photoshop 5.0 and Main Event PhotoScripter 1.0.

Photoshop is published by Adobe Software, Inc., which can be reached at http://www.adobe.com/.

PhotoScripter is published by Main Event Software, which can be reached at http://www.mainevent.com/.

Creating and exporting graphical text

Well, now that you've got a scriptable Photoshop, what are you going to do with it?

Good question.

Well, in Web development (and many other lines of work), people use Photoshop to produce many graphics that might each vary just a little.

This script, **Code 17.1**, creates a yellow oval and draws blue text on top of it before exporting the image as an interlaced GIF. Simply set the list variable myMastheads to the list of strings you want to produce as graphics, and the script will create a series of interlaced GIF images using a minimal color palette. **Figure 17.2** shows our document in Photoshop after the first item of text has been drawn and the image has been flattened in the conversion process. You can draw any shapes you want besides filled ellipses by using the draw command.

To create and export graphics and text:

1. tell application
   → "Adobe Photoshop® 5.0"
      activate

   We start by bringing Photoshop to the front.

2. set myFolder to (choose folder)

   Next, we prompt the user to select a folder and we save a reference to the folder in the variable myFolder.

3. set myMastheads to {"Hello Earthlings!", "What's Up?"}

   Now we define the list of strings to rasterize on top of the drawing layer in myMastheads.

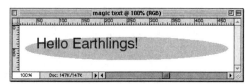

Figure 17.2 Our document in Photoshop after the first item of text has been drawn and the image has been flattened in the conversion process.

Code 17.1 This script creates a yellow oval and draws blue text on top of it before exporting the image as an interlaced GIF with the smallest possible color palette.

```
tell application "Adobe Photoshop® 5.0"
    set myFolder to (choose folder)
    set myMastheads to
    → {"Hello Earthlings!", "What's Up?"}
    set myFont to "Helvetica"
    set mySize to 30.5
    set myTextColor to RGB color
    → {red:0.0, green:0.0, blue:204.0}
    set myObjectColor to RGB color
    → {red:255.0, green:204.0, blue:0.0}
    set myFileInfo to
    → {caption:"Copyright 1998 Ethan"}
    activate
    set myNewDoc to make new document with
    → properties {name:"magic text",
    → color space:RGB mode,
    → width:500 as pixels,
    → height:100 as pixels,
    → resolution:72 as density,
    → fill contents:white}
    set the file info of myNewDoc to
    → myFileInfo
    repeat with i from 1 to number of items in
    → myMastheads
        set mymasthead to item i of myMastheads
        make new layer
        set selection to ellipse
        → {25, 25, 475, 75}
        set the current foreground color to
        → myObjectColor
        fill selection filling with foreground
        → color with antialiasing
        set the current foreground color to
        → myTextColor
```

Code continues on next page

Code 17.1 *continued*

```
                    code

    make new text layer with properties
    → {text:mymasthead,
    → position:{10 as pixels, 50 as pixels},
    → font:myFont, size:mySize,
    → alignment:left justify,
    → leading:mySize, tracking:0.0,
    → auto kerning:true,
    → antialiasing:true,
    → rotating edges:true,
    → orientation:horizontally,
    → is vertical:false, writing system:0}

    delete layer "Background" of current
    → document

    convert current document to indexed
    → color mode
    → {palette:web,
    → dither method:diffusion,
    → color matching quality:better,
    → preserving exact colors:true}
    → with flattening layers

    convert current document to RGB mode

    convert current document to indexed
    color mode
    → {palette:exact,
    → color matching quality:better,
    → preserving exact colors:true}
    → with flattening layers

    save current document in file
    → (myFolder & i & ".gif" as text) as
    → Compuserve GIF {interlacing:true}

    convert current document to RGB mode

  end repeat
end tell
```

4.   `set myFont to "Helvetica"`

We use this variable, `myFont`, to define the font to use with our graphical text.

5.   `set mySize to 30.5`

This variable, `mySize`, sets the point size for our graphical text.

6.   `set myTextColor to RGB color`
       `→ {red:0.0, green:0.0,`
       `→ blue:204.0}`

`myTextColor` defines the color (blue) that we'll use for our text. RGB colors are defined by a record with properties `red`, `green` and `blue`. Values for each property range from 0 to 255.

7.   `set myObjectColor to RGB color`
       `{red:255.0, green:204.0,`
       `→ blue:0.0}`

`myObjectColor` defines the color that we'll use for our filled oval. In this case, yellow, since 100% red plus 80% green yields a nice rich yellow RGB color.

8.   `set myFileInfo to`
       `→ {caption:"Copyright 1998`
       `→ Ethan"}`

Here we do something very sly. We set the variable `myFileInfo` to be a caption field for our image with a copyright statement in a string. This information will be saved with our GIF image and stay attached to it when it is transmitted over the Web!

9.   `set myNewDoc to make new`
       `→ document with properties`
       `→ {name:"magic text",`
       `→ color space:RGB mode,`
       `→ width:500 as pixels,`
       `→ height:100 as pixels,`
       `→ resolution:72 as density,`
       `→ fill contents:white}`

Here we create a new Photoshop RGB document named "magic text" that is 500 pixels wide by 100 pixels tall. We start out with the document filled with white and set at a resolution of 72 dpi. The `make` command returns a reference to our new document that we store in the variable myNewDoc.

10. `set the file info of myNewDoc`
        `↪ to myFileInfo`

Now we set the `file info` property of our new document to the variable `myFileInfo` where we saved the caption information!

11. `repeat with i from 1 to number`
        `↪ of items in myMastheads`

Then we begin a loop through each of the text strings stored in the list variable myMastheads.

12. `set mymasthead to item i of`
        `↪ myMastheads`

Here we store the current item from our list in mymasthead.

13. `make new layer`

Now we have Photoshop create a new layer.

14. `set selection to ellipse`
        `↪ {25, 25, 475, 75}`

We set the current selection to an ellipse defined by the list {left,top,right,bottom}.

15. `set the current foreground`
        `↪ color to myObjectColor`

Now we set Photoshop's foreground color to the object color we stored in myObjectColor.

16. `fill selection filling with`
        `↪ foreground color with`
        `↪ antialiasing`

We fill the current selection with the foreground color, antialiasing the edge of the selection.

17.
```
        set the current foreground
        → color to myTextColor
```

Now we set Photoshop's foreground color to the text color we stored in myTextColor.

18.
```
        make new text layer with
        properties {text:mymasthead,
        position:{10 as pixels,
        → 50 as pixels},
        → font:myFont,
        → size:mySize,
        → alignment:left
        → justify,
        → leading:mySize,
        → tracking:0.0,
        → auto kerning:true,
        → antialiasing:true,
        → rotating edges:true,
        → orientation:horizontally,
        → is vertical:false,
        → writing system:0}
```

We create a new text layer using variables to define the text to draw, its font, and its point size. We set the text to start appearing at 10 pixels from the left and 50 pixels from the top of the current document. We set the alignment on the text to left, set the leading to the same as the point size, turn on antialiasing, and draw the text horizontally.

19.
```
        delete layer "Background" of
        → current document
```

Now we delete the old, useless Background layer.

20.
```
        convert current document to
        → indexed color mode
        → {palette:web,
        → dither method:diffusion,
        → color matching quality:better,
        → preserving exact
        → colors:true}
        → with flattening layers
```

We convert the image to the Web palette, flattening any layers in the process.

21.
```
convert current document to
  → RGB mode
```
Now we convert back to RGB for a moment to pull a little trick.

22.
```
convert current document to
indexed color mode
{palette:exact,
  → color matching
  → quality:better,
  → preserving exact
  → colors:true}
  → with flattening layers
```
Here is the trick. We convert back to an indexed palette using the same exact method to create a palette that includes only those Web colors that our image actually uses. This can make files significantly smaller.

23.
```
save current document in
  → file (myFolder & i &
  → ".gif" as text) as
  → Compuserve GIF
  → {interlacing:true}
```
Now finally we save the interlaced GIF image with a new file name using the suffix .gif.

24.
```
convert current document to
  → RGB mode
  end repeat
end tell
```
Next, we convert back to RGB mode for the next cycle of the loop.

Code 17.2 This script saves each layer in the Photoshop document you drop on the script application as a separate PICT file.

```
                    code
on open (myFile)
    set myNewFile to myFile as string
    tell application "Adobe Photoshop® 5.0"
        activate
        open myFile
        repeat with i from 1 to number of
        → layers in current document
            select layer i of current document
            show layer i of current document
            → with hiding others
            set myFinalFile to (myNewFile & " "
            → & (name of layer i of current
            → document)) as string
            save document 1 as PICT file
            → {resolution:pixel depth 32,
            → JPEG quality:maximum} in file
            → myFinalFile with making copy
            → without appending file extension
        end repeat
        close document 1 saving no
    end tell
end open
```

Figure 17.3 Photoshop's Layers palette looks like this as the script runs, cycling through the layers as it saves them to separate PICT files.

Exporting each layer of a document as a separate file

Have you ever had a huge Photoshop file filled with layers that were really wonderful? So wonderful that you wanted to make each layer its own file to start the creative process with a cleaner slate? This script will do the trick. Just drop your many-layered Photoshop file onto the script application icon after you save **Code 17.2** as an application! **Figure 17.3** shows Photoshop's Layers palette as it looks when the script is running, cycling through the layers as it saves them to separate PICT files. **Figure 17.4** shows the new files in the folder's Finder window, with a new file for each separate layer of the original file.

To export each layer of the current document as a separate file:

1. `on open (myFile)`

   Our `on open` handler stores the file reference passed to it in the variable `myFile`.

2. `set myNewFile to myFile as string`

   Next, we save the path to our file as a string in the variable `myNewFile`.

3. `tell application`
   `→ "Adobe Photoshop® 5.0"`
   `   activate`

   Now we bring Photoshop to the front.

4. `    open myFile`

   We have Photoshop open the file referenced by the variable `myFile`.

5. `    repeat with i from 1 to`
   `→ number of layers in current`
   `→ document`

   Then we start looping through each layer in the document we've opened.

6.   `select layer i of current`
        `→ document`

We make the layer i in our loop the active layer.

7.   `show layer i of current`
        `→ document with hiding`
        `→ others`

We show the layer i, turning others off.

8.   `set myFinalFile to`
        `(myNewFile & " " &`
        `→ (name of layer i of`
        `→ current document))`
        `→ as string`

We create a new file name made up of the original file name and the layer's name. We store this in the variable `myFinalFile`.

9.   `save document 1 as PICT file`
        `→ {resolution:pixel depth 32,`
        `→ JPEG quality:maximum}`
        `→ in file myFinalFile with`
        `→ making copy without`
        `→ appending file extension`
           `end repeat`

Now we save the visible layer as a PICT file with the new file name.

10.   `close document 1 saving no`
        `end tell`
`end open`

Finally, after our loop is finished, we close the original document without saving our changes to it.

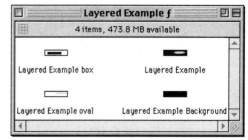

Figure 17.4. The new files in the folder's Finder window, showing a file for each separate layer of the original file.

Code 17.3 This script turns all image files in the folder you drop on the script application into separate layers in a new Photoshop file.

```
                      code
on open (myFolder)

    set myFiles to list folder myFolder
    → without invisibles

    set myFirstFile to (myFolder & item 1 of
    → myFiles) as string

    set myFolder to myFolder as string

    tell application "Finder"

        set myNewFile to (duplicate alias
        → myFirstFile)

    end tell

    tell application "Adobe Photoshop® 5.0"

        activate

        open myNewFile

        flatten current document

        repeat with i from 2 to number of items
        → in myFiles

            set myFile to (myFolder & item i of
            → myFiles) as string

            open alias myFile

            flatten current document

            set the selection to all pixels

            copy

            close current document saving no

            paste

            set the name of current layer to
            → (item i of myFiles as string)

        end repeat

    end tell

end open
```

Figure 17.5 Photoshop's Layers palette as it appears while the script runs.

Importing a folder full of files into a document as layers

Sometimes you want to do the opposite of what we did in the previous script—turn a bunch of flattened image files into layers in a single file. **Code 17.3** lets the user drop a folder of image files onto its script application icon to make one new file in Photoshop. The script cycles through each file in the folder, flattening it and making it a new layer with the same name as the original file. **Figure 17.5** shows Photoshop's Layers palette as it looks while the script runs.

To import a folder full of files into a new document as layers:

1. `on open (myFolder)`

Our `on open` handler stores the reference to the folder dropped on it in the variable `myFolder`.

2. `set myFiles to list folder myFolder without invisibles`

Next we store the list of items in the folder `myFolder` in the variable `myFiles`. We use `without invisibles` to ignore invisible files.

3. `set myFirstFile to (myFolder & item 1 of myFiles)`

Now we'll get the name of the first file in the list `myFiles`. We'll start with this file in our layer-building process.

4. `set myFolder to myFolder as string`

We make sure that `myFolder` holds the path to the folder as a string.

5. `tell application "Finder"`
    `set myNewFile to (duplicate alias myFirstFile)`
    `end tell`

Here we have the Finder duplicate the file we stored a path to in myFirstFile. We store the reference the Finder returns in myNewFile. It points to the new duplicated file that we'll have Photoshop open first.

6.
```
    tell application
→ "Adobe Photoshop® 5.0"
     activate
```
Now we bring Photoshop to the front.

7.
```
     open myNewFile
```
We have Photoshop open the new duplicated file that we stored a reference to in the variable myNewFile.

8.
```
      flatten current document
```
Then we have Photoshop flatten the document we just opened.

9.
```
      repeat with i from 2 to
→ number of items in myFiles
```
Now we loop through all the other files that follow the first one in the list of files we stored in myFiles.

10.
```
       set myFile to
→ (myFolder & item i of
→ myFiles) as string
```
We store the path to the file from the current item in the loop in myFile.

11.
```
       open alias myFile
```
We have Photoshop open the current file in the loop, which we've stored in myFile.

12.
```
       flatten current document
```
Photoshop flattens the document.

13.
```
       set the selection to all
→ pixels
```
We select the entire document.

14.
```
       copy
```
We copy the entire document.

15.
```
close current document
saving no
```
We close the document without saving any changes.

16.
```
paste
```
Now the current document is again the one we started with so we paste in the copy of the document just opened as a new layer.

17.
```
set the name of current
⇥ layer to (item i of
⇥ myFiles as string)
     end repeat
   end tell
 end open
```
We set the name of the new layer just created to the same name as the file that was the source for its image, then close the loop.

Adding transparency to grayscale images

One of the wonderful features of Photoshop is its ability to use an alpha channel so that layers can have levels of transparency. But when you scan something from a scanner, you get a fully opaque image without any transparency in it.

Code 17.4, will batch processing a folder full of grayscale image files (such as line art scans), eliminating the backgrounds so that the shapes float on a transparent layer. **Figures 17.6** and **17.7** show before and after views of an image containing shapes that needed to be filled with white and then placed on a transparent layer .

To add transparency to a folder full of grayscale images:

1. `property whiteX : 10`
`property whiteY : 10`

These properties define where our script will use the magic wand to click on a white pixel.

2. `on open (myFolder)`

Our on open handler stores the folder reference it receives in myFolder.

3. `set myFiles to list folder`
`→ myFolder without invisibles`

Now we store the list of items in the folder myFolder in myFiles.

4. `repeat with myFile in myFiles`

We begin a loop through each item in myFiles, placing the current item in myFile.

5. `set myCurrentFile to`
`→ (myFolder & myFile )`
`→ as string`

Now we construct the path to the current file in the loop as a string and store it in the variable myCurrentFile.

Figure 17.6 An opaque grayscale image ready to be converted to a transparent masked image.

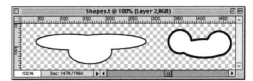

Figure 17.7 The same image made transparent and with all closed shaped masked in white.

Code 17.4 This script converts opaque grayscale images, such as those created by scanning line art, to transparent masked images.

```
property whiteX : 10
property whiteY : 10
on open (myFolder)
    set myFiles to list folder myFolder
    → without invisibles
    repeat with myFile in myFiles
        set myCurrentFile to
        → (myFolder & myFile) as string
        tell application "Finder"
            set myKind to kind of alias
            → myCurrentFile
        end tell
        if myKind ≠ "folder" then
            makeTransparent(myCurrentFile)
        else
            tell me to open (myCurrentFile as
            → alias)
        end if
    end repeat
end open
on makeTransparent(myFile)
    tell application "Adobe Photoshop® 5.0"
        activate
        open alias myFile
        convert document 1 to grayscale mode
        → without flattening layers
```

Code continues on next page

Code 17.4 *continued*

```
┌─────────────────────────────────────────┐
│ ▦▦▦▦▦▦▦▦▦▦ code ▦▦▦▦▦▦▦▦▦▦▦          ▦ │
├─────────────────────────────────────────┤
    set the selection to all pixels
    copy
    paste
    invert channel 1 of document 1
    set the selection to channel 1 of
    → document 1
    set myLayer to (make new layer at
    → document 1)
    fill the selection filling with black
    → color
    delete layer 1 of document 1
    delete layer "Background" of document 1
    set the selection to the magic point
    → {whiteX as pixels, whiteY as pixels}
    expand by 1 as pixels
    modify the selection using the inverse
    → selection
    set myLayer to (make new layer at
    → document 1 with properties
    → {blending mode:multiply mode})
    fill the selection filling with white
    merge layers document 1
    set myNewFile to myFile as string
    set myNewFile to myNewFile & ".t"
    save document 1 in file myNewFile
    close document 1 saving no
  end tell
  tell application "Finder"
    set the label index of alias myNewFile
    → to 1
  end tell
end makeTransparent
```

6.
```
    tell application "Finder"
      set myKind to kind of
      → alias myCurrentFile
    end tell
```

Now we have the Finder return in myKind the kind of item that we are currently looking at.

7.
```
if myKind ≠ "folder" then
    makeTransparent(myCurrentFile)
```

If the item isn't a folder it's a file, so we call our handler makeTransparent to convert the image.

8.
```
    else
      tell me to open
      → (myCurrentFile as alias)
    end if
  end repeat
end open
```

Otherwise, if the item is a folder, we call our own open handler with a reference to the folder.

9. `on makeTransparent(myFile)`

Our handler makeTransparent receives a reference to the file it should try to convert in the variable myFile.

10.
```
    tell application
    → "Adobe Photoshop® 5.0"
      activate
```

Now we bring Photoshop to the front.

11. `open alias myFile`

We open the current file referenced by myFile.

12.
```
    convert document 1 to
    → grayscale mode without
    → flattening layers
```

We have Photoshop convert the image to grayscale without flattening its layers.

13.

```
set the selection to all
 ↦ pixels
copy
paste
```

We select the entire document, copy it, and paste it to create a new layer that is the same as the flattened image.

14.

```
invert channel 1 of document 1
```

Then we invert the color channel of our image.

15.

```
set the selection to
 ↦ channel 1 of document 1
```

We select all of the white pixels in our inverted image completely and select the gray ones with some transparency.

16.

```
set myLayer to (make new
 ↦ layer at document 1)
fill the selection filling
 ↦ with black color
```

Now we create a new layer and fill the selection from step 15 with black.

17.

```
delete layer 1 of document 1
delete layer "Background"
 ↦ of document 1
```

Now we can delete the two layers created in our process.

18.

```
set the selection to the
 ↦ magic point {whiteX as
 ↦ pixels, whiteY as pixels}
```

We magic wand the new transparent image, expecting to click on a completely transparent pixel. We do this to begin the process of filling any closed shapes with white as a mask that we can use to color in our shapes later. You may need to change the values in whiteX and whiteY depending on your image.

19.

```
expand by 1 as pixels
```

We expand the magic wand's selection by one pixel to eat into the black lines.

20.
```
      modify the selection using
      → the inverse selection
```
Then we invert our selection so that we now have selected the interiors of any closed shapes in the document.

21.
```
      set myLayer to (make new
      → layer at document 1 with
      → properties {blending
      → mode:multiply mode})
```
We create a new layer with its blending mode set to multiply.

22.
```
      fill the selection filling
      → with white
```
Now we fill the selection still current from step 20 with white.

23.
```
      merge layers document 1
```
We merge the white layer and black layer of the document to create a transparent layer with filled closed shapes.

24.
```
      set myNewFile to myFile as
      → string
      set myNewFile to myNewFile &
      → ".t"
```
Here we set myNewFile to a new file name by adding a suffix .t to the original file name.

25.
```
      save document 1 in file
      → myNewFile
```
Now we save the new document with our new file name from the previous step.

26.
```
      close document 1 saving no
   end tell
```
We close the document without saving changes over the original.

27.
```
   tell application "Finder"
      set the label index of alias
      → myNewFile to 1
   end tell
end makeTransparent
```
Finally, we have the Finder set the label of the new file to the first label.

Creating animations

One of the most interesting possibilities opened up by PhotoScripter is the ability to script filters and lighting effects. This script, **Code 17.5**, takes an image, duplicates it to a new layer, applies a filter to it, then repeats the process five times. **Figures 17.8** and **17.9** show a document before and after being processed with this script.

To create an animation in a series of layers by repeated filtering:

1. `tell application`
   `→ "Adobe Photoshop® 5.0"`
   `activate`

   First we bring Photoshop to the front.

2. `set the selection to all pixels`
   `copy`
   `paste`

   We select the entire current document, copy it, and paste it to create a new layer with a copy of the original image.

3. `repeat with i from 1 to 5`

   Now we start a loop that we'll cycle through five times.

4. `paste`

   We paste the current image in the clipboard into a new layer.

5. `set the selection to all`
   `→ pixels`

   Now we select that entire image.

6. `→ filter current document`
   `applying twirl {angle:20}`

   We apply the twirl filter to the current selection using a twirl angle of 20 degrees.

7. `copy`
   `end repeat`
   `end tell`

   Finally, we copy the processed image to the clipboard before continuing our loop.

Code 17.5 This script creates a series of layers for use as an animation.

```
tell application "Adobe Photoshop® 5.0"
   activate
   set the selection to all pixels
   copy
   paste
   repeat with i from 1 to 5
      paste
      set the selection to all pixels
      filter current document applying twirl
      → {angle:20}
      copy
   end repeat
end tell
```

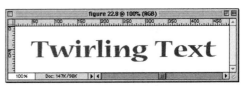

Figure 17.8 Our original image file with some red graphical text in it.

Figure 17.9 The final layer of our document after the script has run, creating six layers, each progressively more filtered.

✔ Combine this script with others

- You could combine this script with the next two scripts to preview and create animated GIFs directly from Photoshop!

CREATING ANIMATIONS

Code 17.6 This script previews an animation created as multiple layers by turning off all layers in the current Photoshop document, then turning on one layer at a time in sequence.

```
code
on run

   tell application "Adobe Photoshop® 5.0"

      activate

      hide every layer of document 1

      set myLayers to number of layers in
      → document 1

      repeat with i from 1 to myLayers by 1

         show layer i of document 1

         if i > 1 then hide layer (i - 1) of
         → document 1

      end repeat

   end tell

end run
```

Figure 17.10
Photoshop's Layers palette as it looks while the script runs.

Previewing an animation created as separate layers

When you've composed an animated scene in Photoshop where each frame in the animation is a separate layer in your document, this script, **Code 17.6**, will preview your animation right in Photoshop by displaying the layers in the document one at a time. If you have a Background layer, this script will ignore it. **Figure 17.10** shows what Photoshop's Layers palette looks like as the script runs.

To preview an animation created as separate layers:

1. `on run`
   `tell application`
   `→ "Adobe Photoshop® 5.0"`
   `activate`

   We start by bringing Photoshop to the front.

2. `hide every layer of document 1`

   We hide every layer of the current document. In the current version of PhotoScripter, this command does not affect the Background layer. To modify this script to deal with the Background layer of a document, refer to it by name as `layer "Background"`.

3. `set myLayers to number of`
   `→ layers in document 1`

   We store the number of layers in our current document in the variable `myLayers`.

4. `repeat with i from 1 to`
   `→ myLayers by 1`

   Then we begin a loop through each layer in the document. If your animation goes in reverse order, change this line to read:
   `repeat with i from myLayers to 1`
   `by -1`

5.
```
        show layer i of document 1
```
Now we have Photoshop make the current layer in our loop visible.

6.
```
        if i > 1 then hide layer
      → (i - 1) of document 1
    end repeat
  end tell
end run
```
Here, we check to see if we're on a layer after the first layer. If we are, we turn off the layer before the current one before closing our loop.

Code 17.7 This script makes a multi-frame GIF animation in GifBuilder from the current layered Photoshop document.

```
on run
    tell application "GifBuilder"
        activate
        new
    end tell
    tell application "Adobe Photoshop® 5.0"
        activate
        show every layer of document 1
        set myLayers to number of layers in
        → document 1
    end tell
    repeat with i from myLayers to 1 by -1
        tell application "Adobe Photoshop® 5.0"
            activate
            select layer i of document 1
            set the selection to all pixels
            copy
        end tell
        tell application "GifBuilder"
            activate
            paste
        end tell

    end repeat
end run
```

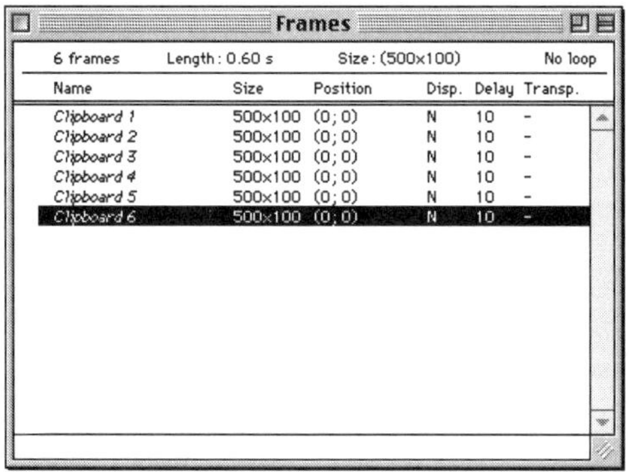

Figure 17.11 The Frames window in GifBuilder after our script has run, creating a six-frame GIF animation from a Photoshop file with six layers.

Exporting a layered document as an animated GIF with GifBuilder

Finally, if you've created a cool frame-based animation as a layered Photoshop document, this script is for you! **Code 17.7** works with GifBuilder to make an animated GIF from the current open document in Photoshop. **Figure 17.11** shows the Frames window in GifBuilder with a six-frame GIF animation created from a six-layer Photoshop file.

To export a layered Photoshop document as an animated GIF with GifBuilder:

1. ```
   on run
       tell application "GifBuilder"
           activate
           new
       end tell
   ```
   We start by having GifBuilder come to the front and clear its animation frames for a new animation.

2. ```
   tell application
   → "Adobe Photoshop® 5.0"
       activate
   ```
   Next, we have Photoshop come to the front.

3. ```
       show every layer of document 1
   ```
   Then we have Photoshop make every layer in the current document visible.

4. ```
       set myLayers to number of
       → layers in document 1
   end tell
   ```
   We store the number of layers in our current document in the variable myLayers.

5. ```
       repeat with i from myLayers to
       → 1 by -1
   ```
   ```

We begin a loop through the layers, starting with the last one and going backward to the first layer.

6.
```
        tell application
    → "Adobe Photoshop® 5.0"
            activate
```

We now bring Photoshop to the front again.

7.
```
        select layer i of document 1
```

We make the current layer in our loop the active layer in Photoshop.

8.
```
            set the selection to all
        → pixels
            copy
        end tell
```

We select the entire image in the active layer and copy it to the clipboard. Note that only non-transparent (opaque) pixels will be copied.

9.
```
            tell application "GifBuilder"
                activate
                paste
            end tell
        end repeat
    end run
```

Now we bring GifBuilder to the front and paste the image from the clipboard to a new frame in the current animation before closing the loop.

SCRIPTING WITH APPLE DATA DETECTORS

Apple Data Detectors work with AppleScripts and a system extension (and scripting addition) to enable your computer to recognize and act on certain types of text information. For example, let's say you have a word processing document that contains several e-mail addresses. Select a range of text and Control-click the selection, and Apple Data Detectors will quickly scan the document, identify all the kinds of information it can understand, and then prompt you with a contextual menu of AppleScript actions you can take based on the addresses. Or if someone sends you a World Wide Web address in an e-mail message, you can use Apple Data Detectors to find the address within the message.

Currently, Apple Data Detectors 1.0.2 can identify data that's in the form of Internet addresses, which includes the following:

◆ E-mail addresses

◆ Web sites

◆ Newsgroup names

◆ File names on FTP sites

◆ Names of remote computers

Creating Apple Data Detector action scripts

The Apple Data Detectors system components include a special scripting addition to allow you to write your own actions. Apple Data Detectors action scripts are simply compiled AppleScript files with a special format for the script description field. The first line defines the detector to use, the second line defines the contextual menu string to display for the action, and subsequent lines define the description for the action as displayed in the Apple Data Detectors control panel. To add new actions to ADD, simply copy your compiled script file to the Apple Data Detectors folder in your System Folder.

Figure 18.1 shows the AppleScript dictionary entries for ADD's scripting addition. **Figure 18.2** shows the Apple Data Detectors folder with the Actions folder for new actions.

✔ If your scripts don't appear

- If your new action scripts don't appear in the control panel's list, delete the Apple Data Detectors Database file, then reopen the control panel to have ADD recatalog all of its actions.

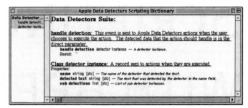

Figure 18.1 The Apple Data Detectors scripting addition's AppleScript dictionary.

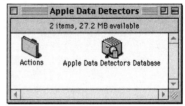

Figure 18.2 The Apple Data Detectors Database file can be deleted when new compiled scripts added to the Actions folder don't show up.

Scripting Apple Data Detectors

All the scripts that follow were designed and tested for Apple Data Detectors 1.0.2.

The Apple Data Detectors package is free.

Apple Data Detectors are published by Apple Computer, Inc., which can be reached at http://swupdates.info. → apple.com/.

CREATING APPLE DATA DETECTOR ACTION SCRIPTS

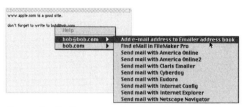

Figure 18.3 Saving an e-mail address in the text of a Stickies note to Claris Emailer.

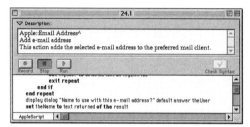

Figure 18.4 The description field of your script is very important to Apple Data Dectectors. The first line must specify the detector to use for this script, the second line is the contextual menu command, and subsequent lines appear as a description in the ADD control panel.

Detecting e-mail addresses and adding them to an address book

This action script will detect an e-mail address and save it in the address book of your preferred mail client. **Figure 18.3** shows an e-mail address in the text of a Stickies note being saved to Claris Emailer.. **Figure 18.4** shows the script's description field in the Script Editor with special Data Detectors information.

✔ Making your script an action script

- Pay close attention to **Figure 18.4**. Make sure the format of your script's description field matches the example shown in the figure.

Code 18.1 This script retrieves the selected e-mail address from ADD.

```
on handle detection myStructure
    set myEmailAddress to detected text of myStructure
    set myParseTree to sub detections of myStructure
    set myUser to ""
    repeat with myEntries in myParseTree
        if the name of myEntries is "user" then
            set myUser to detected text of myEntries
            exit repeat
        end if
    end repeat
    display dialog "Name to use with this e-mail address?" default answer myUser
    set myName to text returned of the result

    makeAddress(myName,myEmailAddress)

end handle detection
```

To detect an e-mail address and add it to your e-mail client's address book:

1. `on handle detection myStructure`

ADD automatically calls this `handle detection` handler in the script whenever a user selects this action script to act on an e-mail address. We store the value passed to the handler in the variable `myStructure`. (Handlers are discussed in Chapter 3.)

2. `set myEmailAddress to detected`
   `→ text of myStructure`
   `set myParseTree to sub`
   `→ detections of myStructure`

The e-mail address is passed to the handler in the `detected text` property of the value it receives.

3. `makeAddress(myName,myEmailAddress)`
   `end handle detection`

Finally, we call our `makeAddress` handler (or function) to create the address book entry in the mail client of our choice.

Check the Internet

Check out the support web site for this book for versions of the script customized for different e-mail clients:
`http://www.peachpit.com/vqs/applescript`

DETECTING E-MAIL ADDRESSES

Code 18.2 This script detects a URL and displays the InterNIC record of its domain.

```
on handle detection myStructure
    set myHostname to detected text of
    → myStructure
    set myHostname to characters
    → ((offset of "." in myHostname) + 1)
    → thru -1 of myHostname as string
    tell application "Finger"
        activate
        geturl ("whois://rs.internic.net/" &
        → myHostname as string)
    end tell
end handle detection
```

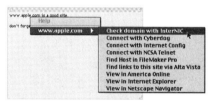

Figure 18.5 Detecting a domain name and calling Finger to display its InterNIC record.

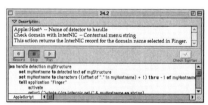

Figure 18.6 The description field of this script in the Script Editor with its definitions for Apple Data Dectectors.

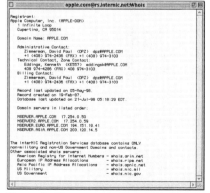

Figure 18.7 The InterNIC record as displayed in Finger.

Detecting a domain name

This action script (**Code 18.2**) will detect a Web URL and then parse the domain name from the URL, calling Finger to display the domain's InterNIC record. **Figure 18.5** shows the script in action. **Figure 18.6** shows the script's description field in the Script Editor with special Data Detectors information. **Figure 18.7** shows the InterNIC domain name record displayed in Finger.

To detect a domain name and display its InterNIC record:

1. on handle detection myStructure
       set myHostname to detected text
       → of myStructure

   ADD calls this handle detection handler when a user selects this action script to act on a Web URL. The URL is passed in the detected text property.

2.   set myHostname to characters
       ((offset of "." in myHostname)
       → + 1) thru -1 of myHostname
       → as string

   Here we strip the host machine name from the string to get the domain name alone. We do this by replacing the whole hostname stored in myHostname with the characters of the hostname from the first character after the period (using offset) through the last character (using -1 to indicate the last character).

3.   tell application "Finger"
           activate
           geturl
           → ("whois://rs.internic.net/"
           → & myHostname as string)
       end tell
   end handle detection

   Now, we have Finger display the InterNIC domain name record via a whois call. See the spread *Returning content from other scriptable applications* in Chapter 11 for more on Finger.

Detecting a URL and displaying links with Alta Vista

This action script (**Code 18.3**) will detect a Web URL in text the user Control-clicks and then send a query URL to Alta Vista via Netscape Navigator. The results will show all sites that link to the original URL. **Figure 18.8** shows the script detecting a URL. **Figure 18.9** shows the script's description field in the Script Editor with special Data Detectors information. **Figure 18.10** shows the Alta Vista query results in Netscape for a selected URL.

To detect a URL and display links with Alta Vista:

1. ```
on handle detection myStructure
    set myHostname to detected text
    → of myStructure
```

   ADD calls this `handle detection` handler when a user selects this action script to act on a Web URL. The URL is passed in the `detected text` property.

2. ```
    tell application
    → "Netscape Navigator™ 4.04"
        activate
        OpenURL
        → ("http://www.altavista.com/
        → cgi-bin/query?pg=q&kl=XX&q=
        → link%3A" & myHostname as
        → string)
    end tell
end handle detection
```

   Now we send a URL to Netscape and query Alta Vista.

✔ Make ADD an entry to your scripts

- Think about integrating the other scripts in this book into a `handle detection` handler to use ADD as a very quick and universal entry point for your scripts!

Code 18.3 This script takes the ADD-passed URL and searches Alta Vista for sites that link to it.

```
on handle detection myStructure
    set myHostname to detected text of
    → myStructure
    tell application "Netscape Navigator™
    → 4.04"
        activate
        OpenURL ("http://www.altavista.com/
        → cgi-bin/query?pg=q&kl=XX&q=link%3A"
        → & myHostname as string)
    end tell
end handle detection
```

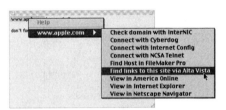

Figure 18.8 Detecting a URL and calling Netscape to query Alta Vista for sites that link to this URL.

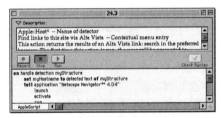

Figure 18.9 The description field of this script in the Script Editor with its definitions for Apple Data Dectectors.

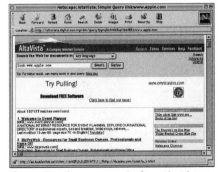

Figure 18.10 The query results from Alta Vista as displayed in Netscape.

USING TIMBUKTU PRO TO CONTROL WINDOWS

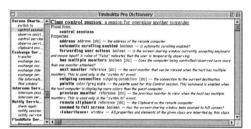

Figure 19.1 Timbuktu's `control session` definition from its AppleScript dictionary.

Figure 19.2 Timbuktu's `exchange session` definition from its AppleScript dictionary.

Scripting Timbuktu Pro

All the scripts that follow were designed and tested for Timbuktu Pro 4.7.1.

These scripts will work with any version 4.x of Tibuktu Pro.

Timbuktu Pro is published by Netopia, which can be reached at `http://www.netopia.com/`.

Timbuktu Pro version 4.0 introduces complete AppleScript support. With it we have a bridge to any Windows PC running Timbuktu Pro for Windows. Through this bridge, we can control and manipulate Windows 95 and NT machines from AppleScript!

Two of Timbuktu Pro's most powerful abilities, to control another machine and to exchange files with it, are fully scriptable. The `control session` and `exchange session` object classes allow our scripts to control every aspect of these abilities. **Figure 19.1** shows Timbuktu's `control session` definition from its AppleScript dictionary, and **Figure 19.2** shows its `exchange session` definition.

✔ Timbuktu is recordable and attachable

- Timbuktu Pro is recordable, so discovering proper syntax is as easy as recording your actions.

- Timbuktu Pro has a Scripts menu that can run your custom scripts directly from the application.

Restarting a Windows NT server

The script shown in **Code 19.1** will restart a Windows NT server. It uses Sändi's Additions to send mouse clicks through Timbuktu Pro to the NT machine. These clicks choose the Start button, select Shut Down, then choose the Restart option before restarting the PC. **Figure 19.3** shows the Control Session window as it looks while our script is running.

This script assumes some very particular things about your Windows NT configuration. The Windows machine you are accessing via Timbuktu must already be logged in, and the Start button must be in the upper-left corner of the screen. You may need to adjust the X and Y coordinates of some MouseClick commands to get this script to work with your PC.

To restart a Windows NT server:

1. `tell application "Timbuktu Pro"`
   `activate`

   We start by bringing Timbuktu Pro to the front.

2. `make new control session`
   `→ connecting to internet address`
   `→ {internet name:"192.0.0.1",`
   `→ platform:platform unknown}`
   `→ connecting as "Controller"`
   `→ with password "x2"`

   Then we connect as the user "Controller" with password "x2" by creating a new control session with our Windows NT machine located at IP address 192.0.0.1. Change the address, user, and password to suit your situation.

3. `delay 4`
   `MouseClick 1 At {10, 10} with`
   `→ LocalCoordinates`

   We pause 4 seconds to wait for the control screen to appear and then click on

Code 19.1 This script restarts a Windows NT server.

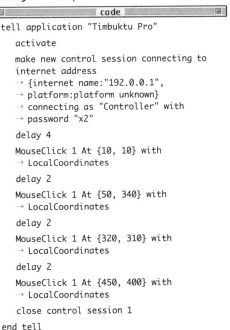

```
tell application "Timbuktu Pro"
    activate
    make new control session connecting to
    internet address
    → {internet name:"192.0.0.1",
    → platform:platform unknown}
    → connecting as "Controller" with
    → password "x2"
    delay 4
    MouseClick 1 At {10, 10} with
    → LocalCoordinates
    delay 2
    MouseClick 1 At {50, 340} with
    → LocalCoordinates
    delay 2
    MouseClick 1 At {320, 310} with
    → LocalCoordinates
    delay 2
    MouseClick 1 At {450, 400} with
    → LocalCoordinates
    close control session 1
end tell
```

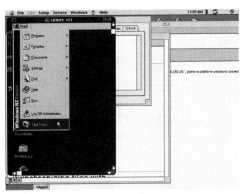

Figure 19.3 The Control Session window showing the script running with the NT server's Start menu opened and Shut Down selected.

the Start button in the upper left of the PC's screen.

4.
```
delay 2
MouseClick 1 At {50, 340} with
→ LocalCoordinates
```
Now we pause 2 seconds and click on the Shut Down item in the Start menu.
```
delay 2
MouseClick 1 At {320, 310} with
→ LocalCoordinates
```
We pause 2 seconds again to wait for the Restart dialog to appear and click on the Restart radio button.

5.
```
delay 2
MouseClick 1 At {450, 400} with
→ LocalCoordinates
```
We pause 2 more seconds and then click on the Restart button.

6.
```
close control session 1
end tell
```
Finally, we close our session in Timbuktu Pro.

✔ Clicking is tricky!

■ Using `MouseClick` is an acquired skill. You will quite likely need to adjust the coordinates in each of the `MouseClick` commands in this script to get it to work reliably on your system. Be patient, this technique is pushing the envelope of what AppleScript can do. If the need to perform this function is great enough, the method will be worth its trouble.

✔ Mac OS 8.5 required

■ The command `delay` is only supported by Mac OS 8.5.

Scripting with Sändi's Additions

This script requires the scripting addition Sändi's Additions. You must have Sändi's Additions installed in your Scripting Additions folder for this script to work.

Sändi's Additions adds a series of commands that simulate mouse clicks and keystrokes.

Sändi's Additions is free for noncommercial use.

Sändi's Additions is published by Alessandro Lüthi, who can be reached at `sandro@swissonline.ch`.

RESTARTING A WINDOWS NT SERVER

Synchronizing a folder on your Mac and PC

This script (**Code 19.2**) synchronizes a local folder on the Mac with a remote folder on a PC, making sure that any files in either the local folder or the remote folder in the current exchange session exist in both folders. Note that PC file names are restricted to 8.3 format (eight characters and a three-letter file extension) in Timbuktu Pro 4.0; this may change in later versions. Since modification dates aren't returned from PC Timbuktu Pro, we don't check for file dates. **Figure 19.4** shows the File Exchange window displaying our script's progress in matching the contents of a folder on the Mac with one on the PC.

To synchronize a folder on your Mac and PC:

1.
```
on run
    tell application "Timbuktu Pro"
        set myFolder1 to local side
        → of first exchange session
        set myFolder2 to remote side
        → of first exchange session
    end tell
```
We start by saving the names of the files in the local panel and remote panel of the File Exchange window in the variables myFolder1 and myFolder2.

2.
```
SyncFolders(myFolder1,
    → myFolder2)
SyncFolders (myFolder2,
    → myFolder1)
end run
```
Now we call our handler SyncFolders once to copy missing files from the remote folder to the local folder, and again to copy missing files from the local folder to the remote folder.

Code 19.2 This script synchronizes a local folder on the Mac with a remote folder on a PC.

```
on run
    tell application "Timbuktu Pro"
        set myFolder1 to local side of first
        → exchange session
        set myFolder2 to remote side of first
        → exchange session
    end tell
    SyncFolders(myFolder1, myFolder2)
    SyncFolders (myFolder2, myFolder1)
end run


on SyncFolders(myFolder1, myFolder2)
    tell application "Timbuktu Pro"
        set myContainer2 to container of
        → myFolder2
        repeat with i from 1 to the number of
        → items in myFolder1
            set myFile to item i of myFolder1
            if (class of myFile is not folder)
            → then
                set myFileName to name of myFile
                if not (exists file myFileName of
                → myContainer2) then
                    set myTransfer to
                    → (transfer myFile to
                    → myFolder2 with replacing)
                    repeat while exists myTransfer
                        try
                            if (transfer status of
                            → myTransfer is finished
                            → with errors) then
                                close myTransfer
                                exit repeat
                            end if
                        on error
                            exit repeat
                        end try
                    end repeat
                end if
            end if
        end repeat
    end tell
end SyncFolders
```

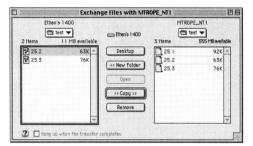

Figure 19.4 Timbuktu's File Exchange window showing our script's progress in matching the contents of a folder on the Mac with one on the PC.

3. `on SyncFolders(myFolder1,`
`   → myFolder2)`

Our handler gets the local and remote folders in the variables `myFolder1` and `myFolder2`.

4. `    tell application "Timbuktu Pro"`
`        set myContainer2 to container`
`            → of myFolder2`

We start our handler by getting the reference of the container for the side of the Transfer window referenced by `myFolder2` and storing it in the variable `myContainer2`.

5. `        repeat with i from 1 to the`
`            → number of items in`
`            → myFolder1`

Then we start repeating through each file item in the other side of the Transfer window.

6. `            set myFile to item i of`
`                → myFolder1`
`            if (class of myFile is not`
`                → folder) then`
`                set myFileName to name`
`                    → of myFile`

Now we check to see if the file is a folder.

7. `            if not (exists file myFileName`
`                → of myContainer2) then`
`                set myTransfer to`
`                    → (transfer myFile to`
`                        → myFolder2 with replacing)`

Now, we construct the equivalent file path on the opposite side of the Transfer window and test for its existence. If it doesn't exist, we start copying it.

8. `if (transfer status of myTransfer`
`    → is finished with errors) then`

Now, we loop until the transfer is complete by testing the `transfer status` property of our Transfer window. Then, we continue looping through the other files.

SCRIPTING MAIL AND LIST SERVERS

Figure 20.1 The entry in AutoShare's AppleScript dictionary for the Send Mail command, which allows your scripts to send mail via EIMS.

Figure 20.2 Eudora Internet Mail Server 2.x includes an AppleScript dictionary with a New User command to add user accounts to the mail server.

In the first half of this chapter, we'll look at the SMTP mail server Eudora Internet Mail Server (EIMS) and its companion list server AutoShare. AutoShare has a complete AppleScript dictionary that allows you total control of mailing lists and sending mail via EIMS. AutoShare works with either the freeware EIMS 1.x or the commercial EIMS 2.x. In the second half of the chapter, we'll look at the integrated mail and list server ListSTAR/SMTP.

AutoShare is a freeware application that has a complete AppleScript dictionary. We'll work with the object classes for lists and users in our scripts for AutoShare. AutoShare can also be used to send e-mail directly via EIMS with the Send Mail command. **Figure 20.1** shows the Send Mail entry in AutoShare's dictionary. EIMS 2.x supports adding user accounts via AppleScript with the New User command. **Figure 20.2** shows the New User entry in EIMS's dictionary.

Converting all list subscribers to non-posting

This script (**Code 20.1**) sets the subscriber option for every subscriber to the list "my-list-name" to non-posting. This effectively makes the mailing list a broadcast-only list. **Figure 20.3** shows the dictionary entry for the sub options record to use with Subscribe List.

To convert all subscribers to a list to non-posting:

1. `set myList to "my-list-name"`

   We begin by storing the name of the mailing list we want to modify in the variable myList.

2. ```
   tell application "AutoShare"
       Subscribe List myList Email "@"
   → Options {Subscriber Post:false}
   → end tell
   ```

   Next, we have AutoShare change all subscribers' Subscriber Post flag to false by using the Subscribe List command.

✔ Using a wildcard

- The @ character acts as a wildcard to represent all subscribers to a list when used in place of an e-mail address.

Code 20.1 This script sets all subscribers to a list to non-posting.

```
set myList to "my-list-name"
tell application "AutoShare"
    Subscribe List myList Email "@" Options
    → {Subscriber Post:false}
end tell
```

Figure 20.3 The Subscribe command has Options that can be used to modify subscribers' account settings.

Scripting AutoShare

All the scripts that follow were designed and tested for AutoShare 2.4.

At the time of publishing, AutoShare 3.0 was about to be released. All the scripts here should work with version 3, which enhances the program's features and AppleScript support.

AutoShare 2.4 is freeware.

AutoShare is published by Mikael Hansen, who can be reached at http://www.dnai.com/~meh/autoshare/.

Scripting Eudora Internet Mail Server

All the scripts that follow were designed and tested for Eudora Internet Mail Server 2.x.

Eudora Internet Mail Server is published by Qualcomm, Inc., which can be reached at http://www.eudora.com/.
```

Code 20.2 This script adds a user to a mailing list in AutoShare.

```
code
set myEmail to "x@x.com"
set myName to "Mister X"
set myList to "my-list-name"
tell application "AutoShare"
    Subscribe List myList Email myEmail
    → Name myName Options {Subscriber
    → Conceal:true, Subscriber Digest:true,
    → Subscriber Mail:false,
    → Subscriber Ack:true,
    → Subscriber Post:false}
end tell
```

Figure 20.4 AutoShare's dictionary definition for Sub Options explains the various subscriber account parameters you can change with the Subscribe command.

Subscribing a user to a mailing list

This script (**Code 20.2**) subscribes a user to a mailing list using the Subscribe command. **Figure 20.4** shows the myriad options available when subscribing a new user.

To subscribe a user to a mailing list:

1. `set myEmail to "x@x.com"`
   `set myName to "Mister X"`
   `set myList to "my-list-name"`

   We begin by setting our e-mail address, username, and list name in the variables myEmail, myName, and myList.

2. `tell application "AutoShare"`
   `    Subscribe List myList Email`
   `    → myEmail Name myName Options`
   `    → {Subscriber Conceal:true,`
   `    → Subscriber Digest:true,`
   `    → Subscriber Mail:false,`
   `    → Subscriber Ack:true,`
   `    → Subscriber Post:false}`
   `    end tell`

   Next, we tell AutoShare to add the new user with the specified e-mail address to the list. We set the subscriber options for the user as well. We set the option Subscriber Conceal to true to hide the subscribers' e-mail addresses from the new user. We set the Subscriber Digest option to true so the new user gets the list's digest version. We set the Subscriber Mail option to false so mail is off. We set the Subscriber Ack option to true so acknowledgements are sent. Finally, we set Subscriber Post to false so the new user can't send messages.

Setting a mailing list's subject line prefix

This script (**Code 20.3**) sets the default prefix for the subject line of every message sent to the mailing list. This prefix will remain in effect until changed. **Figure 20.5** shows the list options available for configuration via AppleScript.

To set a mailing list's subject line prefix:

1. ```
tell application "AutoShare"
    SetList Options
    → {Subject Prefix:"[New List]",
    → List:"my-mail-list"}
    end tell
```

    We tell AutoShare to set the subject prefix of list "my-mail-list" to "[New List]".

## ✔ The many list options

■ **Figure 20.5** shows the tremendous number of list options that can be set using SetList.

**Code 20.3** This script sets a mailing list's subject prefix.

```
tell application "AutoShare"
    SetList Options {Subject Prefix:"[New
    → List]", List:" my-mail-list "}
end tell
```

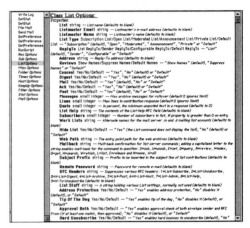

Figure 20.5 AutoShare's List Options properties allow you to change many settings for your mailing lists with the SetList command.
```

Code 20.4 This CGI script adds a user account to EIMS 2.x when it receives form data for the text fields named "domain", "user", "password", and "name".

```
                    code
on handle CGI request myURL ¬

    searching for mySearchArgs

    set myArgList to (tokenize mySearchArgs
    → with delimiters {"&", "="})

    set myDomain to (offset in list myArgList
    → of "domain" with returning next item)

    set myUser to (offset in list myArgList of
    → "user" with returning next item)

    set myPassword to (offset in list
    → myArgList of "password" with returning
    → next item)

    set myName to (offset in list myArgList of
    → "name" with returning next item)


tell application "EIMS Server"

try

    New User {domain:myDomain,
    → username:myUser, password:myPassword,
    → fullname:myName, accountEnabled:true,
    → forwardType:forwardNone}

on error

end try

end tell


set crlf to  (ASCII character 13) &
→ (ASCII character 10)

set myHTML to "HTTP/1.0 200 OK" & crlf &
→ "Server: MacHTTP/2.0" & crlf &
→ "MIME-Version: 1.0" & crlf &
→ "Content-type: text/html" & crlf & crlf

    set myHTML to myHTML &
    → "<HTML><BODY><P>Your account has been
    → created.</BODY></HTML>"

return myHTML

end handle CGI request
```

Adding a user account to EIMS 2.x

This CGI script (**Code 20.4**) adds a user account to Eudora Internet Mail Server 2.x. Only versions 2 and above of EIMS support AppleScript. These versions are commercial products. **Figure 20.6** shows the script-created new user's information in EIMS Admin.

To add a user account to EIMS 2.x:

1. on handle CGI request myURL ¬
    searching for mySearchArgs

    We begin our CGI handler by putting the searching for property into our variable mySearchArgs. searching for contains the reply string from the URL. The reply string value is all of the text that follows the question mark in a GET URL. See Chapter 11 for more details on creating CGI scripts.

2.   set myArgList to
       → (tokenize mySearchArgs with
       → delimiters {"&", "="})

    ACME Script Widgets adds the statement tokenize, which returns a list from a string given list item delimiters, in this case the ampersand and the equals sign. We convert the string mySearchArgs into a series of items in a list, following the format: {name, value}.

3.   set myDomain to (offset in list
       → myArgList of "domain" with
       → returning next item)
       set myUser to (offset in list
       → myArgList of "user" with
       → returning next item)
       set myPassword to (offset in
       → list myArgList of "password"
       → with returning next item)
       set myName to (offset in list
       → myArgList of "name" with
       → returning next item)

We set variables for the domain name, username, password, and name. We retrieve the values for fields named "domain", "user", "password", and "name" with ACME Script Widgets' offset in list statement. Using offset in list with the modifier returning next item gives us the item in the list right after each field name, where its value is stored.

4. tell application "EIMS Server"
    New User {domain:myDomain,
    → username:myUser,
    → password:myPassword,
    → fullname:myName,
    → accountEnabled:true,
    → forwardType:forwardNone}
end tell

Now we tell EIMS Server to create the new user with the New User command.

Figure 20.6 EIMS Admin displays a window for the new user our script created.

Scripting with ACME Script Widgets

This script requires the scripting addition ACME Script Widgets. You must have ACME Script Widgets installed in your Scripting Additions folder for this script to work.

ACME Script Widgets is shareware. It costs $29 for a single-user license.

ACME Script Widgets is published by ACME Technologies, which can be reached at http://www.acmetech.com/.

Figure 20.7 ListSTAR/SMTP lets you send mail from your scripts to individual users or entire address lists with the StarNine Send command.

Scripting ListSTAR/SMTP

ListSTAR/SMTP is a full-fledged SMTP server and list server. The SMTP server is designed primarily to support the list server. ListSTAR has an extensive AppleScript dictionary and comes with some compiled script libraries of useful routines.

ListSTAR supports user, list, and service object classes. We'll work with all three in our scripts. **Figure 20.7** shows the ListSTAR entry for the StarNine Send command, which is used to send SMTP mail.

Scripting ListSTAR/SMTP

All the scripts that follow were designed and tested for ListSTAR/SMTP 1.2.

ListSTAR/SMTP is published by StarNine Technologies, which can be reached at http://www.starnine.com/.

Subscribing a user to a mailing list

This script (**Code 20.5**) subscribes a user to an existing ListSTAR mailing list. For the purposes of our example, we'll add a user named John Doe with the e-mail address john@doe.com to a list named Test. **Figure 20.8** shows ListSTAR's Address List window with our new user added to the "Test" list.

To subscribe a user to a mailing list:

1.
```
set myList to "Test"
set myName to "John Doe"
set myEmail to "john@doe.com"
```
We begin by setting the list name, user-name, and e-mail address in the variables myList, myName, and myEmail.

2.
```
tell application "ListSTAR Server"
    set myAddressRecord to
    → ({freeFormName:myName,
    → eMailAddress:myEmail}
    → as StarNineAddress)
```
ListSTAR needs a properly formatted address record in order to send mail, so we first tell ListSTAR to create a StarNineAddress record for the new user and set the values for the name (myName) and e-mail address (myEmail).

3.
```
    StarNine Subscribe myList
    → addresses myAddressRecord
    end tell
```
Then we subscribe the user to the list with the StarNine Subscribe command.

Code 20.5 This script subscribes a new user to a mailing list.

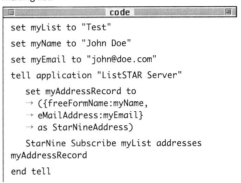

```
set myList to "Test"
set myName to "John Doe"
set myEmail to "john@doe.com"
tell application "ListSTAR Server"
    set myAddressRecord to
    → ({freeFormName:myName,
    → eMailAddress:myEmail}
    → as StarNineAddress)
    StarNine Subscribe myList addresses
myAddressRecord
end tell
```

Figure 20.8 ListSTAR's Address List window with our new user added to the Test list.

Code 20.6 This script sends a mail message to all subscribers to a mailing list.

```
                     code
set mySubject to "Subject Name"
set myBody to "Welcome new user!"
tell application "ListSTAR Server"
   activate
   set myListAddress to actualName of
   → item 1 of (Address Lists name "Test")
   set myMailAddress to
   → ({AddressList:myListAddress}
   → as StarNineAddress)
   StarNine Send "Test" to myMailAddress
   → subject mySubject body myBody
end tell
```

Figure 20.9 ListSTAR's Mail Information window displaying the outgoing mail sent to all addresses on the Test list.

Sending mail to a mailing list's subscribers

This script (**Code 20.6**) sends a mail message to every subscriber on a mailing list. **Figure 20.9** shows ListSTAR's Mail Information window displaying the outgoing mail sent to all addresses on the Test list.

To send a mail message to a mailing list's subscribers:

1. `set mySubject to "Subject Name"`
`set myBody to "Welcome new user!"`

First, we set the subject line and body of the outgoing message in variables.

2. `tell application "ListSTAR Server"`
`activate`
`set myListAddress to actualName`
`→ of item 1 of (Address Lists`
`→ name "Test")`

Next, we tell ListSTAR to come to the front and retrieve the full pathname to the address list file.

3. `set myMailAddress to`
`→ ({AddressList:myListAddress}`
`→ as StarNineAddress)`

Now we set our outgoing mail address in the variable `myMailAddress` to the address list file stored in `myListAddress` so that all recipients on the list get the message.

4. `StarNine Send "Test" to`
`→ myMailAddress subject`
`→ mySubject body myBody`
`end tell`

Finally, we send the message with the `StarNine Send` command.

Enabling and disabling a mailing list

This script (**Code 20.6**) will enable or disable a ListSTAR mailing list. A disabled mailing list is effectively put on hold until it is enabled again. **Figure 20.10** shows ListSTAR's dictionary entries for commands dealing with lists.

To enable or disable a mailing list:

1. `set myList to "Test"`

We begin by setting the list name in the variable myList.

2. `set mySetting to button returned of`
`→ (display dialog "Change List`
`→ Status for " & myList buttons`
`→ {"Disable", "Enable", "Cancel"})`

Now we ask the user whether they want to disable or enable the list.

3. `tell application "ListSTAR Server"`
`    if mySetting is "Disable" then`
`        Disable Service myList`
`    else`
`        Enable Service myList`
`    end if`
`end tell`

Then we tell ListSTAR to disable or enable the list based on the user's choice.

✔ Freezing a list in an emergency

■ Using this script to disable a mailing list is an effective way to put the list on hold in an emergency when you need to keep mail from coming in or going out.

Code 20.7 This script enables or disables a mailing list.

```
set myList to "Test"
set mySetting to button returned of
→ (display dialog "Change List Status for "
→ & myList buttons {"Disable", "Enable",
→ "Cancel"})
tell application "ListSTAR Server"
    if mySetting is "Disable" then
        Disable Service myList
    else
        Enable Service myList
    end if
end tell
```

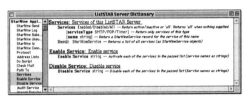

Figure 20.10 ListSTAR's AppleScript dictionary includes commands for retrieving all lists and for enabling and disabling lists.

MARIONET FOR SCRIPTING THE INTERNET

Marionet is an application that provides a complete AppleScript interface to almost every protocol on the Internet. It gives developers and power users the ability to create custom Internet solutions in AppleScript.

Marionet is a faceless background application that receives requests to connect to Internet servers and returns results in sessions.

In this chapter, we'll use Marionet to convert DNS names and IP addresses, send mail, get FTP files, retrieve newsgroup articles, and return HTML data from a Web server.

Scripting Marionet

All the scripts that follow were designed and tested for Marionet 1.1.1.

At the time of publishing, Marionet was available from IncWell only in a bundle with their CGI development product FlameThrower. Marionet alone is more than worth the retail price of FlameThrower.

Marionet is published by IncWell Digital Media Group, which can be reached at `http://www.incwell.com/`.

Scripting Marionet

Marionet is controlled exclusively from AppleScript (unless you use IncWell's SuperCard and FlameThrower or Apple Computer's HyperCard to control it). Marionet's AppleScript dictionary is vast in the scope of Internet protocols it supports. The list includes:

◆ **Chat:** This proprietary protocol lets you create your own chat server.

◆ **FTP:** File Transfer Protocol is the Internet standard for exchanging files with servers.

◆ **NNTP:** NNTP is the protocol that newsgroups speak. With access to NNTP servers, you can get and send newsgroup messages.

◆ **Gopher:** Gopher servers are all over the Internet. A script can search any one of them using this protocol.

◆ **HTTP:** With HTTP you can access Web servers directly to retrieve raw files and monitor or mine data from Web sites.

◆ **SMTP** and **POP:** You can access mail servers directly with the SMTP and POP protocols.

Marionet works on a session model: Before commands are sent, a session is opened and it is referenced with each command until the session is closed. Marionet runs as an asynchronous application, so a scripting addition known as MarionetSync is required to have your script wait for Marionet's results before continuing execution. MarionetSync is available at no charge on the Web.

Figure 21.1. The main window of the Marionet Manager application showing the status of this machine's copy of Marionet.

✔ Quitting Marionet

■ IncWell provides an application called Marionet Manager that lets you check whether your copy of Marionet is running and also lets you quit Marionet. **Figure 21.1** shows Marionet Manager's main window.

Scripting with MarionetSync

All the scripts in this chapter require the scripting addition MarionetSync. You must have MarionetSync installed in your Scripting Additions folder for this script to work.

MarionetSync adds the `MarionetSync` command to make Marionet operate synchronously and wait for results before continuing script execution.

MarionetSync is free for noncommercial use.

MarionetSync is published by IncWell Digital Media Group, which can be reached at `http://www.incwell.com/`.

Code 21.1 This script resolves a DNS name to an IP address.

```
code
on WaitForMarionet(myWaitTime)
    MarionetSync myWaitTime
    set myResults to the result
    return myResults
end WaitForMarionet
on run
    set myDomain to text returned of
    → (display dialog "Domain Name to resolve:
    → " default answer "")
    tell application "Marionet™ 1.1.1"
        set mySessionData to session begin
        set mySession to the status text of
        → mySessionData
        dns name to address mySession name
        → myDomain
        set myResults to my WaitForMarionet(30)
        set myStatus to the errorStatus of the
        → error data of myResults
        if myStatus is ok then
            set myAddress to record1 of the
            → aeData of myResults
        else
            set myAddress to " name server error"
        end if
        session end mySession
    end tell
    display dialog myDomain & "=" & myAddress
end run
```

Figure 21.2 The dialog displayed by our script with the results from Marionet.

Resolving a DNS name to an IP address

This script (**Code 21.1**) prompts the user for a domain name and then returns the IP address that the name resolves to. **Figure 21.2** shows the dialog displayed by our script with the IP address results.

To resolve a DNS name to an IP address:

1. on WaitForMarionet(myWaitTime)

   This handler is used to pause and wait for Marionet to finish processing a command and then get the results. The value passed to it is stored in myWaitTime and is used by our function to determine how long (in seconds) to wait for results.

2. MarionetSync myWaitTime

   We call the MarionetSync command that pauses our script for a not to exceed a duration of myWaitTime seconds waiting for Marionet to return the results of the session's command.

3. set myResults to the result
   return myResults
   end WaitForMarionet

   When the results are returned, this handler passes them back.

4. on run
   set myDomain to text returned of
   → (display dialog "Domain Name
   → to resolve:" default answer "")

   We begin our on run handler by prompting the user for a hostname to resolve to an IP address.

5. tell application "Marionet™
   → 1.1.1"
       set mySessionData to session
       → begin
       set mySession to the status
       → text of mySessionData

RESOLVING A DNS NAME TO AN IP ADDRESS

Next, we start talking to Marionet and begin a new session, storing the session ID. The session ID is generated by Marionet to facilitate the tracking of a session.

6.
```
dns name to address mySession
→ name myDomain
```

Now we tell Marionet to resolve the DNS name to an IP address.

7.
```
set myResults to my
→ WaitForMarionet(30)
```

Then we call our handler WaitForMarionet to wait for results from Marionet, retrieving the results in the variable myResults.

8.
```
set myStatus to the
→ errorStatus of the error
→ data of myResults
```

Here we check to see if the command was completed without error.

9.
```
if myStatus is ok then
    set myAddress to record1 of
    → the aeData of myResults
else
    set myAddress to " name
    → server error"
end if
```

If it was completed without an error, we retrieve the IP address returned and store it in the variable myAddress. If an error occurred, we put an error string in the variable.

10.
```
    session end mySession
end tell
```

Then we close the session with Marionet.

11.
```
display dialog myDomain & "=" &
→ myAddress
end run
```

Finally, we display the domain name and resolved IP address.

✔ Going the other way

■ To resolve IP addresses to their corresponding domain names, change the code in step 6 to this:
```
dns address to name mySession
→ address myDomain
```

Code 21.2 This script send a mail message directly via an SMTP server.

```
on WaitForMarionet(myWaitTime)
    MarionetSync myWaitTime
    set myResults to the result
    return myResults
end WaitForMarionet
    on run
    set myServerName to "mail.sending.com"
    set myRecipient to "test@test.com"
    set mySender to "me@sending.com"
    set mySubject to "Greetings"
    set myBody to "Hello from Marionet!"
    tell application "Marionet™ 1.1.1"
        set mySessionData to session begin
        set mySession to the status text of
        → mySessionData
        set myMessage to "To: " & myRecipient &
        → (ASCII character 13)
        set myMessage to myMessage & "From: " &
        → mySender & (ASCII character 13)
        set myMessage to myMessage & "Subject:
        → " & mySubject & (ASCII character 13)
        → & (ASCII character 13)
        set myMessage to myMessage & myBody
        send mail mySession server name
        → myServerName from ¬
            mySender address list {myRecipient}
            → message myMessage
        set myResults to my WaitForMarionet(30)
        set myStatus to the errorStatus of the
        → error data of myResults
        if myStatus is ok then
            set myFlag to "Successful"
        else
            set myFlag to "Failed"
        end if
        session end mySession
    end tell

    display dialog myFlag
end run
```

```
206.14.230.10=sgi.mediatrope.com

              [ Cancel ]  [  OK  ]
```

Figure 21.3 The entry for the send mail command from Marionet's AppleScript dictionary.

Sending mail directly via an SMTP server

This script (**Code 21.2**) sends a mail message directly via an SMTP server using a mail account on that server. When you send mail directly via an SMTP server you have total control of the message's header. This can be very useful for creating mail that has different Reply-To fields, among other things. The sidebar shows many of the fields that you can define in your mail message header. **Figure 21.3** shows Marionet's dictionary entry for the send mail command.

To send mail directly via an SMTP server:

1. on run
        set myServerName to
        → "mail.sending.com"
        set myRecipient to
        → "test@test.com"
        set mySender to "me@sending.com"
        set mySubject to "Greetings"
        set myBody to "Hello from
        → Marionet!"

We begin our on run handler by setting the mail server name, recipient address, sender address and subject line, along with the body text in the variables myServerName, myRecipient, → mySender, mySubject, and myBody.

2.   set myMessage to "To: " &
        → myRecipient &
        → (ASCII character 13)

Here we format our message to include the appropriate header information. We start with the required To field to define who gets this message.

3.   set myMessage to myMessage &
        → "From: " & mySender &
        → (ASCII character 13)

SENDING MAIL DIRECTLY VIA AN SMTP SERVER

We set the From field to the value in our variable mySender.

4.
```
    set myMessage to myMessage &
    → "Subject: " & mySubject &
    → (ASCII character 13) &
    → (ASCII character 13)
```

We set the Subject field to the value in our variable mySubject. Then we append two return characters to indicate that the header is finished.

5.
```
    set myMessage to myMessage &
    → myBody
```

Finally, we append the body text stored in myBody to our message.

6.
```
    send mail mySession server
    → name myServerName from
        mySender address list
        → {myRecipient} message
        → myMessage
```

Now we tell Marionet to send the mail message using the server and account information stored in the variables.

7.
```
    set myResults to my
    → WaitForMarionet(30)
```

Then we call our handler to wait for results from Marionet.

✔ Making a broadcast mailing list

■ To create a broadcast mailing list, try adding a repeat loop to this script that goes through a list of recipients and sends each one a message.

Typical mail header fields

cc: Secondary, informational recipients; cc stands for carbon copy.

bcc: Recipients not to be disclosed to other recipients; bcc stands for blind carbon copy.

Reply-To: This header indicates where the sender wants replies to go.

References: This is a reference to other related messages.

Keywords: Specifies search keys for data base retrieval.

Comments: Contains comments to the message.

MIME-Version: An indicator that this message is formatted according to the MIME standard, and an indication of which version of MIME is used.

Content-Type: Indicates the format of the content (character set, etc.). Note that the values for this header are defined in different ways. Look for the MIME-Version header to understand if Content-Type is to be interpreted according to RFC 1049 or according to MIME. The MIME definition should be used in generating mail.

See the Internet RFC (Request for Comments) 2076 for more header fields. This file can be found at `http://` `→ www.cis.ohio-state.edu/htbin/rfc/`.

Code 21.3 This script uses Marionet to send a file via FTP.

```
on WaitForMarionet(myWaitTime)
   MarionetSync myWaitTime
   set myResults to the result
   return myResults
end WaitForMarionet
   on run
   set myServer to "ftp.test.com"
   set myUser to "joe"
   set myPassword to "x2"
   set myDirectory to "disk2"
   set myFile to (choose file with prompt
→ "Select file to send via FTP")
   tell application "Finder"
     set myFileName to name of myFile
   end tell
   set myFile to myFile as string
   tell application "Marionet™ 1.1.1"
     set mySessionData to session begin
     set mySession to the status text of
→ mySessionData
     put ftp file mySession local path
→ myFile url (myServer & "/" &
→ myDirectory & "/" & myFileName) &
→ transfer type "binary" user myUser
→ password myPassword
     set myResults to my WaitForMarionet(30)
     set myStatus to the errorStatus of the
→ error data of myResults
     if myStatus is ok then
       set myFlag to "File Transferred"
     else
       set myFlag to "Error"
     end if
     session end mySession
   end tell
   display dialog myFlag
end run
```

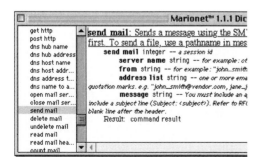

Figure 21.4 The dialog displayed by our script after a successful transfer.

Sending a file via FTP

This script (**Code 21.3**) uses Marionet to send a file via FTP. **Figure 21.4** shows the dialog displayed by our script after a successful transfer.

To send a file via FTP:

1. on run
       set myServer to "ftp.test.com"
       set myUser to "joe"
       set myPassword to "x2"
       set myDirectory to "disk2"

We begin our on run handler by setting the FTP server name, username, password, and directory in variables.

2.   set myFile to (choose file with
       → prompt "Select file to send
       → via FTP")

We also prompt the user to select the local file to send via FTP.

3.   tell application "Finder"
         set myFileName to name of
       → myFile
       end tell

Now we have the Finder return the name of the file, which we store in myFileName.

4.   set myFile to myFile as string

We resave the full path to the file as a string in myFile.

5. put ftp file mySession local path
       → myFile url (myServer & "/" &
       → myDirectory & "/" & myFileName)
       → transfer type "binary" user
       → myUser password myPassword

Now we tell Marionet to send the file to the server myServer and directory myDirectory with the put ftp command. We use a transfer type of "binary" to keep the file contents preserved; we could also use "text" to send text files.

Retrieving a newsgroup's article list with NNTP

This script (**Code 21.4**) retrieves an article list for a newsgroup from a specified news server. **Figure 21.5** shows the local file with all article listings saved by Marionet.

To retrieve a newsgroup's article list from a news server:

1.
```
on run
    set myServer to
    → "nntphost.domain.com"
    set myGroup to "group.name.alt"
    set myFile to (new file)
    set myFile to myFile as string
```

We begin our on run handler by setting the NNTP server name and newsgroup name in variables. We also prompt the user to select a new file to save our article listing into. You'll need to change myServer to point to your news server and myGroup to name the newsgroup you want to look at.

2.
```
    open news server mySession
    → named myServer
    set myResults to my
    → WaitForMarionet(30)
```

Now we tell Marionet to open the news server stored in myServer and then call our wait handler to wait for results from Marionet.

3.
```
    set myStatus to the
    → errorStatus of the error
    → data of myResults
    if myStatus is ok then
        select newsgroup mySession
        → named myGroup
        set myResults to my
        → WaitForMarionet(30)
```

If the last command was successful, we tell Marionet to find the newsgroup

Code 21.4 This script retrieves an article listing for a newsgroup from a news server.

```
on WaitForMarionet(myWaitTime)
    MarionetSync myWaitTime
    set myResults to the result
    return myResults
end WaitForMarionet
    on run
    set myServer to "nntphost.domain.com"
    set myGroup to "group.name.alt"
    set myFile to (new file)
    set myFile to myFile as string
    tell application "Marionet™ 1.1.1"
        set mySessionData to session begin
        set mySession to the status text of
        → mySessionData
        open news server mySession named
        → myServer
        set myResults to my WaitForMarionet(30)
        set myStatus to the errorStatus of the
        → error data of myResults
        if myStatus is ok then
            select newsgroup mySession named
            → myGroup
            set myResults to my
            → WaitForMarionet(30)
            set myStatus to the errorStatus of
            → the error data of myResults
            if myStatus is ok then
                set myData to tokenize
                → (the record1 of the aeData of
                → myResults) with delimiters
                → {space}
                set myStart to item 3 of myData
                set myEnd to item 4 of myData
                list news articles mySession
                → local path myFile start with
                → article myStart end with
                → article myEnd
                set myResults to my
                → WaitForMarionet(30)
            end if
        end if
        session end mySession
    end tell
end run
```

Figure 21.5 Our local file saved by Marionet with the list of newsgroup articles returned by the script.

stored in myGroup and then call our wait handler again.

4.
```
set myResults to my
→ WaitForMarionet(30)
set myStatus to the errorStatus
→ of the error data of myResults
if myStatus is ok then
    set myData to tokenize
        → (the record1 of the aeData
        → of myResults) with
        → delimiters {space}
    set myStart to item 3 of
        → myData
    set myEnd to item 4 of myData
```

If the last command was successful, we retrieve the starting and ending article numbers from the results returned by Marionet.

5.
```
list news articles mySession local
    → path myFile start with article
    → myStart end with article myEnd
set myResults to my
    → WaitForMarionet(30)
```

Now we tell Marionet to retrieve a list of all news articles from the news server and save it in a local file, then call our wait handler one last time.

Retrieving files from a Web server with HTTP

This script (**Code 21.5**) retrieves a file from an HTTP server. This file can be HTML or any other file type that HTTP can access. **Figure 21.6** shows the text of our retrieved HTML file for this example script.

To retrieve a file from a Web server:

1. on run
```
    set myURL to text returned of
    → (display dialog "Select URL to
    → retrieve:" default answer
    → "http://www.apple.com/
    → index.html")
```
We begin by prompting the user for a URL to retrieve.

2.
```
    set myFile to (new file)
    set myFile to myFile as string
```
Then we prompt the user for a new file to save the retrieved data into. We convert the variable myFile, which holds our file name, to a string so that we can pass it to Marionet later.

3.
```
    get http mySession local path
    → myFile url myURL
```
Now we tell Marionet to retrieve the URL via HTTP and save it in the local file stored in the variable myFile.

4.
```
    set myResults to my
    → WaitForMarionet(30)
```
Then we call our handler to wait for results from Marionet.

Code 21.5 This script retrieves a file from an HTTP server.

```
on WaitForMarionet(myWaitTime)
    MarionetSync myWaitTime
    set myResults to the result
    return myResults
end WaitForMarionet
  on run
    set myURL to text returned of
    → (display dialog "Select URL to
    → retrieve:" default answer
    → "http://www.apple.com/index.html")
    set myFile to (new file)
    set myFile to myFile as string
    tell application "Marionet™ 1.1.1"
        set mySessionData to session begin
        set mySession to the status text of
        → mySessionData

        get http mySession local path myFile
        → url myURL
        set myResults to my WaitForMarionet(30)
        set myStatus to the errorStatus of the
        → error data of myResults
        if myStatus is ok then
            set myFlag to "File Retrieved"
        else
            set myFlag to "Error"
        end if
        session end mySession
    end tell

    display dialog myFlag
end run
```

Figure 21.6 The text of our retrieved file from the URL http://www.apple.com/index.html.

THE BIG PROJECT: A WEB SERVER MONITOR

Figure 22.1 Ensure that Marionet is running by checking Marionet Manager.

Figure 22.2 Acid Jazz has a simple AppleScript dictionary.

In this chapter, we'll create a stand-alone script application that monitors a Web server to ensure that it is running. This script project will use AppleScript's built-in `on idle` handler to trigger our code every 90 seconds. We'll use either Marionet or Anarchie Pro to retrieve an HTML file. Then, we'll make sure that the page returned has an expected string in it. If the string is not found, our script will use Acid Jazz, a shareware phone dialing application, to send a page to a pager.

This script could be expanded to test more than one server and perform actions other than paging if it detects a server failure. Chapter 23 will expand on this script to make it a complete application in FaceSpan with a full-fledged user interface.

We'll use Marionet (or Anarchie Pro) and Acid Jazz in this script. You can use Marionet Manager to make sure your copy of Marionet is up and running. **Figure 22.1** shows the Marionet Manager application.

You should open Acid Jazz and ensure that its preferences are configured for your particular modem and port before your script tries to dial out on the modem. **Figure 22.2** shows Acid Jazz's simple AppleScript dictionary.

Monitoring a Web server by retrieving a file

This script consists primarily of an on idle handler that runs every 90 seconds. It retrieves a file from a HTTP server and checks to make sure it contains a certain string. If it doesn't, something is probably wrong, so then the script sends out a page to notify the Webmaster. **Figure 22.3** shows the HTML data returned by Marionet in a test run of this script.

To monitor a Web server by testing file retrieval:

1. `property myURL : "www.server.com"`
   → `property myMatchString :`
   → `"Welcome to our home page"`

   We begin by setting the URL we're going to test and the string to search for.

2. `on WaitForMarionet(myWaitTime)`

   This handler is used to pause and wait for Marionet to finish processing a command and then get the results. The value passed to it is stored in myWaitTime and is used by our function to determine how long (in seconds) to wait for results.

3. `MarionetSync myWaitTime`

   We call the MarionetSync command that pauses our script for a (not to exceed) a duration of myWaitTime seconds waiting for Marionet to return the results of the session's command.

4. `set myResults to the result`
   `return myResults`
   `end WaitForMarionet`

   When the results are returned, this handler passes them back.

5. `on idle`

   Our on idle handler is run by AppleScript every 90 seconds thanks to the handler returning the value 90 at its end in step 10.

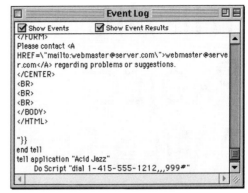

Figure 22.3. The Script Editor's Event Log shows the HTML data returned by Marionet and the script's request to Acid Jazz to dial a pager with the code 999.

Scripting Acid Jazz

All the scripts that follow were designed and tested for Acid Jazz.

Acid Jazz can be found at
`http://www.macinsearch.com/`
→ `infomac2/communication/`
→ `acid-jazz-12v2.html`.

Acid Jazz is published by Kevin Jundt.

Code 22.1 Our Web server monitor script .

```
code
property myURL : "www.server.com"
property myMatchString : "Welcome to our
→ home page"

on WaitForMarionet(myWaitTime)
   MarionetSync myWaitTime
   set myResults to the result
   return myResults
end WaitForMarionet


on idle
      tell application "Marionet™ 1.1.1"
         set mySessionData to session begin
         set mySession to the status text of
         → mySessionData
         get http mySession url myURL
         set myResults to my
         → WaitForMarionet(30)
         set myStatus to the errorStatus of
         → the error data of myResults
         if myStatus is not ok then
            set myHTML to ""
         else
            set myHTML to record2 of the
            → aeData of myResults
         end if
         if myHTML does not contain
         → myMatchString then
            tell application "Acid Jazz"
               Do Script "dial 1-415-555-
               → 1212,,,999#"
            end tell
         end if
         session end mySession
      end tell
   return 90
end idle
```

6.
```
tell application "Marionet™ 1.1.1"
   set mySessionData to session
   → begin
   set mySession to the status
   → text of mySessionData
```
Next, we begin talking to Marionet with a new session, storing the session ID.

7.
```
   get http mySession url myURL
```
Now we tell Marionet to return the file from the HTTP server.

8.
```
   set myResults to my
   → WaitForMarionet(30)
```
Then we call our handler WaitForMarionet to wait for results from Marionet.

9.
```
   set myStatus to the errorStatus
   → of the error data of myResults
```
We get the error result string from Marionet's results record that we stored in myResults.

10.
```
   if myStatus is not ok then
      set myHTML to ""
   else
      set myHTML to record2 of the
      → aeData of myResults
   end if
```
If the command was not successful, we set the variable myHTML to a null string. If the command succeeded, we retrieve the file data from Marionet's results record stored in myResults and put it into myHTML.

11.
```
   if myHTML does not contain
   → myMatchString then
      tell application "Acid Jazz"
         Do Script "dial
         → 1-415-555-1212,,,999#"
      end tell
   end if
```
Next, we check our returned data for the match string stored in myMatchString.

If it isn't found, we use Acid Jazz to dial the phone number 1-415-555-1212, pause by sending commas, then send the pager code 999.

12.
```
        session end mySession
    end tell
  return 90
end idle
```

Finally, we end our session with Marionet and conclude our `idle` handler, returning 90 to let AppleScript know we want the handler to run again in 90 seconds. You can change this value to determine how often the Web site is tested.

✔ Moving on and making it better

■ Continue on to Chapter 23 when you're done here! You'll learn how to make this script into a full-fledged application with its own easy-to-use interface.

Making it work with Anarchie Pro

◆ To make this script work with Anarchie Pro 3.0 instead of Marionet, delete all of steps 2 through 4 and also delete the lines in step 12 that read:
```
session end mySession
end tell
```

◆ Replace steps 6 through 10 with the following code:
```
set (my myCounter) to 0
set mytempfile to (path to me as
→ string)&" Temp File"
  tell application "Anarchie Pro"
    webfetch alias mytempfile url
    → myURL
end tell
set myfileref to (open for access
→ alias mytempfile)
set myHTML to (read myfileref)
close access myfileref
```

GIVING YOUR SCRIPTS A FACE

Figure 23.1 The FaceSpan Project window.

FaceSpan is a cutting-edge interface design and rapid application development tool. It gives you the power to build and customize Macintosh applications quickly and easily using AppleScript as the underlying programming language for the entire application. Using FaceSpan, you can create simple interfaces such as floating tool palettes that give you quick access to your favorite scripts. Or, you can create more sophisticated applications that integrate the features of a group of other applications that you control via AppleScript from your FaceSpan project.

Bringing one of your scripts into FaceSpan to give it a complete interface is not hard to do. It is one of the easiest and most rewarding AppleScripting experiences available.

In this chapter, we'll move our Web server monitor script from Chapter 22 into FaceSpan.

Figure 23.1 shows FaceSpan's Project window. You'll see this window once you've created a new project.

Scripting FaceSpan

All the scripts that follow were designed and tested for FaceSpan 3.0.

FaceSpan is published by Digital Technology International, which can be reached at http://www.facespan.com.

Creating a window with controls

We'll begin our new project by creating a window and some controls to hold the user-configurable values of our script. First we'll need to create a new window in the Project window. Once we have our new window, we'll add three text boxes with editable text and labels, two buttons, and a text box with locked text.

Make your window look like the one in **Figure 23.2**, naming each of the text boxes and buttons as shown there. The code here was written using references to these object names, and won't work if it doesn't find them.

To create a window with controls:

1. Create a new window from the Project window. Name it "Main" and set its title property to "Server Monitor".

2. Now create a text box with editable type, name it "url", and create a label with the same title.

3. Now create a text box with editable type and a scrollbar, name it "matchstring", and create a label for it.

4. Create a text box with editable type, name it "phone", and create a label for it.

5. Create a text box with uneditable type, name it "status", and set it to read "Server Monitoring on...".

6. Create a button and name it "Stop" with the same text for its title.

7. Create a button and name it "Monitor" with the same text for its title.

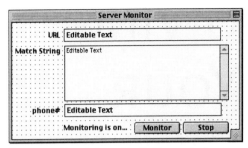

Figure 23.2 Our window with all of the controls we need.

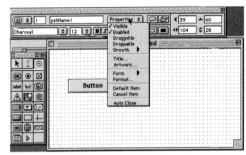

Figure 23.3 Changing a button's title by choosing the title property from the editing palette's pop-up menu.

✔ Changing object properties

■ FaceSpan's object editing palette gives you complete control over the selected object's properties. **Figure 23.3** shows a user about to edit a button's title property by selecting it from a pop-up menu of properties.

CREATING A WINDOW WITH CONTROLS

Figure 23.4 The Project Script button in the Project window.

Entering the project script

The project script is the main code for our FaceSpan script application. You can easily start converting a stand-alone script to a FaceSpan project by pasting your script into the project script in FaceSpan. We'll do that with our server monitor script from Chapter 22. Let's paste that script into our project script and modify it to take advantage of the controls and window we've created. Click the Project Script button to open the project script and paste in your script from the last chapter. In the steps below, we'll cover every line of code again. Steps 1, 5, and 14 through 19 cover new code additions. **Figure 23.4** shows the Project Script button in the Project window.

To enter your project script:

1. `property myURL : "www.server.com"`
`property myMatchString : "Welcome`
`→ to our home page"`
`property myPhone : "555-1212,,,999"`
`property myRunning : true`

    We begin by setting our URL to test and the string to search for as well as the phone number to dial. We also set a flag to decide whether to test the server at all.

2. `on WaitForMarionet(myWaitTime)`

    This handler is used to pause and wait for Marionet to finish processing a command and then get the results. The value passed to it is stored in `myWaitTime` and is used by our function to determine how long (in seconds) to wait for results.

3. `MarionetSync myWaitTime`

    We call the `MarionetSync` command that pauses our script for a not to exceed a duration of `myWaitTime` seconds waiting for Marionet to return the results of the session's command.

4.
```
   set myResults to the result
   return myResults
end WaitForMarionet
```

When the results are returned, this handler passes them back.

5.
```
on idle
   if myRunning then
      set myURL to textbox "url" of
      → window "main"
      set myMatchString to textbox
      → "matchstring" of window
      → "main"
      set myPhone to textbox "phone"
      → of window "main"
```

Whenever our on idle handler is run by AppleScript, we first test our flag to see whether to monitor the server at all. If we're monitoring the server, we set our properties from the text boxes in our window.

6.
```
      tell application
      → "Marionet™ 1.1.1"
         set mySessionData to
         → session begin
         set mySession to the
         → status text of
         → mySessionData
```

Next, we reset the counter variable and begin talking to Marionet with a new session, storing the session ID.

7.
```
         get http mySession url myURL
```

Now we tell Marionet to return the file from the HTTP server.

8.
```
         set myResults to my
         → WaitForMarionet(30)
```

Then we call our handler WaitForMarionet to wait for results from Marionet.

Code 23.1 Our FaceSpan project script.

```
┌─────────────────── code ───────────────────┐
property myURL : "www.server.com"
property myMatchString : "Welcome to our
→ home page"
property myPhone : "555-1212,,,999"
property myRunning : true


on WaitForMarionet(myWaitTime)
   MarionetSync myWaitTime
   set myResults to the result
   return myResults
end WaitForMarionet


on idle
   if myRunning then
      set myURL to textbox "url" of window
      → "main"
      set myMatchString to textbox
      → "matchstring" of window "main"
      set myPhone to textbox "phone" of
      → window "main"
      set textbox "status" of window
      → "main" to "Checking server..."
      tell application "Marionet™ 1.1.1"
         set mySessionData to session begin
         set mySession to the status text
         → of mySessionData
         get http mySession url myURL
         set myResults to my
         → WaitForMarionet(30)
         set myStatus to the errorStatus
         → of the error data of myResults
         if myStatus is not ok then
            set myHTML to ""
         else
            set myHTML to record2 of the
            → aeData of myResults
         end if
         if myHTML does not contain
         → myMatchString then
            tell application "Acid Jazz"
               Do Script "dial " & myPhone
               → & "#"
            end tell
         end if
         session end mySession
      end tell
```

Code continues on next page

Code 23.1 *continued*

```
                    code
            set textbox "status" of window
              → "main" to "Monitoring is on..."
        end if
    return 90
end idle

on quit
    set myURL to textbox "url" of window "main"
    set myMatchString to textbox
      → "matchstring" of window "main"
    set myPhone to textbox "phone" of window
      → "main"
    continue quit
end quit

on run
    open window "main"
    set textbox "url" of window "main" to
      → myURL
    set textbox "matchstring" of window "main"
      → to myMatchString
    set textbox "phone" of window "main" to
      → myPhone
    set textbox "status" of window "main" to
      → "Monitoring is on..."
    set the enabled of push button "monitor"
      → of window "main" to not myRunning
    set the enabled of push button "stop" of
      → window "main" to myRunning
end run

on chosen myObj
    copy name of myObj to myMenuItem
    copy title of menu of myObj to myMenu
    if index of menu of myObj = 1 then
        display dialog "Server Monitor - my own
          → AppleScript creation"
    else if myMenu is "File" then
        if myMenuItem = "Quit" then
            quit
        end if
    end if
end chosen
```

9.
```
set myStatus to the errorStatus of
  → the error data of myResults
```
We get the error result string from Marionet's results record that we stored in myResults.

10.
```
if myStatus is not ok then
    set myHTML to ""
else
    set myHTML to record2 of the
      → aeData of myResults
end if
```
If the command was not successful, we set the variable myHTML to a null string. If the command succeeded, we retrieve the file data from Marionet's results record stored in myResults and put it into myHTML.

11.
```
if myHTML does not contain
  → myMatchString then
    tell application "Acid Jazz"
    Do Script "dial " & myPhone
      → & "#"
    end tell
end if
```
Next, we check our returned data for the match string stored in myMatchString. If it isn't found, we use Acid Jazz to dial the phone number.

12.
```
    session end mySession
end tell
```
Finally, we end our session with Marionet.

13.
```
            set textbox "status" of
              → window "main" to
              → "Monitoring is on..."
        end if
    return 90
end idle
```
After the script has run and we have results back, instead of just finishing the script we use FaceSpan to display the results by setting the status text box to

show monitoring is active before ending the on `idle` handler. We return a value of 90 to let AppleScript know we want this handler to run again in 90 seconds.

14.
```
on quit
    set myURL to textbox "url" of
    ⇢ window "main"
    set myMatchString to textbox
    ⇢ "matchstring" of window "main"
    set myPhone to textbox "phone"
    ⇢ of window "main"
    continue quit
end quit
```

On a quit, we set our properties to the current values of the window's text boxes so the settings are preserved across separate launches of the application (properties' values are preserved this way in all AppleScript and FaceSpan applications).

15.
```
on run
    open window "main"
    set textbox "url" of window
    ⇢ "main" to myURL
    set textbox "matchstring" of
    ⇢ window "main" to
    ⇢ myMatchString
    set textbox "phone" of window
    ⇢ "main" to myPhone
    set textbox "status" of window
    ⇢ "main" to "Monitoring is
    ⇢ on..."
```

On a run, we set our window's text boxes to the application's property values.

16.
```
    set the enabled of push button
    ⇢ "monitor" of window "main" to
    ⇢ not myRunning
    set the enabled of push button
    ⇢ "stop" of window "main" to
myRunning
end run
```

We set the buttons' `enabled` property to the settings in our variable `myRunning`.

17.
```
on chosen myObj
    copy name of myObj to
      ⇥ myMenuItem
    copy title of menu of myObj to
      ⇥ myMenu
```

The on chosen handler is a FaceSpan event that allows our project script to respond to menu selections by the user.

18.
```
    if index of menu of myObj = 1
      ⇥ then
        display dialog "Server
          ⇥ Monitor - my own
          ⇥ AppleScript creation"
    else if myMenu is "File" then
        if myMenuItem = "Quit" then
            quit
        end if
    end if
end chosen
```

Here we quit if the Quit menu item is selected. We display an About dialog box if the About item is selected.

✔ Using Anarchie Pro instead

■ It can be done! See Chapter 22 for details on using Anarchie Pro 3.0 instead of Marionet.

Adding scripts to window controls

Now, we're ready to add scripts to our window's two buttons to control the flag that determines whether or not server monitoring is active. **Figure 23.5** shows how to open a script for the currently selected object in FaceSpan.

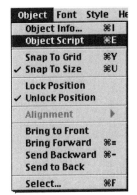

Figure 23.5 Opening the object script from the Object menu.

To add a script to our window's Monitor button:

1. Select the Monitor button and then choose Object Script from the Object menu. Enter **Code 23.2**.

2. `on hilited myObj`

   FaceSpan sends a `hilited` event to the button after the user has clicked it. Our handler to deal with `hilited` receives a reference to the button that was clicked in the variable `myObj`.

3. `    set myRunning to true`

   We set the monitoring flag variable `myRunning` to `true` so our main code will know to start monitoring the server.

4. `    set textbox "status" of window`
   `    → "main" to "Monitoring is`
   `    → on..."`
   `    set the enabled of myObj to false`
   `    set the enabled of push button`
   `    → "stop" of window "main" to`
   `    → true`
   `end hilited`

   Next, we set the text in the status text box, disable the button that was clicked, and then enable the Stop button.

Code 23.2 The script for our Monitor button.

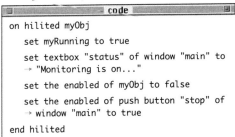

```
on hilited myObj
    set myRunning to true
    set textbox "status" of window "main" to
    → "Monitoring is on..."
    set the enabled of myObj to false
    set the enabled of push button "stop" of
    → window "main" to true
end hilited
```

Code 23.3 The script for our Stop button.

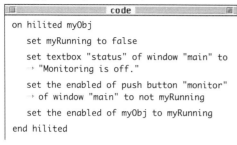

```
on hilited myObj
    set myRunning to false
    set textbox "status" of window "main" to
    → "Monitoring is off."
    set the enabled of push button "monitor"
    → of window "main" to not myRunning
    set the enabled of myObj to myRunning
end hilited
```

To add a script to our window's Stop button:

1. Select the Stop button and then choose Object Script from the Object menu. Enter **Code 23.3**.

2. `on hilited myObj`

Our handler to deal with `hilited` receives a reference to the button that was clicked in the variable `myObj`.

3. `set myRunning to false`

We set the monitoring flag variable `myRunning` to `false` so our main code will know to stop monitoring the server.

Saving a project as an application

Finally, we can save our FaceSpan project. **Figure 23.6** shows FaceSpan's Save As... dialog configured to save the current project as a stand-alone application. **Figure 23.7** shows our project running as a stand-alone application.

To save a project as an application:

◆ When you're ready to save our project as a stand-alone application, choose Save As... from the File menu.

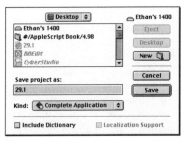

Figure 23.6 FaceSpan's Save As... dialog set to save our project as a complete application.

Figure 23.7 Our project running as a stand-alone application.

DEBUGGING
APPLESCRIPT

AppleScript can be easy to write. AppleScript looks like simple written English in its most elegant object-model form. However, with the myriad applications supporting AppleScript, unique commands and unusual implementations have left many scripters struggling to get the syntax exactly right.

In this chapter, we'll look at the debugging tools of Apple's free Script Editor and three other commercial AppleScript editors: Scripter, Script Debugger, and FaceSpan.

The functioning of your AppleScripts can also be affected by how your system software is configured. We'll conclude this chapter with a look at the System Folder components that AppleScript requires to work properly in Systems 7.x, 8, and 8.5.

Debugging with the Script Editor

The Script Editor has two very basic debugging tools available for your use. The Event Log window allows you to watch the Apple Events sent to other applications and the results those applications return. The Result window shows the most recent evaluated result of an expression. These windows are invaluable tools for debugging scripts in the Script Editor. **Figure 24.1** shows the Event Log window and **Figure 24.2** shows the Result window.

Figure 24.1 The Event Log window displays all events sent to other applications and any results those events return.

To use the Script Editor to debug your scripts:

1. Always test your scripts in the Script Editor before saving them. When an error occurs during execution, the Script Editor will conveniently highlight the offending line of code in your script.

2. Leave the Event Log window open at all times when you run scripts from within the Script Editor.

3. Open the Result window to quickly see the results of running a single line of code in the Script Editor.

4. Use AppleScript's special `stop log` and `start log` commands in your script to hide and show selected portions of your code's activity in the Event Log, instead of having to look at all the results of your entire script.

5. Insert temporary `display dialog` commands into your script to display the contents of variables during your script's execution. Once your script is debugged, you can easily delete any of these commands.

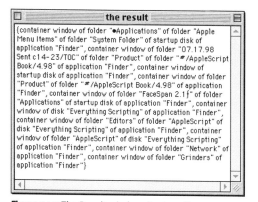

Figure 24.2 The Result window displays the most recent result returned from any executed script.

6. In Mac OS 8.5, you can insert temporary say commands into your script to have AppleScript speak the contents of variables during execution instead of using display dialog.

7. For the best error handling, add complete try statements to your scripts that deal intelligently with errors. See *Error handling* in Chapter 3 for more information.

Debugging with Scripter

Scripter 2.0, from Main Event Software, offers the most unique suite of AppleScript debugging tools available. The application palette lets you put the dictionaries of the programs you script most often just a click away. **Figure 24.3** shows the application toolbar in Scripter.

Scripter's Build a Command window, shown in **Figure 24.4**, uses AppleScript dictionaries to help you construct legal command syntax based on a program's own dictionary definitions. In addition, Scripter's unique ability to call handlers from Call Boxes within the editor lets you test your CGI handlers while editing! **Figure 24.5** shows the Call Box window ready to test a CGI handler.

To use Scripter to debug your scripts:

1. Assign your most frequently scripted programs space on the application palette for quick access to dictionaries.

2. Use the Build a Command window to help understand command syntax when scripting.

3. Test your CGI handlers inside Scripter by calling them from Scripter's Call Box.

4. All of the debugging techniques recommended for the Script Editor will also work in Scripter.

✔ Tip

■ Scripter does not compile on run handlers, which are optional anyway in AppleScript. If you use scripter, be sure to omit any on...run...end...run lines you might have.

Figure 24.3 Scripter's application palette allows quick access to specific dictionaries for reference and command building.

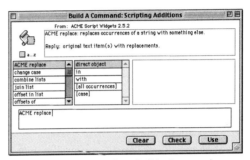

Figure 24.4 Scripter's unique Build a Command window walks you through the construction of proper syntax by using the application's dictionary.

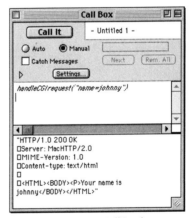

Figure 24.5 Scripter's Call Box lets you test your handlers live from within the editor!

Scripter

Scripter 2.0 is published by Main Event Software, which can be reached at http://www.mainevent.com/.

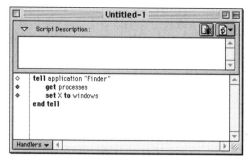

Figure 24.6 Script Debugger's Script window with two debugging breakpoints set.

Figure 24.7 Script Debugger's Data window lets you monitor the values of any variables or properties in your script.

Figure 24.8 Script Debugger's Dictionary window enhancements include a graphical object model display.

Debugging with Script Debugger

Script Debugger, from Late Night Software, is the only AppleScript editor that is itself scriptable. It also includes a nice assortment of debugging tools. The Script window includes breakpoints, which let you indicate a point in code at which you want execution to be halted, as shown in **Figure 24.6**. The Data window, shown in **Figure 24.7**, lets you track the current value of any variable or property you type in. Script Debugger's Dictionary is not nearly as sophisticated as Scripter's Build a Command interface, but is a nice enhancement over the Script Editor. **Figure 24.8** shows the Dictionary window.

To use Script Debugger to debug your scripts:

1. Use breakpoints to interrupt script execution or pause so you can step line by line through your code as it runs, checking values and monitoring for errors.

2. Add important variable and property names to the Data window to track your script's activities more closely.

3. All of the debugging techniques recommended for the Script Editor will also work in Script Debugger.

Script Debugger

Script Debugger is published by Late Night Software, which can be reached at http://www.latenightsw.com/.

Debugging with FaceSpan

FaceSpan is not just a complete application development environment for AppleScript; it also includes script editing and debugging capabilities. FaceSpan's Dictionary window (**Figure 24.9**) shows all events and objects as text that can be dragged and dropped into the Script window. The Dictionary also remembers the dictionaries of applications you use. In FaceSpan's Script window, shown in **Figure 24.10**, there are pull-down menus for objects and events that enable you to insert script code quickly and easily.

To use FaceSpan to debug your scripts:

1. Keep the Dictionary window open for quick syntax reference and drag-and-drop script construction.

2. Use the Script window pull-downs to insert FaceSpan events and objects.

3. Open FaceSpan's Message window all the way to see the Event Log.

4. All of the debugging techniques recommended for the Script Editor will also work in FaceSpan.

Figure 24.9 FaceSpan's Dictionary window displays an application's statements and object classes as text that can be dragged and dropped.

Figure 24.10 FaceSpan's Script window has pull-downs to help you build code for events and objects.

FaceSpan

FaceSpan is published by Digital Technology International, which can be reached at http://www.facespan.com/.

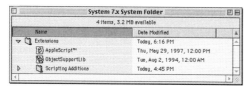

Figure 24.11 Proper system software configuration for Mac OS 7.x.

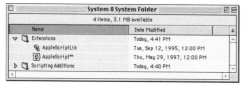

Figure 24.12 Proper system software configuration for Mac OS 8.

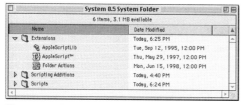

Figure 24.13 Proper system software configuration for Mac OS 8.5.

Proper system software configurations for AppleScript

As AppleScript has matured, its System Folder components and their placement have changed slightly from Mac OS 7.x to Mac OS 8 and again in Mac OS 8.5. **Figures 24.11** through **24.13** show the minimum required System Folder components and their proper placement for each System.

✔ Mac OS 8.x and the Scripting Additions folder

- Beginning with version 8.0 of the Mac OS, the Scripting Additions folder migrated to live right inside of the System Folder. Prior versions of the system expected the Scripting Additions folder to be inside of the Extensions folder.

- If you can't seem to use commands from scripting additions, or scripts won't run or compile properly, check the location of the Scripting Additions folder. Some software installers add a Scripting Additions folder to the Mac OS 8.x Extensions folder, confusing AppleScript. You can solve this problem by moving any scripting additions or dialects to the real Scripting Additions folder right inside of the System Folder. Be sure to delete the extra Scripting Additions folder.

✔ ObjectSupportLib Tip

- The ObjectSupportLib file is required in Mac OS 7.x versions of AppleScript. However, some versions of this file are faulty and will prevent AppleScript scripts from running properly. ObjectSupportLib versions 1.0.4 and 1.1.1 break some applications' Apple Events handling.

- Delete any copy of ObjectSupportLib
  from your System Folder if you're running
  any version of Mac OS 8.

- Go to the Technical Information Library
  at `http://til.info.apple.com/` and
  search on "objectsupportlib" to find
  more details.

✔ Late breaking news about AppleScript

- Mac OS 8.5 marks a new era of change
  and improvement for AppleScript.
  Visit this book's Web site at `http://`
  → `www.mediatrope.com/applescript/`
  for the latest news on AppleScript or
  search the Apple Technical Information
  Library (TIL) using Sherlock. Search on
  the term "applescript."

APPLESCRIPT REFERENCE

This appendix covers just about every one of AppleScript's standard commands, control statements, handlers, references, operators, variable and property assignments, and constants.

For information on other commands, statements, and objects see the dictionary for the specific application or scripting addition.

Visit www.apple.com to find Adobe Acrobat versions of the official AppleScript Language Guide and other useful AppleScript documentation for downloading and printing.

Commands

Optional terms are shown in square brackets: [optional].

Underlined placeholder terms (such as **reference**) are meant to be replaced with appropriate information. See the last section, *Placeholder definitions*, for a detailed definition of each placeholder term.

Each command definition includes an example code snippet with description.

activate

```
activate
```

```
tell application "FreeHand 8.0" to activate
```
We tell FreeHand to become the frontmost application.

close

```
close reference
```

```
close reference saving in reference
```

```
tell application "Fetch" to close transfer
→ window 1
```
We tell Fetch to close the current transfer window.

copy

```
copy expression to variable
```

```
copy 4*2 to x
```
We copy the results of the calculation 4 times 2 into the variable x, which will contain 8 after this line is executed.

count

```
number of objectClass in reference
```

```
count every objectClass in reference
```

```
set x to {1,2,3}
get number of items in x
```
We put the list {1,2,3} into the variable x. Then we retrieve the count of items in the list contained by x. The result will be 3.

delete

```
delete reference
```

```
tell application "Finder" to delete file "Temp"
→ of folder "Files" of startup disk
```
We tell the Finder to delete the file named Temp found in the folder Files on our startup disk.

duplicate

```
duplicate reference
```

```
duplicate reference to reference
```

```
tell application "Photoshop 5.0" to duplicate
layer 1 of document 1
```
We tell Photoshop to duplicate the first layer of our current document.

exists

```
exists reference
```

```
reference exists
```

```
tell application "Finder"
    if disk "HD" exists then beep
end tell
```
We tell the Finder to have our computer beep if a volume named HD is mounted on our Desktop.

get

```
get expression
```

```
get expression as objectClass
```

```
get "My name "&return&"is Mac." as string
```
Returns this string to the result:
```
My name
is Mac
```

launch

```
launch
```

```
tell application "Netscape Navigator 4" to launch
```
Tells Netscape to behave as if it were double-clicked from the Finder.

make

```
make [new] objectClass at reference
```

```
make [new] objectClass at reference
→ with properties
→ { propertyName: propertyValue
→ [,propertyName: propertyValue]...}
```

```
make [new] objectClass at reference
→ with data value
```

```
tell application "Finder" to make new folder at
→ startup disk with properties {name: "New"}
```
We tell the Finder to create a new folder named New on the startup disk.

move

```
move reference to reference
```

```
tell application "Photoshop" to move selection
→ to {10 as pixels,10 as pixels}
```
We tell Photoshop to move the current selection to the coordinates 10 pixels in the x plane and 10 pixels in the y plane.

open

```
open reference
```

```
open listOfReferences
```

```
tell application "QuarkXpress" to open alias
→ "HD:Quark Doc"
```
We tell Quark to open a file named Quark Doc on the volume named HD.

print

```
print reference
```

```
tell application "Claris Emailer 2.0" to print
→ window 1
```

We tell Emailer to print the frontmost window to the current default printer.

quit

```
quit
```

```
tell application "Microsoft Word 98" to quit
```

We tell the Word application to quit.

run

```
run
```

```
run reference
```

```
tell application "FileMaker Pro 4.0" to run
```

We tell the FileMaker application to run.

save

```
save reference in reference
```

```
tell application "FreeHand 8.0" to save in file
→ "HD:image.jpg" as JPEG
```

We tell FreeHand to save the current document as a JPEG with the file name image.jpg on the volume HD.

set

```
set variable to expression
set reference to expression
```

```
tell application "Finder" to set the name of
→ file "Test" of startup disk to "New Test"
```

We tell the Finder to rename the file named Test on our startup drive to New Test by having the Finder set the name property of the file.

Control statements

if

```
if boolean then statement
if boolean [ then ]
[ statement ]…
[ else if boolean [ then ]
   [ statement ]…]…
[ else
   [ statement ]…]
end [ if ]
```

```
if 2>3 then beep
```

This statement will not result in a beep being generated, since the Boolean test 2>3 results in false. See *Comparisons and control statements* and the following spreads in Chapter 3 for more information on if.

repeat

```
repeat
   [ statement ]…
   [ exit repeat ]…
end [ repeat ]
repeat integer [ times ]
   [ statement ]…
end [ repeat ]
repeat while boolean
   [ statement ]…
end [ repeat ]
repeat until boolean
   [ statement ]…
end [ repeat ]
repeat with variable from integer to
→ integer [ by integer ]
   [ statement ]…
end [ repeat ]
repeat with variable in list
   [ statement ]…
end [ repeat ]
```

```
repeat with x from 1 to 10
   display dialog x
end repeat
```

This code will generate a loop that runs for 10 cycles, incrementing the value in the variable x from 1 to 10.

tell

```
tell reference to statement
tell reference
   [ statement ]…
end [ tell ]
```

```
tell application "Sherlock" to quit
```

Sends the quit command to the application Sherlock.

try

```
try
[ statement ]…
on error
[ variable]
[ number variable]
[ from variable]
[ partial result variable]
[ to variable]
   [ statement ]…
end [ try ]
```

```
try
   quit
on error myErr
   display dialog myErr
end try
```

This `try` statement will execute the error handler if the `quit` command fails, displaying a dialog showing the error message string. See *Error handling* in Chapter 3 for more information.

with timeout

```
with timeout [ of ] integer seconds
    [ statement ]…
end [ timeout ]
```

```
with timeout of 50 seconds
    tell application "Netscape Navigator 4.0"
        OpenURL "http://www.apple.com/"
    end tell
end timeout
```

We tell Netscape to open the URL http://
→ www.apple.com/, allowing up to 50 seconds for the operation to be completed. See *Waiting with timeout* in Chapter 3 for more.

considering

```
considering attribute
→ [,attribute. and attribute]
→ [ but ignoring attribute
→ [,attribute… and attribute] ]
    [ statement ]…
end considering
```

```
considering case
    if "Help" starts with "H" then beep
end considering
```

This code will generate a beep since our string does start with a capital H and we are conducting the comparison with case sensitivity turned on.

ignoring

```
ignoring attribute
→ [,attribute… and attribute]
→ [ but considering attribute
→ [,attribute… and attribute] ]
    [ statement ]…
end ignoring
```

```
ignoring application responses
    tell application "Finder" to duplicate alias
    → "HD:My Folder"
    tell application "Finder" to duplicate alias
    → "HD:My Other Folder"
end ignoring
```

By ignoring application responses we have the Finder duplicate two folders simultaneously by having our script not wait for a response from each of the `duplicate` commands.

Attributes for considering and ignoring

application responses

If ignored, AppleScript won't wait for responses from applications before proceeding to the next statement in a script. Any results or errors returned are ignored.

case

If considered, AppleScript makes string comparisons with case sensitivity.

diacriticals

If ignored, AppleScript ignores diacritical marks in string comparisons.

expansion

If ignored, AppleScript sees æ, Æ, œ, and Œ as single characters and not equal to the character pairs ae, AE, oe, and OE.

hyphens

If ignored, AppleScript ignores hyphens in string comparisons

punctuation

If ignored, AppleScript ignores punctuation marks in string comparisons.

white space

If ignored, AppleScript ignores spaces, tab characters, and return characters in string comparisons.

Handlers

on

```
on subroutineName
→ ( [ variable1 [,variable2]…] )
    [ statement ]…
    [ return expression ]…
end [ subroutineName ]
```

```
on showScore(score)
display dialog score
end showScore
```

You can create your own functions, or subroutines, within your scripts. These custom handlers can receive values and return resulting values. This example shows a dialog that displays the value passed to it. See *Handlers* in Chapter 3.

on idle

```
on idle
    [ statement ]…
end [idle]
```

```
on idle
    set x to x+1
end idle
```

This built-in handler will execute every 30 seconds by default while your script application is running.

on open

```
on open (reference)
    [ statement ]…
end [open]
on open (listOfReferences)
    [ statement ]…
end [open]
```

```
on open (myfiles)
    tell application "Finder" to reveal myfiles
end open
```

This built-in handler is executed when your script is saved as an application and items are dropped onto the application's icon in the Finder. References to the items dropped onto the application are passed to the handler. This example will have the Finder show all items dropped onto the script application. See *Making drag-and-drop applications with <u>on</u> <u>open</u>* in Chapter 3 for more.

on quit

```
on quit
    [ statement ]…
    [continue quit]
end [quit]
```

```
on quit
    close access myfile
    continue quit
end quit
```

This built-in handler is executed when your script application receives the quit Apple Event before your script application does its own quit routines. Include a continue quit statement at the end of your handler to be sure AppleScript gets a chance to properly quit your script. This example closes the file referenced by myfile before quitting.

on run

```
on run
    [ statement ]…
end
```

```
on run
    display dialog "Hello World"
end
```

This built-in handler is executed whenever your script is run, whether from the Script Editor or as a compiled script or stand-alone script application. If you have loose code in your script, AppleScript will assume that code is your implied on run handler. You can't have both loose code and an explicit on run handler in a script. See *Using <u>on</u> <u>run</u> and saving scripts as applications* in Chapter 3 for more.

References

ID

<u>objectClass</u> ID <u>IDvalue</u>

```
tell application "FileMaker Pro 4.0" to get cell
"Name" of record ID myID
```

We tell FileMaker Pro to return the value in the field Name for the record with the ID value stored in the variable myID.

Index

first <u>objectClass</u>
second <u>objectClass</u>

third <u>objectClass</u>
fourth <u>objectClass</u>
fifth <u>objectClass</u>
sixth <u>objectClass</u>
seventh <u>objectClass</u>
eighth <u>objectClass</u>
ninth <u>objectClass</u>
tenth <u>objectClass</u>
<u>integer</u> st <u>objectClass</u>
<u>integer</u> nd <u>objectClass</u>
<u>integer</u> rd <u>objectClass</u>
<u>integer</u> th <u>objectClass</u>
last <u>objectClass</u>
front <u>objectClass</u>
back <u>objectClass</u>
middle <u>objectClass</u>
some <u>objectClass</u>
every <u>objectClass</u>
every <u>objectClass</u> from <u>reference</u> to
→ <u>reference</u>
<u>objectClass</u> from <u>reference</u> to <u>reference</u>
<u>objectClass</u> <u>integer</u> through <u>integer</u>
<u>objectClass</u> <u>integer</u> thru <u>integer</u>
<u>objectClass</u> <u>integer</u> through <u>integer</u>
<u>objectClass</u> <u>integer</u> thru <u>integer</u>

```
set x to {1,2,3,5}
get the third item of x
```

This code generates the result of 3.

Name

<u>objectClass</u> named <u>string</u>

```
tell application "Finder" to get label index of
→ file named "My File" of startup disk
```

We tell the Finder to return the label index property for a file looked up by name.

Property Matching

<u>reference</u> whose
<u>reference</u> where

```
tell application "Finder" to get name of every
→ item of startup disk where kind is "folder"
```

The result of this code is a list of the names of every item on our startup disk's top directory that is a folder.

Relative

<u>objectClass</u> before <u>reference</u>
<u>objectClass</u> front of <u>reference</u>
<u>objectClass</u> in front of <u>reference</u>
<u>objectClass</u> after <u>reference</u>
<u>objectClass</u> back of <u>reference</u>
<u>objectClass</u> in back of <u>reference</u>

in <u>reference</u> in <u>reference</u>
of <u>reference</u> of <u>reference</u>

set x to character 2 of word 3 of "Hey you there"

This code generates the result h.

Operators

Operators are covered in detail in *Understanding operators* in Chapter 3. Comparison and containment operators are covered elsewhere in Chapter 3.

Arithmetic Operators

OPERATOR	MEANING	EXAMPLE	VALID VALUE TYPES
^	Raise to the power of	2^4=16	number
*	Multiply	1*3=3	number
+	Add	2+7=9	date, number
-	Subtract	5-2=3	date, number
/	Divide	8/2=4	number
div	Divide without remainder	11 div 2=5	number
mod	Divide returning remainder	11 mod 2=1	number

Logical Operators

OPERATOR	MEANING	EXAMPLE
and	Returns true is both tests are true	x and y returns true only if x is true and y is true.
or	Returns true is either test is true	x or y returns true as long as either x or y is true.
not	Returns true if test is false; returns false if test is true	not x returns false is x is true.

Containment operators

contains

<u>list</u> contains <u>list</u>
<u>record</u> contains <u>record</u>
<u>string</u> contains <u>string</u>

does not contain

<u>list</u> does not contain <u>list</u>
<u>record</u> does not contain <u>record</u>
<u>string</u> does not contain <u>string</u>

ends with

<u>list</u> ends with <u>list</u>
<u>string</u> ends with <u>string</u>

is in

<u>list</u> is in <u>list</u>
<u>record</u> is in <u>record</u>
<u>string</u> is in <u>string</u>

is not in

<u>list</u> is not in <u>list</u>
<u>record</u> is not in <u>record</u>
<u>string</u> is not in <u>string</u>

starts with

<u>list</u> starts with <u>list</u>
<u>string</u> starts with <u>string</u>

Comparison operators

=

equal
equals
equal to
is
is equal to
<u>expression</u> = <u>expression</u>

≠

does not equal
doesn't equal
is not
is not equal to
isn't
isn't equal to
<u>expression</u> ≠ <u>expression</u>

<

comes before
is less than
is not greater than or equal to
isn't greater than or equal to
less than
<u>date</u> ≤ <u>date</u>
<u>integer</u> ≤ <u>integer</u>
<u>real</u> ≤ <u>real</u>
<u>string</u> ≤ <u>string</u>

>

comes after
greater than
is greater than
is not less than or equal to
isn't less than or equal to
<u>date</u> ≥ <u>date</u>
<u>integer</u> ≥ <u>integer</u>
<u>real</u> ≥ <u>real</u>
<u>string</u> ≥ <u>string</u>

≤

```
<=
```
does not come after
doesn't come after
is less than or equal to
is not greater than
isn't greater than
less than or equal to
date ≤ date
integer ≤ integer
real ≤ real
string ≤ string

≥

```
>=
```
does not come before
doesn't come before
greater than or equal to
is greater than or equal to
is not less than
isn't less than
date ≥ date
integer ≥ integer
real ≥ real
string ≥ string

Concatenation operator

&

string & string
list & list

Variable and property assignments

Variable assignment

copy expression to variable
copy reference to variable
set variable to expression
set variable to reference

`set x to 10`

This code stores the value 10 in the variable x.

Global variable declaration

global variable [, variable]...

`global k`

This code establishes the variable k as a global variable whose value will be directly accessible from all handlers in your script.

Local variable declaration

local variable [, variable]...

`local z`

This code establishes the variable z as a local variable. There is never a need to explicitly define local variables, since they are automatically declared when a value is assigned to them.

Script property assignment

property propertyName : expression

`property myname: "John Doe"`

This code establishes the property myname and assigns the string value John Doe to the property. Property values survive across separate executions of a script and are handy places to store preference settings for a script's behavior.

Constants

current application
reference
The default target application.

false
boolean
The Boolean false value.

it
reference
The default target.

me
reference
The current script. Used in tell me in order to call handlers of the current script.

pi
real
The value π (approximately 3.14159).

result
any value type or class
The result returned by the most recently executed command or expression.

return
string
A return character: ASCII character 13.

space
string
A space character: ASCII character 32.

tab
string
A tab character: ASCII character 9.

text item delimiters

```
AppleScript's text item delimiters
text item delimiters of AppleScript
list
```

The `text item delimiters` property is a list of the delimiters used by AppleScript to coerce lists to strings and to get text items from strings.

true

```
boolean
```

The Boolean `true` value.

Placeholder definitions

attribute

A characteristic that can be considered or ignored by invoking the `considering` and `ignoring` statements. Example:

```
considering case
    set myflag to "help" contains "E"
end considering
```

boolean

A logical value of either `true` or `false`. Boolean is a value type or class. The results of comparisons are always Boolean values. Example:

```
set x to true
```

date

The AppleScript value type, or class, that specifies a time, day, month, and year.

expression

Any series of words or terms that have a value. Examples:

```
"s" & "mith"
(2^3)+9.5-myVariable
```

integer

A positive or negative number without any decimal component. Integer is a value type or class. Example:

```
set z to 2 as integer
```

list

An ordered collection of values. Lists are enclosed by curly brackets and each pair of items is separated by a comma. List is a value type or class. Example:

```
{1,4,5,"e",1}
```

objectClass

A category of objects that have similar properties and elements and respond to similar commands. Examples:

```
characters, words, lines, paragraphs
windows, documents, files
```

propertyName

When user-defined, a name for a container used to store a value. Properties are like variables, but their values are per-sistent and are saved when a script is run. Objects also have properties that can be set and read. Example:

```
get the label index of alias "HD:My File"
```

propertyValue

When user defined, the value for a container used to store a value. Properties are like variables, but their values are persistent and are saved when a script is run. Objects also have properties that can be set and read. Example:

```
make new folder with properties {name: "Hey"}
```

real

A number that can include a decimal component. Real is a value type or class. Example:

```
set q to 2.475 as real
```

record

An unordered collection of properties. Properties are referenced by a name and stored as a name-value pair. Record is a value type or class. Example:

```
set b to {name: "Me", address:"100 Main Street"}
as record
```

reference

A phrase that specifies one or more objects using standard reference forms. Applications, documents, windows, and all other objects can be referenced by variables. A reference is a value type or class. Example:

```
set x to the current location
```

statement

A series of words or terms in your script that contain a request for an action or evaluate an expression. Example:

```
put 2*4 into x
```

string

An ordered series of characters. String is a value type or class. Example:

```
set r to "hello" as string
```

subroutine

A combination of statements that are executed in response to a user-defined handler. Example:

```
on showscore(score)
    display dialog score
end showscore
```

value

Data that can be manipulated and stored in scripts. Value types, or classes, include: boolean, constant, data, date, integer, list, real, record, reference, and string. Examples:

```
"me"
set y to 1
```

variable

A named container used to store a value. Examples:

```
set x to "me" as string
set y to 1
```

To Learn More About AppleScript

In this appendix, you'll find out where to learn more about AppleScript. World Wide Web sites, America Online resources, mailing lists, and newsgroups are all included. We'll also look at ISO Productions' unique *Everything CD for Macintosh Scripting*.

There are many wonderful scripting additions and scriptable applications that could not be covered in this book. Wander the Web and check out some of the online AppleScript resources to continue your discovery of the powers of AppleScript.

Don't Forget

As the owner of this book you get free access to even more AppleScript information, including detailed coverage of applications like BBEdit, Creator 2 and Macromedia Freehand on the Peachpit Press AppleScript for the Internet web site. Visit this URL today!

```
http://www.peachpit.com/vqs/
→ applescript/
```

AppleScript resources on the World Wide Web

Check out these Web sites to further your AppleScript education:

- http://applescript.apple.com/
  Apple's official AppleScript Web site.

- http://www.scriptweb.com/
  A very complete reference to Mac scripting, with a database of scripting additions (OSAX).

- http://www.script.org/
  The AppleScript Language Association's (ASLA) Web site.

- http://www.its.unimelb.edu.au/ma/
  → public/macscrpt/
  Macscrpt mailing list Web archives.

- http://www.latenightsw.com/
  The Web site of Last Night Software, creators of Script Debugger.

- http://www.mainevent.com/
  The Web site of Main Event Software, creators of Scripter and PhotoScripter.

- ftp://mirror.apple.com/mirrors/
  → gaea.scriptweb.com/
  Apple's mirror site for the GAEA scriptweb archive of AppleScript files. Includes many scripting additions, shareware, and utilities.

- http://oasis.bellevue.k12.wa.us/
  → cheeseb/
  The AppleScript Sourcebook, a Web site maintained by Bill Cheeseman.

- http://www.facespan.com/
  The FaceSpan Web site.

✔ America Online

- America Online has a good shareware and freeware software library. Search for "AppleScript" to see what's new.

AppleScript newsgroups and mailing lists

Check out these mailing lists for the latest AppleScript info:

- The Macscrpt mailing list: To subscribe, send e-mail to listserv@dartmouth.edu. Put "SUB MACSCRPT" and your name in the body of the message.

- Apple's AppleScript mailing lists: Visit http://www.lists.apple.com/ → Applescript.html to find out how to subscribe to Apple's AppleScript mailing lists.

Everything CD for Macintosh Scripting

ISO Productions has put together a great many AppleScript resources on a single CD-ROM called the *Everything CD for Macintosh Scripting*. The disk includes an Adobe Acrobat PDF file of the 400+ page AppleScript Language Guide, which by itself is worth the price of the CD.

Everything CD for Macintosh Scripting is published by ISO Productions, which can be reached at http://www.isoproductions.com/.

INDEX

A

Acid Jazz 301
Acid Jazz scripting 302
ACME Script Widget
    scripting 183, 208, 286
    doing without 183
action scripts 271
additions, scripting 2, 7
additions, scripting, beware 11
additions, scripting folder 11
Adobe Photoshop 234, 249
aliases adding to UNIX server 171-173
Alta Vista, detecting URL with 274
America Online 332
Anarchie 151
    retrieving entire site's files via HTTP 163
    retrieving directory with FTP 157
    retrieving file via FTP 154
    retrieving file via HTTP 162
    scripting 153
Anarchie Pro 304
Anarchie Pro instead of FaceSpan 311
animation 246-248
    creating 264
    moving text 248
    previewing as separate layers 265-266
    with GIFBuilder 267
Appearance, customizing in OS 8.5 60-61
Apple Data Detectors 269
    as entry point 274
    creating action scripts 270
    if scripts don't appear 270
    scripting 270
Apple Events 3
AppleScript for the Internet 6
AppleScript
    browser runs downloaded 104
    defining as handler 33
    dictionary
    how it works 3
    late news 322
    making work with Internet Explorer 106
    newsgfoups 332
    reference 323-330
    resources on World Wide Web 332
    running from browser, 102-106
    what it does 4
applets 40
application, saving project as 314
application, stand alone script 301
application, script tips 40
applications
    commercial editing 9
    drag-and-drop 41
    recordable 2
    returning content 102
    scriptable 7, 10
Application Switcher, customizing in OS 8.5 58-59
AutoShare 281
AutoShare scripting 282

B

batch process 51
BBEdit 235
browser cache, clearing with Internet Explorer 99
browser, running downloaded AppleScripts 104
browser, running AppleScripts from 102-106
button Monitor 312
button Stop 313

C

CGI 179
    defined 4
    making HTML page 184

replies sending with WebSTAR 194-195
saving 180
charts, graphical creating 239
Claris Emailer 271
clip2gif
creating and exporting text 238
creating graphical charts 239
making interlaced GIF images 244-245
scripting 237
ClipboardToHTML scripting 227
commands 14
delay 277
find 220
Find 9
if...then...else 24
if...then 13
long 35
MouseClick 277
one-liners 35
OpenURL 89
repeat while 13
replace 220
subscribe 283
summarize 66
using 35
using else with if 25
with timeout 32
common gateway interface (see CGI)
comparisons, advanced 26
comparisons, combining 27
configurations
easier switch in OS 8.5 77
switching TCP with Location Manager 70
system software for AppleScript 321
TCP/IP, creating in OS 8.5 72-73
TCP/IP, switching 76-77
TCP/IP, toggling between two 76
connections
PPP maintaining 80
PPP making 79
Remote Access making 81-82
control panel, scripting TCP/IP 71
content returning from scriptable applications 192
content returning via redirection 192
control panel
customizing Appearance 60-61
customizing Apple Menu Options 56
Location Manager 77
scripting Users & Groups 84-86
cookies file, Netscape Navigator 100-101
creator types 46-47
changing file 46
discovering 47
CyberStudio 219

scripting 219
converting styled text 226-227
modifying text, fonts and styles 220

D
database
content creating new record 205
content finding records in 201
content getting data from record in 203
content, sorting records in 202
Database, Test 205
DataComet 165
DataComet scripting 166
debugging 315
with FaceSpan 320
with Script Debugger 319
with Script Editor 316
with Scripter 318
Decode URL 180
Decode URL scripting 182
Desktop printers
in OS 8.5
stopping queues 67
starting queues 68
dictionaries 10
directory, retrieving directory via FTP 155-157
DNS name resolving to IP address 293
document exporting text 235
domain name detecting 273
domain names 192
drag-and-drop 245
droplets, making 41

E
e-mail adding addressed to book 271-272
EIMS 2.x adding user account 285
EIMS 281
EIMS scripting 282
elements 14
Emailer
faxing mail with faxSTF 126-128
scripting 108
Encode URL 180
Encode URL scripting 91.182
EPS files exporting pages 234
error handling 31
errors, ignoring
errors, intercept with try 31
Eudora Internet Mail Server (see EIMS)
Eudora Pro 137
filing mail based on keywords 138-141
forwarding mail w/keywords 144-145
scripting 137

sending replies w/keywords 142-143
Eudora, converting mail 108-114
Event Log 246
extension, system 3

F

FaceSpan 12, 170, 301, 320
    changing object properties 306
    debugging with 320
    entering project script 307-311
    scripting 305
    using Anarachie Pro instead 311
faxSTF 126
faxSTF, scripting with 128
Fetch 151
    scripting 152
    updating directory via FTP 158-161
fields mail header 296
FIFO 180
File Buddy 10
File Exchange, customizing in OS 8.5 62-64
FileMaker Pro 199
file, moving 44
file, other ideas for testing for existence 48
file, testing for existence 48
file, users pick 37
file-sharing status, changing 83
FileMaker different tricks 202
FileMaker merging data w/templates 206-208
FileMaker Pro 107
    copying mail data to 131-133, 146-147
    creating mailing list 134-135, 148-149
    creating sample database 131, 147
    faster record creation 133
    mailing list with Outlook Express 135
    scripting 200
    syntax issue 201
files
    creating from scratch 53-54
    EPS 234
    finding and searching with Sherlock 65-66
    finding end 53
    HTTP retrieving from Web server 300
    importing tab-delimited as table 225
    making HTML template 207
    retrieving via FTP 154
    searching with Finder 65
    searching with Sherlock 65
    searching with summarize 66
    sending via FTP 152-153
Finder 43
    customizing 55-56
    searching for files and folders 65-66

Finger l.5 192
Frontier language 5
folder actions 57
    scripts 57
    using in OS 8.5 57
folders
    creating at user's request 52
    creating on Desktop 52
    duplicating items added 57
    learning to batch process 51
    making 52
    mounting network volumes in OS 8.5 52
    moving 44
    renaming all files 49-51
    synchronizing on Mac and PC 278-279
    users pick 37
FTP
    modifying 153
    retrieving directory 155-157
    retrieving directory with Anarchie 157
    retrieving files 154
    retrieving with Anarchie 154
    sending files 152-153. 297
    updating directory with Fetch 158-161
    working with Anarchie 153

G

GET understanding data 181-183
GET versus POST 89. 192
GIF creating animated 246-248
    converting with Web-safe palette 241-242
    format converting files 240
    images making interlaced 243-245
GIFBuilder
    constructing animated GIF 247-248
    exporting layered document 267
    scripting 237
GoLive CyberStudio (see CyberStudio)
graphical text creating and exporting 250-254
grayscale images 260
grayscale images, adding transparency 260-263

H

handlers 33-34
    as functions 34
    calling 34
    defining AppleScript 33
    defining multiple variables 34
    defining on open 41
    defining run 39-40
    one handle CGI request 180
    on run...end run 39
    on...end 39
    saving as application 40

INDEX

HTML
batch exporting Word documents 215-217
converting styled text 226
files, logging errors 222-224
files, merging data with templates 206-208
files, printing entire folder 92-93
making template file 207
page to call CGI 184
source code importing and formatting 231-233
HTTP
retrieving entire site's files with Anarchie 163
retrieving file with Anarchie 162
retrieving files from Web server 300
hyperlinks modify script to create 221
Hypertext Transfer Protocol (see HTTP)

I

IAC 5
Interapplication Communication (see IAC)
Internet Explorer
clearing cache 99
making AppleScripts work with 106
printing local HTML files 94-96
retrieving HTML source code 98
scripting 90
submitting form data from 90-91
Internet, converting scripts for transmission
103-104
Internet, searching with Sherlock 66
InterNIC record 273
InterNIC, query results 192
IP address resolving DNS name to 293

J

JavaScript 231

K

kaywords
faxing mail with fxSTF 126-128
filing mail w/Eudora Pro 138-141
forwarding mail 124-125
importing mail into Microsoft Word 129-130
mail 118-121
sending replies 122-123
sending replies w/Eudora Pro 142-143
working with Outlook Express 121
kiosk mode 97

L

languages, compliant script 5
Lasso 199
layers creating animations 264

layers exporting as separate file 255-256
layers importing folder 257-259
libraries, saving script 33
lists, defined 20
lists, importance of 20
lists, types of 21
ListSTAR mailing list 288
ListSTAR/SMTP 281
ListSTAR/SMTP scripting 287
Location Manager, switching sets in OS 8.5 69-70
Location Manager, using to switch TCP
configurations 70
logic, 24
logic, conditional 4
loops
counting repeat 29
exiting from infinite 29
infinite 28
moving through list with repeat 30
repeat 28-30
skipping and going in reverse 30
using conditional repeat 30

M

Mac OS 8.5 (see OS 8.5)
MacPerl 5
MacTCI 5
MacroMaker 2
Macromedia FreeHand 234
MagicCookies 100
mail file, UNIX, anatomy of 115
mail
header fields 296
copying in FileMaker Pro 131-133, 145-147
creating mailing list in FileMaker Pro 134-135
creating mailing list w/FileMaker Pro 148-149
filing based on keywords 118-121
filing w/Eudora Pro 138-141
forwarding with Eudora Pro 144-145
forwarding with keywords 124-125
importing into Microsoft Word w/ keywords
129-130
replying based on keywords 122-123
replying w/Eudora Pro using keywords 142-143
mailing lists
enabling and disabling 290
freezing 290
making broadcast 296
subject line prefix 284
subscribing to ListSTAR 288
user subscribing 283
Marionet 291
quitting 292
scripting 291, 292

MarionetSync 292
Microsoft Internet Explorer 87
Microsoft Word scripting 209
Microsoft Word, importing mail w/keywords,
      129-130
Monitor button 312
monitoring Web server 302-304
Movie Player 62, 64
multi-homing, enabling with TCP/IP 74-75

N

Netscape 54
Netscape Navigator 87
      clearing browser cache 99
      deleting cookies file 100-101
      printing local HTML files from 92-93
      putting into kiosk mode 97
      scripting 88
      submitting form data 88-89
NNTP retrieving newsgroup's list 298-299

O

objects 14, 22-34
      application 22
      drawing 237
      examples 22
      model 23
ObjectSupportLib tip 321
Okey Dokey Pro 94, 128
Okey Dokey Pro scripting 96
on-line, more info 6
Open Scripting Architecture (see OSA)
Open Scripting Architecture eXtension
      (see OSAX)
Open Transport 71
operators 16
operators, using logical 27
options list 284
OS 8.5
      and CGIS 180
      creating TCP/IP configuration 72-73
      customizing Appearance 60-61
      customizing Application Switcher 58-59
      customizing File Exchange 62-64
      easier switch for configurations 77
      mounting network volumes 52
      quickly opening URL 89
      Sherlock 65-66
      switching sets with Location Manager 69-70
      tips 38
      using folder actions 57
      with Desktop printers, 67-68
OS 8.x and Scripting Additions folder 321

OSA 5
OSAX 11
OT/PPP scripting 78
Outlook Express
      issues with 128
      mailing list with FileMaker Pro 135
      making Emailer work with 114
      making importing work 129
      scripting 108
      working with forwarding 125
      working with keywords 121
      working with keyword replies 123
      working with QuickMail Pro 117

P

palettes 240
      controlling color 240
      Photoshop Layers 255
      Web-safe 241
parameters, additional for Remote Access 82
parsing POST data 184-188
parsing server variables 189
parsing URL reply string 181
Peachpit Press support url 6
PhotoScripter 249
Photoshop Layers palette 255
Photoshop scripting with PhotoScripter 249
Point-to-Point Protocol (see PPP) 73
POST 88
POST parsing data 184-188
PPP, maintaining connection 80
PPP, making connection 79
project saving as application 314
properties 15
protocols, Internet 292

Q

Quark making new document 233
QuarkXPress 4, 229
QuarkXPress scripting 230
QuickMail Pro
      converting mail with 116-117
      scripting 116
      working with Outlook Express 117

R

records, defines 21
records, importance of 20
records, types of 21
redirection, returning content
Remote Access
      additional parameters 82

Commands 78
control panel, scripting the OT/PPP and
    Remote Access 78
connection, making 81-82
resource fork, flattening 105
resource, read/write, scripting with 106

S

Sandi's Additions scripting 93, 277
Script Daemon scripting 177
Script Daemon, Telnet to your Mac 177
Script Debugger 9, 319-320
Script Editor 7-9
    debugging with 316
    finding 9
    windows 8
    windows Dictionary 9
    windows Event Log 8
    windows Result 8
    windows Script 8
script, convert for transmission over Internet
    103-104
script , modify to create hyperlinks 221
Scripter 31, 318
Scripter, debugging with 318
scripting
    Acid Jazz 302
    ACME Script Widgets, 183, 208, 286
    Anarchie 153
    Apple Data Detectors 270
    clip2gif 237
    ClipboardToHTML 227
    CyberStudio 219
    DataComet 166
    Decode URL 182
    EIMS 282
    Encode URL 91, 182
    Eudora Pro 137
    FaceSpan 305
    faxSTF 128
    Fetch 152
    FileMaker Pro 200
    Finger 193
    GIFBuilder 237
    ListSTAR/MTP 287
    Marionet 291, 292
    Microsoft Word 209
    Okey Dokey Pro 96
    OT/PPP and Remote Access 78
    Photoshop with photoScripter 249
    QuarkXPress 230
    QuickMail Pro 116
    Sandi's Additions 93, 277

Script Daemon 177
TCP Config 77
Timbuktu 275
WebSTAR 195
XCMD OSAX Lite/FAXstf 128
Scripting Additions folder and OS 8.x 321
scripts, making action 271
scripts, ways to save 42
scroll bars, secret trick 61
server restarting Windows NT 276-277
Sherlock 322
Sherlock, finding files and searching the Web
    65-66
Sherlock, searching Internet 66
SMTP server sending mail directly 293-296
source code, parsing search results 98
source code, retrieving with Internet Explorer 98
spam mail 142
statements
    comparisons and control 24-25
    try 31
    try...on error 32
    tell 13
Stop button, adding script 313
strings 27
subscribers, converting to non-posting 282
subscribers, sending mail 289
support url for Peachpit Press 6

T

Tango 199
targets 14
TCP Config 77
Timbuktu Pro 275
Timbuktu Pro scripting 275
Telnet 177

U

UNIX
    changing script to restart 170
    converting mail 108-114
    mail file, anatomy of 115
    reading passwd file 166-170
    server adding mail aliases 171-173
    server restarting 166-170
    server retrieving environment variable 174-176
URL, parsing reply string 181
url, Peachpit Press support 6
Users & Groups
    control panel 84-86
    adding existing users 85-86
    dealing with passwords 85
    making new user 84-85

INDEX

users
      account adding to EIMS 2.x 285
      asking for choice, 37-38
      interacting with 12, 36
      pick an application 38
      pick a file 37
      pick a folder 37
      subscribing to mailing list 283

V

values 17-19
      coercion 17r 18
      constant 19
      incorrect 18
      more types 19
      setting other 19
      to compare 24
      to set string 17
      types 17
      unit types in OS 8.5 17
variables 15
variable, environment 174
variables, parsing server 189
Visual Basic for Applications 209

W

waiting, how long 32
waiting, with timeout 32
WebSTAR
      creating protected realms 196-197
      scripting 195
      sending partial CGI replies 194-195
wildcard, using 282
windows
      controls adding scripts 312-313
      creating with controls 306

      Event Log 83, 166, 316
      FaceSpan's Project 305
      Fetch's Misc. Preferences 151
      Frame 267
      Script Editor Dictionary 9
      Script Editor Event Log 8
      Script Editor Result 8
      Script Editor Script 8
Windows NT server restating 276-277
Word 98 129, 209
      batch processing 212-214
      recording script 210-211
Word documents, batch exporting as HTML
            215-217
World Wide Web , Apple Script resources 332

X

XCMD OSA Lite/FAXstf, scripting 128

Y

Yves Piguet 237

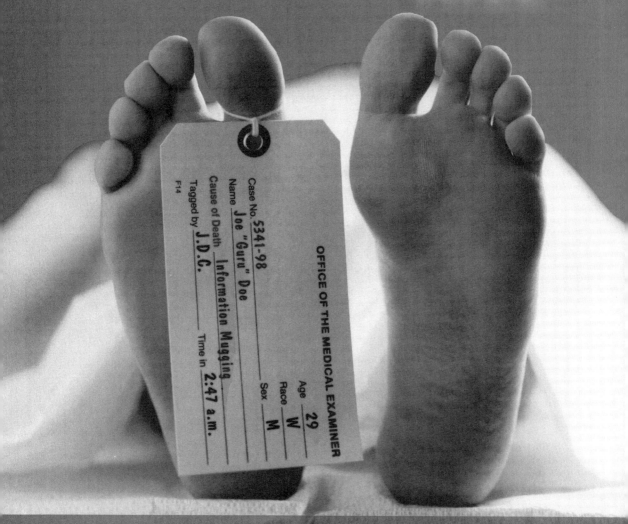